**PENGUIN BOOKS**

# MALTA: THE THORN IN ROMMEL'S SIDE

Laddie Lucas rose in two years from Aircraftman 2nd Class, the lowest rank in the Royal Air Force, to command of No. 249 (Fighter) Squadron at the height of the Battle of Malta in 1942. He was then 26.

In three tours of operational flying, interspersed with two spells as a Command Headquarters staff officer, Lucas led two Spitfire squadrons and a wing on the Western Front in 1943 before switching to command a Mosquito squadron during the Allied drive through north-west Europe in 1944 and 45. He was awarded the DSO and bar, DFC and French Croix de Guerre.

A Tory MP for ten years in the 1950s, Lucas was obliged by his business commitments to refuse ministerial office when offered it in 1957 by Harold Macmillan, then Prime Minister. Married with two sons and five grandchildren, he was one of the country's best-known amateur golfers, captaining Cambridge, England and Great Britain and Ireland against the United States. He retired in 1976 from the chairmanship of a public company to turn again to writing. *Malta: The Thorn in Rommel's Side* is Lucas's ninth published work in a successful run as an author, his early experience as a Fleet Street journalist standing him in good stead.

D0790302

# LADDIE LUCAS

# MALTA: THE THORN IN ROMMEL'S SIDE

## SIX MONTHS THAT TURNED THE WAR

PENGUIN BOOKS

PENGUIN BOOKS

Published by the Penguin Group
Penguin Books Ltd, 27 Wrights Lane, London w8 5tz, England
Penguin Books USA Inc., 375 Hudson Street, New York, New York 10014, USA
Penguin Books Australia Ltd, Ringwood, Victoria, Australia
Penguin Books Canada Ltd, 10 Alcorn Avenue, Toronto, Ontario, Canada m4v 3b2
Penguin Books (NZ) Ltd, 182–190 Wairau Road, Auckland 10, New Zealand

Penguin Books Ltd, Registered Offices: Harmondsworth, Middlesex, England

First published by Stanley Paul & Co. Ltd 1992
Published in Penguin Books 1993
1 3 5 7 9 10 8 6 4 2

Photographs from private collections are credited individually in the photograph sections.
The author and publishers would also like to thank the following for allowing the use of
copyright photographs: Associated Press, Hulton-Deutsch Collection, Robert Hunt
Library, *Illustrated London News*, Imperial War Museum, Italian Defence Archives,
National Archives, Washington

Typeset by Datix International Limited, Bungay, Suffolk
Set in 10/12 pt Monophoto Ehrhardt
Printed in England by Clays Ltd, St Ives plc

To the groundcrews at Takali, indomitable in adversity, who sweated it out
under a Mediterranean sun and kept the
aircraft flying.

*Battle of Malta*
*Spring and summer 1942*

Their shoulders held the sky suspended;
They stood, and earth's foundations stay.
*A. E. Housman*

# CONTENTS

## PART FOUR
### MASTERING THE AXIS

# ACKNOWLEDGEMENTS

I must thank those who have helped me to secure the accuracy and authority of the Malta story.

To Group Captain Ian Madelin, head of the Royal Air Force's Air Historical Branch at the Ministry of Defence in Whitehall, and to his colleague, Sebastian Cox, I am specially indebted for their interest and aid during the preparation of the manuscript. Similarly, I acknowledge the complementary help offered by John Andrews at the Ministry of Defence Library, by Michael Chapman and others on the staff. All have been patient with my repeated needs.

I have, moreover, good reason to be grateful to the National War Museum Association in Malta and those who voluntarily and selflessly serve it. Here, I thank particularly Frederick Galea, the chairman, and John Agius whose knowledge of those rough Mediterranean days of 1942 is positively encyclopaedic.

Then there are those friends and comrades who, fifty years ago, contributed so much to victory and who, half a century later, have given me the benefit of that priceless experience.

From Canada I must mention Gerry de Nancrede, Bob Middlemiss, Roderick Smith, John Sherlock and, before his recent and untimely death, Frank Jones, who so often flew as my No. 2 in 249 Squadron. I am indebted to them as I am to Barbara McNair, widow of Robert, who has allowed me to include her late husband's emotive account of the bombing of the Point de Vue Mess, in Rabat, in March 1942.

From New Zealand I recognize the help which has come from Harry Coldbeck, the photographic reconnaissance pilot, and his compatriot, Jack Rae, another valued 249 Squadron member – as, indeed, I do the assistance which Lex McAuley, the distinguished Australian author, has so willingly dispensed, thus enabling me to confirm certain relevant facts about his countrymen's unforgettable contribution to the Malta battle.

In securing the Fleet Air Arm record, I remember particularly the help provided by two fine fighting officers – the late Sir Frank Hopkins and another good friend, David Foster, who, after his extended service in the Western Desert, moved on to Malta before transferring to the Pacific theatre where he led the historic attacks on the oil refineries at Palembang in Sumatra – one of the longest operational stretches I can recall in World War II.

Here at home, I have leant heavily upon Tony Holland, a stalwart of No. 603, the City of Edinburgh Squadron, at the peak of the Malta fighting and also upon Tony Spooner, chronicler of Adrian Warburton, whose long service with 69, the general reconnaissance Squadron during the battle, has given him a special insight into the island story.

I acknowledge, too, the help offered by Lord James Douglas-Hamilton, author of *The Air Battle for Malta*, whose uncle, Squadron Leader Lord David Douglas-Hamilton, commanded 603 Squadron at Takali while I was first a flight commander and then CO of 249 on the same airfield. Likewise, I remember gratefully Angela Daborn, sister of Raoul Daddo-Langlois, an officer of outstanding worth who was one of my two flight commanders in 249 Squadron. In her lifetime, Angela allowed me access to her late brother's private papers, thereby enhancing the memory of his exceptional record.

I must also mention the cooperation I have received from James Somerville and Bill Moodie, two redoubtable Scots, who assisted me with the references to the worth and courage of our Takali groundcrews without whose support victory would certainly not have been gained.

My thanks are also due to Christopher Shores, the air historian, for his permission to include a reference to 249 Squadron's World War II victories from his work, *Aces High*, a potent confirmation of the unit's wartime achievements.

Finally, I must record my appreciation of the help given by two former opponents who have since become my friends. I am particularly grateful to the Luftwaffe's Eduard Neumann, the highly-regarded *Kommodore* of Jagdgeschwader 27, supporting General Rommel and his Afrika Korps in the Western Desert and in the advance to Egypt in the summer of 1942. He has given me his own first-hand assessment of Malta's strategic importance in the context of the North African and Mediterranean campaigns.

In the same breath I also thank Generale Francesco Cavalera, a young Regia Aeronautica fighter pilot in the Malta battle, who, in the peace which followed, rose to become the professional head of the Italian Air Force and then the Chief of his country's Defence Staff, an appointment never before held by an airman.

By offering their advice so willingly, the two have contributed notably to the balance of the battle story.

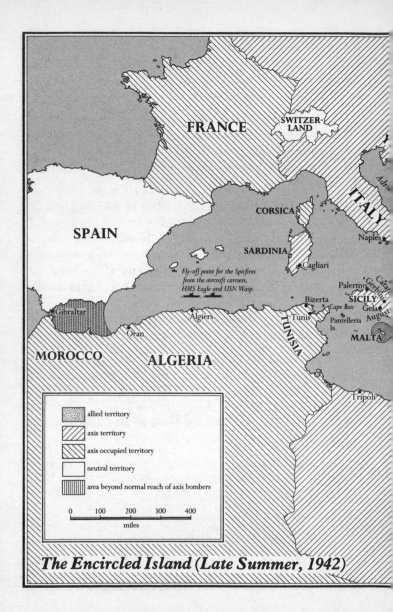

The Encircled Island (Late Summer, 1942)

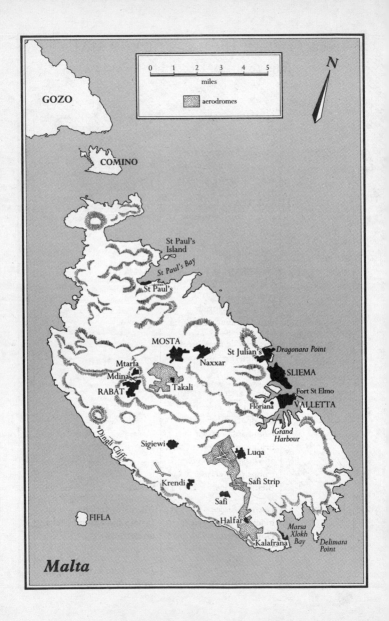

**Malta**

# WORLD WAR II – BATTLE FOR MALTA
## June 10, 1940–December 31, 1942

| | Global events | Malta milestones |
|---|---|---|
| **1940**<br>April 9 | Hitler's forces invade Norway after overrunning Denmark. 'Phoney War' ends. Unyielding Norwegian resistance despite traitor Quisling's call to lay down arms. | |
| May 10 | Neville Chamberlain resigns: Winston Churchill becomes Prime Minister and forms National Coalition Government. | |
| | German Panzers break through the Low Countries. | |
| May 12 | Heroic attack by 12 Royal Air Force Blenheims of 2 Group, Bomber Command, on two bridges over Albert Canal at Maastricht as enemy troops pour across. Six Blenheims lost. | |
| June 10/11 | German forces within 35 miles of Paris: French Government moves to Tours. | Mussolini declares war on Britain and France. Malta on alert. |
| | | Italian bombers (SM 79s) with fighter escort |

|  | *Global events* | *Malta milestones* |
|---|---|---|
|  |  | (Mc 200s), attack Grand Harbour, Halfar and Kalafrana. |
|  |  | Station Fighter Flight of Sea Gladiators (Faith, Hope and Charity) in action. |
| June 14 | German troops march down the Champs Elysées: Nazi swastika hoisted over Eiffel Tower. |  |
| June 16 | Paul Reynaud, French Premier, resigns: Marshal Pétain succeeds and seeks armistice. |  |
| June 18 | Churchill declares that Britain will fight on alone. |  |
| June 22 | France surrenders in the Forest of Compiègne. | Flight Lieutenant George Burges, in Faith, destroys first Italian bomber over Island. |
| June 23 | General Charles de Gaulle, now in London, resolves to raise Free French forces to fight alongside Britain. |  |
| July 1 | Battle of Britain begins. |  |
| July 3 | Royal Navy destroys large part of French Fleet at Oran. A thousand French sailors killed. |  |
| July 10 | Reichsmarschall Hermann Goering orders Luftwaffe to attack Channel shipping and ports in |  |

| | *Global events* | *Malta milestones* |
|---|---|---|
| | south-east and southern England. | |
| July 23 | Home Guard formed. 250,000 volunteers come forward in a week. | |
| August 2 | | *Operation Hurry*: First delivery of 12 fighter Hurricanes from carrier, HMS *Argus*, all aircraft arrive on Island. |
| August 20 | Fighter Command of Royal Air Force now fighting for its life. Churchill tells House of Commons, 'Never in the field of human conflict has so much been owed by so many to so few.' Supply of pilots – not aircraft – now critical. | |
| August/ September | | *Operation Hats*: First convoy of three merchantmen, with Naval escort, arrives from Alexandria. 40,000 tons of supplies delivered. |
| September 7 | German High Command's fatal decision to switch Luftwaffe's attack from Fighter Command airfields and sectors on to London and other cities. | |
| September 15 | Royal Air Force claims 185 enemy aircraft destroyed. (Figure revised to 56 post-war). | |

| | Global events | Malta milestones |
|---|---|---|
| October 13 | Battle of Britain ends in victory for Allies. Battle of Atlantic now begins in earnest. | |
| November 5 | Franklin D. Roosevelt re-elected President of the United States for unparallelled third four-year term. | |
| November 11 | | Fleet Air Arm Swordfish from HMS *Illustrious*, after photographic reconnaissance by Glenn Martin Marylands from Malta, attack Italian Fleet at Taranto, Southern Italy. Brilliant success: transfers balance of Naval power in Mediterranean irrevocably in Allies' favour. |
| November 17 | | *Operation White*: Second delivery of twelve Hurricanes from HMS *Argus*: only four arrive on Island: eight aircraft run out of fuel: dreadful cock-up. |
| 1941 January | | Prolonged Axis blitz on HMS *Illustrious* en route Malta: 126 members of crew killed, 91 wounded. Heroic action by ship repairers, AA gunners, Naval personnel, and RAF fighters in face of violent enemy assault on ship in Grand Harbour. |

|  | *Global events* | *Malta milestones* |
|---|---|---|
|  |  | Carrier made seaworthy, proceeds to Alexandria under own steam on January 23. |
| January 2 | Luftwaffe bombs neutral Eire. |  |
| January 14 | Lord Woolton, Food Minister, introduces sweeping new price controls on selected foodstuffs to prevent profiteering. Average British family now living on weekly budget of less than £5. |  |
| January 22 | Commonwealth troops under General Wavell advance through Libya and capture Tobruk. |  |
| February 14 | General Erwin Rommel's Afrika Korps arrive in Tripoli to shore up Italian forces in Western Desert. Luftwaffe arrives in strength in North Africa. |  |
| March 11 | United States signs Lease-Lend Agreement with British Government. 'Give us the tools,' says Churchill, 'and we will finish the job.' |  |
| March 17 | Ernest Bevin, Minister of Labour, calls on 'The Women of Britain' to man the factories: invited 100,000 volunteers to come forward. |  |

| | Global events | Malta milestones |
|---|---|---|
| March 21 | Opening of Luftwaffe's spring blitz on London: Buckingham Palace targeted; St Paul's Cathedral survives. | |
| April 16 | 500 enemy aircraft raid capital in biggest raid yet. | |
| April 27 | | *Operation Dunlop*: 24 Hurricanes delivered from carrier, HMS *Ark Royal*: twenty-three arrive in Malta. |
| May 10 | Rudolf Hess, Hitler's Deputy, lands in Scotland by parachute from Messerschmitt 110. Brings peace feelers. Asks to see Duke of Hamilton. Duke says: 'He can wait until the morning.' | |
| May 11 | London blitz builds up. Chamber of House of Commons destroyed: MPs now meet in House of Lords. 20,000 Londoners killed and 25,000 badly wounded in war so far. Liverpool, Glasgow and Clydebank, Belfast, Southampton, Portsmouth and Plymouth all feel weight of Nazi attacks. | |
| May 19 | | Lieut.-General Sir William Dobbie appointed Governor and C-in-C. |

|          | *Global events*                                                                                                                                                                                      | *Malta milestones*                                                                                                                                     |
|----------|------------------------------------------------------------------------------------------------------------------------------------------------------------------------------------------------------|--------------------------------------------------------------------------------------------------------------------------------------------------------|
| May 20   | Germans launch airborne assault on island of Crete.                                                                                                                                                 |                                                                                                                                                        |
| May 27   | Battleship *Bismarck*, pride of the German Navy, is sunk in the Atlantic after dramatic chase of some four days. Royal Navy thus avenges earlier loss of the 42,000-ton battlecruiser HMS *Hood*.    |                                                                                                                                                        |
| June 1   |                                                                                                                                                                                                    | Air Vice-Marshal Hugh Lloyd appointed Air Officer Commanding in succession to Air Commodore F. H. M. Maynard.                                           |
| June 14  |                                                                                                                                                                                                    | *Operation Tracer*: forty-eight Hurricanes dispatched from carriers *Ark Royal* and *Victorious*. Forty-five arrive on island.                          |
| June 22  | Hitler, disregarding Friendship Pact, attacks Russia. Panzers advance. Second fatal move of World War II.                                                                                            |                                                                                                                                                        |
| July     |                                                                                                                                                                                                    | *Operation Substance*: Convoy from Gibraltar comprising six merchantmen with Naval escort delivers 65,000 tons of supplies to Island.                   |
| July 8   | P. G. Wodehouse, British author, broadcasts from Germany to United States: fury of British media.                                                                                                   |                                                                                                                                                        |

|  | *Global events* | *Malta milestones* |
|---|---|---|
| July 26 | General Douglas MacArthur placed in overall command of United States' forces in Far East. | Italian E-boats' intrepid attempt to penetrate Grand Harbour and Marsamxett and destroy ships in harbour and submarine base at Manoel Island. Radar cover effective. Guns from St Elmo and Ricasoli in action. Coastal batteries and Hurricanes later engage. Force wiped out. Eighteen Italians taken prisoner. |
| August 14 | Britain and the United States sign historic Atlantic Charter. | |
| September | | *Operation Halberd*: Convoy from Gibraltar comprising nine merchantmen, one carrier, three battleships, five cruisers and eighteen destroyers deliver 85,000 tons of supplies. One merchantman lost, one battleship damaged. |
| October 20 | German land forces at gates of Moscow; but now comes the Soviet winter. | |
| November | | Field Marshal Albert Kesselring and Luftflotte II transferred from Eastern Front to Sicily in preparation for all-out aerial assault on Malta. |

|  | *Global events* | *Malta milestones* |
|---|---|---|
| November 13/14 | | *Ark Royal* torpedoed and sunk by German U-boat after aircraft delivery to Malta. Heavy blow for reinforcing operations. |
| December | | *Operation Herkules*: Axis code name for invasion of Island: now in active preparation. General Kurt Student to be in command of airborne forces. |
| December 2 | All British unmarried women between ages of 20 and 30 called up. Age for men eligible for call-up lowered to 18½ and raised to 50. Boys and girls between 16 and 18 also to register. | |
| December 7 | Washington reports Japanese attack on Pearl Harbor. Tokyo declares war on United States and Britain. Japanese troops advance strongly in south-east Asia. | |
| 1942 February | | *Operation MF5*: Convoy from Alexandria comprising three merchantmen, three cruisers and sixteen destroyers: whole force obliged to turn back to Alexandria on February 14. No supplies delivered. |

| | Global events | Malta milestones |
|---|---|---|
| February 11/12 | Daring Channel dash by German Navy. *Scharnhorst*, *Gneisenau* and *Eugen* leave Brest and, in broad daylight, run the gauntlet of shore batteries and aircraft through Straits of Dover to reach ports in north-west Germany. | |
| February 13 | | Forty-two internees deported to Uganda, via Cairo, under Emergency Powers (Removal of Detained Persons) Ordinance, 1942. Sir Arturo Mercieca, former Chief Justice and President of Court of Appeal, among the number. |
| February 15 | Fall of Singapore. General Percival surrenders forces to advancing Japanese. | |
| February 28 | | *Operation Spotter*: First attempt at flying off Spitfires from HMS *Eagle* to Malta thwarted by fault with (untested) overloaded fuel tanks. Appalling error. Fleet returns to Gibraltar: Navy greatly displeased. |
| March 7, 21, 29 | | *Operations Spotter, Picket I* and *Picket II*: Thirty-one Spitfires successfully delivered to Malta from *Eagle*: all aircraft arrive safely. |

|  | *Global events* | *Malta milestones* |
|---|---|---|
| March 21 |  | Luftwaffe scores direct hit on Point de Vue Hotel, Rabat (Officers' Mess). Five pilots and an intelligence officer are killed in attack. |
| March 20–25 |  | *Operation MW10*: Convoy from Alexandria comprising four merchantmen, five cruisers and seventeen destroyers. Two merchantmen, *Pampas* and *Talabot*, sunk in Grand Harbour; a third, *Breconshire*, is towed last miles to Island and then sunk. Only 5000 tons of supplies saved. |
| March 27 | British commandos from destroyer *Cambletown* storm U-boat base at St Nazaire in south-west France. |  |
| March 28 | 200 aircraft of Bomber Command raid Baltic port of Lubeck. Royal Air Force stepping up deep-penetration offensive against Germany. |  |
| April |  | Blitz reaches climax. Royal Opera House, Valletta, and other historic buildings destroyed. Total tonnage of bombs dropped by Luftwaffe in *March* and *April* is *twice* that dropped |

|  | *Global events* | *Malta milestones* |
|---|---|---|
|  |  | on London in worst *year* of blitz. Fliegerkorps II flies 9599 sorties against Island in April (4992 in March). |
| April 9 |  | Nazi bomb penetrates dome of Mosta Church, near Takali, while congregation at worship. Fails to explode. Third largest suspended dome in world remains miraculously intact. |
| April 12 |  | Only a handful of aircraft now left serviceable to fly. Aircrew filling sandbags and building 'blast pens' for aircraft with Army. |
| April 14 |  | Royal Navy's submarine, *Upholder*, and Lt Cdr David Wanklyn VC, lost on 25th and culminating mission. *Upholder* has sunk 128,353 tons of shipping – 53,648 tons more than any other ship in 10th Submarine Flotilla. Flotilla now forced, by weight of air attack, to quit base at Manoel Island. |
| April 15 |  | King George VI awards George Cross 'to the Island Fortress . . . [for] heroism . . . that will long be famous in history'. |

| | *Global events* | *Malta milestones* |
|---|---|---|
| April 18 | In Pacific, US B-25s, led by James Doolittle (later General), bomb Tokyo from USN carrier *Hornet*. | |
| April 20 | | *Operation Calendar*: US Navy's carrier *Wasp* delivers, by personal arrangement between Prime Minister Churchill and President Roosevelt, forty-seven Spitfires of 601 and 603 Squadrons, forty-six arriving on Island. Massive enemy retaliation. Only seven aircraft left serviceable on ground forty-eight hours later. Malta's nadir. |
| April 21 | | Photographic reconnaissance of Sicily by NZ's Flight Lieutenant Harry Coldbeck reveals 1500 400 yards glider strips being prepared at Gerbini in readiness for airborne assault on Malta. |
| April 23 | | Thirty-ninth General Hospital at St Andrews destroyed by Ju 87s and Ju 88s: other hospitals extensively damaged. |
| April 26 | | British Ultra (Intelligence) organization's decoding of German Enigma ciphers discloses plans for |

|  | *Global events* | *Malta milestones* |
|---|---|---|
|  |  | withdrawal of Fliegerkorps II's units from Sicily and transfer to North Africa, Crete and elsewhere. |
| May 2 |  | Ultra confirms two Luftwaffe *gruppen* already withdrawn from Sicily. Chiefs of Staff in London reassure Malta Governor regarding danger of invasion 'which can now be discounted'. |
| May 7 |  | Field Marshal Viscount Gort VC takes Oath of Office as Governor of Malta in succession to Sir William Dobbie. |
| May 9 |  | *Operation Bowery*: US Navy's carrier *Wasp* and Royal Navy's carrier *Eagle*, operating together, delivery sixty-four Spitfires, sixty reaching Island safely. |
| May 10 |  | Violent Luftwaffe reaction: furious air battles fought over Island, sixty-three enemy aircraft being destroyed or damaged by fighters or AA gunners. |
|  |  | HMS *Welshman*, Royal Navy's 40-knot mine-laying cruiser, carrying vital supplies, makes yet another all-or-nothing dash for Malta and |

| | *Global events* | *Malta milestones* |
|---|---|---|
| | | reaches Grand Harbour safely, unloads and makes off, seven hours later, for Gib. |
| | | Kesselring reports to German High Command: 'my task [neutralizing Malta] now completed' discloses enemy's poor intelligence service and, with it, unwise timing. |
| May 17 | | Petty pilfering among civilian airfield workers prompts Wing Commander E. J. ('Jumbo') Gracie, Station Commander, Takali, to erect gibbets beside perimeter as warning threat to would-be culprits. Pictures reach London's *Daily Mirror*. Air Ministry intervenes. |
| May 18 | | *Operation LB*: Eagle delivers further sixteen Spitfires, all sixteen reaching Island safely. Heavy reinforcements (seventy-six aircraft) in last nine days, and resultant victories over Island, mark turning point in battle for control of Malta. |
| | | Subsequently, between June 3 and October 29, carriers *Eagle* (sunk by U-boat on 11 August with |

| | *Global events* | *Malta milestones* |
|---|---|---|
| | | loss of 230 crew) and/or *Furious* deliver 226 more Spitfires to Island, 213 arriving safely. |
| | | Stringent food-rationing restrictions tightened yet again. Sale of bread and sandwiches in canteens 'discontinued until further notice'. |
| May 19 | | Axis spy, Borghi Pisani, a Maltese in Italy, lands by motor torpedo boat near Dingli Cliffs. Captured, tried, sentenced to death and hanged 0734 on 28 November. |
| May 26 | Britain signs 20-year Pact with Soviet Union. Stalin says: 'The close collaboration of our two countries after the war is assured.' | |
| May 31 | A thousand aircraft of Royal Air Force's Bomber Command 'devastate' 600 acres of Cologne. Opening of War Cabinet's prolonged policy of 'area saturation bombing' of German cities to destroy civilian morale and so weaken enemy's industrial effort. | |
| June 7 | Following success in Battle of the Coral Sea, Admiral Nimitz routs the | |

| Global events | Malta milestones |
|---|---|
| | Japanese Navy in brilliant carrier engagement in decisive Battle of Midway: establishes US Navy's supremacy in Pacific. |
| June 11–16 | *Operation Vigorous*: Convoy from Alexandria comprising eleven merchantmen, one dummy battleship, eight cruisers, twenty-six destroyers, four corvettes, two minesweepers and two rescue ships forced by presence of Italian Fleet to return to Egypt. Losses – one cruiser and five destroyers: no supplies delivered. |
| | *Operation Harpoon*: Convoy from Gibraltar comprising six merchantmen, one battleship, with cruisers, twenty-six destroyers, four corvettes, two minesweepers and two rescue ships heavily attacked for four days. Two merchantmen reach Grand Harbour. Losses – one cruiser, five destroyers and four merchantmen. 25,000 tons of supplies delivered, saving Malta from starvation for further two–three months. |

|  | *Global events* | *Malta milestones* |
|---|---|---|
|  |  | Rationing now at peak. Hunger of Garrison and people worsening. |
| July 1–14 | Sebastopol, Russian fortress on Black Sea, falls to Germany's 11th Army under General von Mannstein. | Renewed Axis blitz against Island timed to coincide with Afrika Korps's advance to Egypt. German High Command shelves *Operation Herkules* following fall of Tobruk on June 21. |
| July 28 |  | Original aircraft hijack. South African Lieut. Edward Strever, with British and NZ crew of ditched Beaufort of 217 Squadron, overpower crew of rescuing Italian Cant seaplane when heading for Italy. Fly floatplane to Malta where Italians made POWs. |
| July/ August |  | Successful all-out attacks by Malta-based bombing and torpedo-carrying aircraft against Axis convoys crossing Mediterranean with supplies for extended Afrika Korps. Big help for British 8th Army in subsequent battles at Alam Halfa and Alamein. |
| August 10–15 |  | *Operation Pedestal*: Santa Maria convoy from Gibraltar comprising fourteen merchantmen with heavy escort of four |

|  | *Global events* | *Malta milestones* |
|--|-----------------|--------------------|
|  |  | aircraft carriers, two battleships, seven cruisers and twenty-four destroyers, first, under Vice-Admiral Neville Syfrett and, second, Rear Admiral Harold Burrough, is pounded continuously for five days by aircraft, U-boats and elements of Italian Fleet. Only five merchantmen reach Island delivering 53,000 tons of supplies out of original total of 85,000. Losses – nine merchantmen, one carrier (*Eagle*), two cruisers, all sunk, and one carrier, the cruisers and three merchantmen damaged. All-out effort by Fleet Air Arm and Royal Air Force in support. |
| August 19 | Allies, under Admiral Mountbatten, raid Dieppe on French Channel coast. Heavy casualties for small gain. |  |
| August 25 | Duke of Kent, younger brother of King George VI, killed in air crash in Scotland. Sunderland flying boat in which he was travelling to Iceland flies into mountain. |  |
| September | Pilots of the three US Eagle Squadrons, Nos 71, 121 and 133 in Royal Air |  |

|  | *Global events* | *Malta milestones* |
|---|---|---|
|  | Force, who volunteered long before Pearl Harbor, begin transferring to US 8th Air Force in UK to form nucleus of famous 4th Fighter Group under Colonel Don Blakeslee. Meanwhile US 8th Bomber Command's daylight offensive against Third Reich begins to roll. |  |
| September 10 | Air Marshal Sir Arthur Harris, C-in-C Royal Air Force's Bomber Command, steps up night offensive against Germany. 100,000 tons of bombs dropped on Dusseldorf 'within the hour'. |  |
| October 10–20 |  | Final Axis blitz, after which bulk of Luftwaffe units in Sicily transferred to North Africa to sustain Rommel and Afrika Korps. Raids on Island taper away. |
| October 31 | Luftwaffe's fighter-bombers attack Canterbury in daylight following on 'Baedeker Raids' on cathedral cities of Coventry, Exeter and York. |  |
| November 7 | Allies land in French North Africa. |  |

| | *Global events* | *Malta milestones* |
|---|---|---|
| | General Eisenhower aims ultimately to join up with British 8th Army advancing from Libya. | |
| November 15–20 | | *Operation Stone Age*: Convoy comprising four merchantmen with escort of five cruisers and seventeen destroyers from Alexandria delivers 35,000 tons of supplies at the expense of one cruiser damaged. Malta's second Great Siege in four centuries is finally raised. |
| November 18 | | *Welshman, Manxman's* counterpart, arrives in Grand Harbour with more essential provisions to help tide the Island over until arrival of next convoy.<br><br>Twelve Spitfire fighter-bombers with two 500 lb bombs slung under wings, escorted by another twelve fighter version aircraft, go on the offensive and attack chemical factory at Pachino in Sicily. |
| November 26 | Russian forces rout General von Paulus's 6th German Army at Stalingrad. 77,000 Germans killed or taken prisoner. | |

| | *Global events* | *Malta milestones* |
|---|---|---|
| December | | *Operation Portcullis*: Convoy comprising four merchantmen with escort of one cruiser, eighteen destroyers and one minelayer, effectively supplies Island with further 55,000 tons of essential cargoes for no loss for first time since 1941. Hunger slowly begins to recede. Belts eased a notch for Christmas. Issue of four candles and eight nightlights to every family. |
| December 31 | Battle of the Atlantic: dramatic drop in U-boat sinkings of Allied shipping. Under 400,000 tons lost in December against peak totals of over 800,000 tons in June and November. New scientific devices taking effect. | Battle officially ends. |

# PART ONE

# 'A PHANTASMA OR A
HIDEOUS DREAM'

# I

# A PLACE IN THE SUN

Three quotes are sufficient to provide the backcloth for the six spring and summer months of 1942 when, in the face of odds of twenty and thirty to one against, and sometimes more, the Royal Air Force fought the Luftwaffe for control of the daylight air over Malta, and saved the day.

The first is Alan Moorehead's. Moorehead, war correspondent extraordinary and chronicler of Field Marshal Lord Montgomery of Alamein, knew the central Mediterranean and Middle Eastern theatre as well as anyone. This accomplished Australian, one of Fleet Street's sparkling wartime jewels, wrote about events in that 'nerve' area straightly – just as he found them. No unnecessary panegyrics, only a compelling clinical portrayal of the facts, told simply but with colour and imagination, and a blessed economy of words. This is what he said about Malta, standing back, twenty-three years after the island contest:

The greatest of the battles for supply fell upon Malta. This was now turned into a hell. Malta was a base for British submarines and aircraft preying on the Axis lines of supply to Libya. In the spring of 1942, the Axis decided to obliterate that base and they wanted to starve it as well. Right through the spring they turned such blitz upon Malta as no other island or city had seen in the war. It was a siege of annihilation. One after another all the other great sieges were eclipsed – England and Odessa, Sebastopol and Tobruk. Malta became the most bombed place on earth.*

The second comment belongs to Lord James Douglas-Hamilton, author, politician, minister of the Crown, whose

---

*Alan Moorehead, *The Desert War*, Hamish Hamilton, London, 1965.

uncle, Squadron Leader Lord David Douglas-Hamilton, had played a squadron commander's part in the battle. With forty years separating him from the island's climacteric, and with his uncle's daily diary to secure the narrative, Douglas-Hamilton has gone to the heart of the strategic argument:

As General Montgomery had acknowledged, the Battle of El Alamein could not have taken place if Malta had fallen earlier in 1942. If the fighter pilots, assisted by the Army, had failed to stave off invasion, or if the Navy had been unable to fend off starvation by resupplying the Island, or if the Maltese population had refused to support the Garrison, the Battle of El Alamein would never have taken place. Supplies would have reached Rommel and the Afrika Korps, for the most part unhindered: the Afrika Korps would rapidly have built up its strength, and would probably have seized the Nile Delta. Certainly the war for North Africa and the Middle East would have taken a different course.[*]

The last reflection is Winston Churchill's. The Prime Minister saw more acutely than anyone at the time what was at stake for Malta, and for the Allies' grand design, as the German Air Force tore at the Island's guts in that dreadful spring of 1942. Writing retrospectively in his history of the Second World War, Churchill recalled the moment when the Garrison came closest to breaking point: 'During March and April all the heat was turned on Malta, and remorseless air attacks by day and night wore the Island down and pressed it to the last gasp . . .'[†]

This, then, was the place in the sun that Raoul Daddo-Langlois (pronounced Rarl Daddo-Longlay) and I came to

[*] Lord James Douglas-Hamilton MP, *The Air Battle for Malta: The Diaries of a Fighter Pilot*, Mainstream Publishing, Edinburgh, 1981; and Airlife, Shrewsbury, 1990.
[†] Winston Churchill, *The Second World War*: vol. IV, *The Hinge of Fate*, Cassell, 1951.

respect, detest and love during the height of the fighting which, in six cataclysmic months, turned the North African, and so the European war.

Wartime amateurs, and volunteers from 66 Squadron, in 10 Group of Fighter Command in the United Kingdom, we had not offered our indispensable services for the defence of Malta. Far from it. Indeed, the circumstances of our posting to the Island in February 1942 lent credence to the clerics' belief that all life here on earth is but a jigsaw puzzle and the Almighty puts its pieces together according to His view of our personal exertions, potential and usefulness.

Easy to see, then, fifty years on, how Daddo-Langlois's and my unplanned arrival in Malta on 17 February 1942, in the fallible quiet of an early spring dawn, was to fit into life's puzzle. At the time, however, such were its totally unpredictable circumstances that, in the jargon of the base-ball park, it looked very much as if the Almighty, in His inscrutable wisdom, had pitched us a curve.

## 2

# THE PAIR WAS BASIC

One here will constant be,
Come wind, come weather.
*John Bunyan*

'Who wants a posting to Burma?' The adjutant of 66 Squadron held up a piece of paper as he casually threw out the question at the pilots, gathering in front of 'A' Flight's dispersal hut before jumping into the truck which would take us to the Mess for lunch.

The Squadron was based at Portreath, on the north coast of Cornwall, and the signal had come through that morning from Headquarters, Fighter Command, relayed by 10 Group: 'Post two pilots forthwith to Air Command Headquarters, India, for service in Burma.' It was early February 1942. The Japanese threat to south-east Asia was growing alarmingly. Singapore was within days of capitulation. Rangoon would catch it next and with its fall the whole of Burma would then be at risk. It was a sombre prospect.

Meanwhile, here at Portreath, a familiar and depressingly thick and damp mist was sweeping quickly inland from the Atlantic. Already the control tower and the other squadrons' dispersals were obscured. Soon the whole of the western end of the Cornish peninsula would be shrouded in a moist, grey, moving gloom. Flying had been abandoned for the day. It was a bleak scene, calculated to lower the spirits of even the keenest squadron pilot. As an antidote, plans were being laid for some of us to dine that evening at nearby Treganna Castle, an agreeable multi-star hotel, owned in those pre-nationalization days by the Great Western Railway. There, the food, even with wartime rationing, was still good. Moreover, the daughters of the well-to-do families which had evacuated themselves to this haven from fashionable addresses in London, and the blitz, always offered an arresting and welcome change from commonplace winter evenings passed in the Mess. For the girls, most of whom had not yet thrown in their attractive lot with one of the Services, the sight of a Royal Air Force uniform with wings, and the top button of a fighter pilot's tunic left symbolically undone, was irresistible.

As the pilots' truck sped round the airfield's perimeter, Daddo-Langlois, who was sitting on the wooden bench next to me, nudged my arm. 'I'm brassed off with this. Why don't we put in for that Burma posting? Nothing could be more boring than this.'

The thought had already crossed my mind when the adjutant read out the signal. Raoul and I had now had seven months with the Squadron. The two previous commanding officers, Athol Forbes and Dizzy Allen, decorated veterans of the Battle of Britain, from whom we had been able to pick up invaluable rudiments of the day-fighting art, had both departed for a well-earned rest. Sixty-six was now a very different unit from the one we had joined the previous summer at Perranporth, just up the coast from Portreath. What's more, the operations from this part of south-west England were humdrum. With our so-called long-range Spitfire IIs, and the extra fuel tank slung, immovably, under the port wing, our offensive activities were necessarily circumscribed. Escorts across 120 miles of English Channel to the Brittany peninsula for Bomber Command's daylight attacks on the German battlecruisers *Scharnhorst* and *Gneisenau*, lying alongside in Brest harbour, were interspersed with mundane and usually uneventful patrols flown round convoys plying their way between the Scillies and Land's End *en route* for Falmouth, Plymouth or one of the other southern ports.

7

Dawn sorties out into the Atlantic in quest of the Luftwaffe's multi-engined Focke-Wulf Condors, operating with the U-boats from south-west France, never seemed to come to anything in return for the expenditure of a fair measure of nervous energy as we listened to the throb of a single Rolls-Royce Merlin engine over miles of ocean.

The fare had been varied the previous summer with occasional transfers from Cornwall up to Coltishall in East Anglia, there to provide the fighter escorts for the Blenheims of 2 Group on their low-level, and almost suicidal missions against enemy naval vessels and heavily defended convoys moving stealthily round the Frisian Islands and close in along the Dutch and Belgian coastlines to Rotterdam or Antwerp. With well over 120 miles of turbulent North Sea to cross, these were just about the most lethal operations which Bomber Command asked their crews to tackle in wartime. If I hadn't seen them at first hand from the relative safety of a Spitfire, I would never have believed the carnage. (These missions were, in fact, repeated from Malta, often by detachments of the same squadrons operating against Axis convoys sailing southwards across the Mediterranean to supply the enemy's land and air forces in Libya. Horrendous casualties also accompanied these attacks. For the crews, it was the hell of a life – while it lasted.)

But now, in deep winter, at this Cornish outpost, the likelihood of any material change in the customary daily diet seemed remote. True, I had been lucky to be given command of a flight in the Squadron after no more than four months with the unit and a bare total of 370 flying hours in my log book. However, having put this initial operational blooding behind (we never realized how fortunate we were to play ourselves in in a relatively 'quiet' Group), the desire to make a change and get a taste of fighting in a really active overseas theatre grew stronger with every week that passed.

'Never fear,' murmured the old sweats, 'but don't volunteer.' The advice cut little ice with a pair of combat-starved fighter pilots. Moreover, Raoul and I had good reason to stick together. All our service had, up till now, been spent in the same units – initially at Cambridge in one of the ground training wings, then in Canada learning to fly under the great Empire and Commonwealth Air Training Plan, and, finally, back in the United Kingdom, at the same Hurricane operational training unit at Debden, in Essex, before joining 66 in Cornwall. Ours was an easy, certain friendship, valued as much by one as by the other.

In Raoul Daddo-Langlois, the Royal Air Force's Volunteer Reserve had acquired a twenty-year-old officer of unusual capability and worth. Bright, personable and smart with a knack of making people do his bidding without working at it, his credentials were undoubtedly aided by his father's example. A product of the Royal Navy Air Service, the parent had transferred to the Royal Air Force after World War I to become one of the Service's outstanding flying boat captains, rising to the rank of group captain before retirement. A natural discipline had thus been handed down from father to son and, with it, the ability to fly aeroplanes precisely and better than the next man.

All these qualities were, however, tempered with an impatient temperament and a laudable desire to engage the enemy, features which were sometimes allowed to impair Raoul's better judgement. He was not good at weathering the periods of boredom which are inseparable from war. All this meant that, with a noticeable independence of mind and an innate honesty, he was not averse to saying directly what was in his head rather than what others might have preferred to hear. These idiosyncrasies, allied to an intense loyalty to his friends, made for the true companion.

There was, of course, much to be said in wartime for having a close comrade with whom to share the risks and the disasters, the triumphs and the gains. Pairs were a characteristic of squadron life. Maybe they owed something to the fact that, in the day-fighting role, the basis of all our operational flying – and the Germans', too, for that matter – was the pair, a pair of aircraft flying 200 yards apart in loose line abreast (the Luftwaffe called it a *rotte*). Each pilot would look inwards for the most part towards his mate. In this way, the whole sky could be covered, thus reducing to the minimum the likelihood of a surprise attack, and yet retaining all the opportunism demanded for offence.

It was a system which required total reliance of one pilot upon the other. In the face of unfavourable odds, and even stark danger, such a disciplined dependence could mean the difference, literally, between life and death. Unbreakable friendships were smelted in the fire of combat . . .

Raoul and I had no difficulty in reaching agreement over the India posting. It was clearly unlikely that a similar opportunity would arise in the near future for the pair of us to volunteer for a busy overseas theatre: for one of us, yes, but for the two, no. The chance must therefore be gripped. Our new CO, whom we barely knew, was away on leave; his second-in-command was commendably decisive. 'None of us would want to see you two go, but it's up to you.'

The adjutant sent our names to Group the same afternoon. 'Burma!' we cried, 'here we come.'

Rather less than a week later, as we were nearing the end of our embarkation leave, and without any warning, the posting was switched from India to Malta. It gave us both a jolt. We would be fighting the Axis powers, with their massive Mediterranean strength, for control of a tiny piece of rock, continuously bombed and isolated in the middle of an unfriendly sea, with no means of escape in the event of invasion. It seemed a doubtful preference to slogging it out with the Japanese in Burma, with a known escape route to India if all went sour.

It was, to be frank, an unsettling change of plan on which neither Raoul nor I was invited to offer an opinion. The die was thus irrevocably cast.

Of such twelfth-hour shifts of fortune are wars invariably made.

# 3

## CANADIAN CRITIC

The Great Western's flyer pulled uncertainly out of Paddington station. It was Friday the 13th and from the start it seemed that the engine driver was determined to give no hostages to superstition on the tedious journey to Plymouth, our point of departure.

Daddo-Langlois and I had been joined in our carriage by R. A. (Bob) Sergeant, another Spitfire pilot of solid worth, with plenty of experience of Fighter Command and 11 Group's sweeps and so-called circuses with the bombers over France. (Sholto Douglas, the C-in-C, in a graphic phrase, had referred to these early offensive operations over occupied territory as 'leaning out over France and touching the enemy'.)

Bob was an English realist and, seemingly, a well-informed one at that. He possessed in good measure what the Service in those days called 'the gen', about our destination and the route to it, about our means of travel and who would be making up the party, about the officer appointed to lead it, and some up-to-the-minute intelligence about what we might expect to find when we reached Malta. The 11 Group grapevine had clearly been at work.

I can't say that any of it exactly raised my confidence in the belief that the last-minute switch in our overseas posting from south-east Asia to the central Mediterranean would necessarily turn out for the best. Any doubts that we might be harbouring were given a definite boost when Bob began reflecting upon our chances of survival. 'I wonder,' he asked, 'how many of the first ten will come back?' I thought for a moment that he might be going to open a book and start calling the odds on the various runners. In the face of the anticipated circumstances, it was undoubtedly a realistic approach, but hardly one to lift expectations.

Yet, for my part, I remained convinced – utterly certain – that no matter what hazards might lurk along the way between the start of this adventure and its conclusion, I would prevail. This was not born of a careless 'I'll be all right, Jack' attitude; nor did it mean that before any operation – most operations – there was not a hideous 'needle' to contend with: it had nothing to do with any of this. It had everything to do with the fact that, quite irrespective of the dangers, I never thought for an instant that I wouldn't survive to see my homeland again. Not only in Malta, but in all three of my tours of operational flying, I always had this certainty of survival, so much so that I did not at any time in those five years of conflict entertain serious thought for the alternative.

I suspect that, with this confidence – faith is probably the right word – in my destiny, responsibility and risks were much easier for me to handle than they must have been for others whose apprehensions were potent and forbidding. For them, a superhuman effort must have been required to overcome, or at least subdue, such doubts.

Fortunately, I sensed this quite early on, so that when, eventually, my turn came to command, I resolved never to forget that while operations did not greatly disrupt the mental processes or feelings of the majority, there would ever be others, less fortunate, who would be thrown into a private hell by even the sight of an operation order. Yet each was a volunteer.

Indeed, when it came to recommending aircrew for decorations, I tried to do my best to recognize – right up to the end of the war – that those who found the going hardest were just as deserving of a favourable recommendation (if not more so) as the ones for whom this disagreeable business was the proverbial 'piece of cake'. I admired them for seeing it through . . .

But now, as the train wound its deliberate way westwards, through Reading, Hungerford, Frome, Taunton, Exeter and on through Totnes to Plymouth, I found some old and all-too-familiar sentiments welling up. I felt, setting out on this enterprise, just as I had as a small boy on leaving my beloved home at Sandwich in East Kent for my first school at Worthing in Sussex, at the beginning of a new term . . .

There was the last look at my prized belongings before leaving the house, the last sight of my parents, bravely waving goodbye as the train pulled away from the station, the last glances at all the old familiar landmarks . . . and the longing for the time when I would see them again. It would be the start of the holidays, and home, and mother's special dishes, and the affections of one's attentive family. Not even the passage of sixteen or seventeen years could banish such childhood dreams. Their reality was still there . . .

*Plus ça change*, I mused as I gazed reflectively out of the carriage window from my corner seat, *plus c'est la même chose*. Then I returned to the reality of the present and shrugged off my maudlin thoughts. The Royal Air Force was made of sterner, more robust stuff. Besides, I was an acting flight lieutenant, no longer a schoolboy in shorts and stockings.

A 15-hundredweight truck took the three of us, and our scanty luggage, to the Grand, an old seaport hotel which had been requisitioned for the duration. Here we, and our fellow-travellers, were to spend the night before setting off early on the morrow. The rest of the small party had already arrived by the time we got there, flown from 11 Group to Roborough – a far superior means of transport. The pilots were gathered in the hotel lounge.

The Canadian squadron leader, whom I did not know, but to whom I would later owe so much, stepped forward as I came perfunctorily to attention. His first action was to flick apart my unbuttoned service greatcoat, which I had not yet removed. A cursory glance inside confirmed the absence of any decoration underneath the wings on my tunic. A look of deprecating disdain showed at once on his face. A flight lieutenant without a gong was hardly worth a damn.

Our first impression of Stan Turner – Squadron Leader Percival Stanley Turner, already with two DFCs – who had joined the Royal Air Force on a short service commission pre-war, was distinctly unpromising. Apparently unforthcoming and uncommunicative, he took no trouble to hide his belief that anyone who came from 10 Group of Fighter Command was largely beyond the pale by comparison with his adherents from 11 Group in south-east England. Talk of Biggin, Kenley and Tangmere, and other 11 Group sector stations, floated easily about the room. Perranporth and Portreath didn't rank. Where were they, anyway? And Daddo-Langlois? That's an extraordinary name, where are you from? It was mostly clipped, monosyllabic, interrogatory conversation, if such it could be called. Talk about putting strangers at their ease!

Turner had already become something of a legend, although Raoul and I did not know it. Maybe this was one reason for the stiff reception. With 242, the Canadian Squadron in the Royal Air Force, he had fought in the shambles of the Battle of France under a poor squadron commander. After France, the Squadron had been sent to Coltishall to refit in 12 Group and find another squadron commander for the Battle of Britain which must soon follow.

When Douglas Bader, of whom he had never heard, turned up to take over the Squadron, Stan had sought out the adjutant. Peter Macdonald was a flight lieutenant from World War I and an MP. 'Say, Peter,' he said, 'who's this guy they've sent us without any legs. We had an ordinary prick in France and now they've given us a guy with tin legs. Christ!'

Many years later, at a dinner in Winnipeg, Douglas recalled how he had addressed 242 in the Squadron's dispersal hut at Coltishall for the first time. He recognized he had taken over a pretty deranged lot and so was laying it on the line and saying what was in his clear and uncluttered mind. He finished by asking whether anyone wanted to say anything. 'Horse shit!' said an unmistakable voice from the back, followed, after a pause, by , 'Sir!'

Turner was soon to make his mark with 242, at Dunkirk and in the Battle of Britain, and he became, in the process, an almost fanatical devotee of Bader and the squadron commander's leadership of 12 Group's Duxford wing. The next year – 1941 – he had followed the 'legless ace' to Tangmere where 242's former CO had been given command of the Spitfire wing in this active 11 Group sector. There, in company with Johnnie Johnson, Hugh Dundas, Ken Holden, Denis Crowley-Milling, Alan Smith and others among Fighter Command's alumni, he had become, in his own idiosyncratic way, a stand-out, eventually taking command of 145 Squadron on merit.

Now this rugged and curiously diffident exponent was being sent out to Malta to sharpen up the Island's flying, what little there was of it considering its paucity of serviceable aeroplanes. For an officer who had already had a basinful – and showed it – it was quite an undertaking. What Turner was able to accomplish in his first month in the Mediterranean deserves a place in the history books. His was an unforgettable contribution of which, at this first meeting, he gave not the slightest hint. It wasn't the prospect of what might be in store for us in Malta which concentrated his critical mind at that moment in Plymouth, but what he regarded as the total ineptitude of the Royal Navy.

In the two previous days, the German navy, taking a

supreme risk, had sailed *Scharnhorst* and *Gneisenau*, with the cruiser *Prinz Eugen*, out of Brest north-eastwards up the English Channel and through the 22-mile-wide Straits of Dover in daylight in one of the great maritime epics of the war. Profiting from a period of dirty weather and poor visibility, they were now safely anchored alongside in their north-west German ports.

It had been an astonishing operation, for the most part covered with courage and skill by hordes of the Luftwaffe's Messerschmitt 109s and Focke-Wulf 190s under the direct personal command of Adolf Galland.

Turner, like everyone else – including the Royal Navy in Plymouth – couldn't believe it. As the news came through, Stan went momentarily quite quiet. 'Shucks!' he said, and made straight for the bar . . .

It's an ill wind . . . This extraordinary escapade had the effect of projecting our leader's acute operational mind, which was by now super-allergic even to the mention of the Luftwaffe's fighter aircraft, well forward to the affairs of the next day. Having told us that we would be leaving early by Sunderland flying boat for Gibraltar, *en route* for Malta, he added a cautionary rider.

'You guys may as well know that we'll be skirting Brest in broad daylight as we head down south for the Bay of Biscay and Gib. But if it helps any, remember that, for this party with the ships, the Hun will have moved all the 109s and 190s from the Brest peninsula up to the Pas de Calais to fly the cover through the Straits. It's unlikely that they will have returned so soon. Breakfast will be at 0530.'

As he mentioned the 109s and the 190s, I noticed that Stan, out of habit, nothing else, swivelled his head round and was searching the ceiling for imaginary aircraft from five o'clock to seven o'clock, 5000 feet above.

There would be plenty of this in the days and the weeks ahead.

# 4

## OUTCLASSED

Know we not that they which run in a race run all, but
one receiveth the prize? So run, that ye may obtain.
*I Corinthians 9:24*

In the run-up to our departure from England, AOC, Malta,
had been loosing off signals right and left to bring home to
the authorities at the Air Ministry in London and Command
headquarters in Cairo the real extent of the Island's worsening air situation. Lloyd's messages were factual, colloquial
in style and invariably direct. They were also effective.
Indeed, so seriously did the hierarchy now regard matters in Malta that, in January, 1942, the Air Officer
Commanding-in-Chief, Middle East, the intellectually able
Air Marshal Sir Arthur Tedder, dispatched Group Captain
Basil Embry to Valletta to make a first-hand, straight-from-
the-shoulder report on the air picture.

Tedder had picked the right man. Embry, owing his
spiritual allegiance to the Pope in Rome, was a devout and
practising Catholic. He was also to become one of the Royal
Air Force's most formidable and successful field commanders. He was observant, decisive and fearless. He expressed
his objective opinions pungently. He was in business to win
and he never minded how many senior toes he trod on in
pursuit of the truth and in obtaining redress if things, in his
judgement, were wrong. There was no one else in the
Middle East at the time better able to provide an unexpur-
gated version of the island story.

There was, however, another reason why Embry was an
inspired choice for the job. He and Hugh Pughe Lloyd

were cast in the same mould and spoke with the same tongue. Furthermore, they had an unbreakable tie between them in having served together in the United Kingdom in 2 Group of Bomber Command, a ruthlessly aggressive entity, at a time when its casualties were at their highest. Each epitomized to a degree the spirit which animated the Group in those lethal days. Lloyd thus knew that he had in Embry not only a friend, but an ally upon whom he could utterly rely to represent the facts with force to London and Cairo.

Embry's island report, incisively accurate and plainly written, was to make an important, and yet largely unsung, contribution to Malta's ultimate victory. Without it, it is at least arguable whether the War Cabinet in London would have been sufficiently alerted to the enemy's favourable aircraft balance.

Making it clear that the Messerschmitt 109F (with the 'G' yet to come) was now 'superior in every respect to the Hurricane II', he went, as one would have expected, to the heart of the problem:

The morale of the pilots seems to be high although the obsolescent Hurricane IIs are having a certain effect on the pilots. I am informed that the German fighter pilots often fly in front of our Hurricanes in order to show off the superiority of the Me 109Fs. This is bound to have an increasingly adverse effect on the morale of the pilots. I therefore consider that every possible step should be taken to make Spitfire Vs and Kittyhawks available with the least delay.*

To drive home the operational impact of this critical imbalance between the performance of the two aircraft, Embry picked a potent comparison: 'Spitfires could climb to 25,000 feet in 15–20 minutes. Hurricanes could only

*Royal Air Force Air Historical Branch Draft Narrative: Malta (unpublished).

reach 15,000 feet by the time a raid had crossed Malta's coast from Sicily.'* He was equally blunt when it came to the squadron and pilot position. 'With constant flying over sea and cramped living conditions, fighter pilots should be changed every six months and squadrons with the Middle East every two or three months.'† He added a rider which, in the event, was to have a profound effect upon the course of the aerial contest: 'A first-class [operations] controller should be appointed.'‡

If any confirmation were needed to underscore the validity of Embry's assessment, it had come with dreadful certainty on 25 January. On this day, twenty-two Hurricane IIs from Nos 126, 185, 242 and 249 Squadrons had been scrambled to intercept an incoming raid in clear skies. Labouring to gain height to meet the advancing marauders, the pilots had been bounced by the 109s sweeping in high, fast and early in their beautifully flown, wide-open sections of four aircraft in line abreast (the Luftwaffe called a section of four aircraft a *schwärme*), with disastrous results.

Of our force of twenty-two aeroplanes, seven had been shot down while three had returned early with mechanical trouble. Four pilots had baled out, two had crash-landed and one had been shot down into the sea and the pilot killed. The Hurricane pilots had made no claims. Thus, as a result of a single first-class bounce, a third of the defenders had been wiped out and a quarter of all the serviceable fighters on the Island at that moment destroyed.

Nor was the disadvantage confined to aircraft. The brave crews of the Air–Sea Rescue launches who were to perform wonders in saving pilots shot down into the sea during the battle, were being subjected to attacks by the free-ranging 109s. On 5 February, less than a fortnight after the previous Hurricane fiasco, a high-speed launch had been attacked by

* ibid.    † ibid.    ‡ ibid.

20

Messerschmitts. Two of the crew members were killed and six others wounded. Thereafter, fighter escorts were provided for the launches when available. But serviceability and other priority needs restricted the aid; and when it could be given there was the ever-present discrepancy between the performance of the attacking aircraft and the defenders.

Embry's positive findings were indeed being vindicated.

It wasn't long before the first-fruits of Group Captain Embry's intervention were to be seen. The Deputy Chief of the Air Staff (DCAS) in London now sent Lloyd what was considered to be a significant message. It was dated 19 February and was in response to the AOC's complaint that no pilot replacements for those now operationally tired and stale had been received 'for months'.

After disclosing that fifteen pilots were being sent out by flying boat and another fifteen would follow as soon as a further aircraft was available, the DCAS added a personal touch: 'I am ensuring with C-in-C, Fighter Command, that they are a really choice lot of pilots.'* Whether the first consignment which was now about to embark at Plymouth for the Island fell into such a category was debatable. What was important was the fact that human reinforcements would arrive in Malta in a matter of a few days.

As we looked out on the grey and bleak waters of the seaplane base at Mountbatten in the early light of 14 February, three or four Sunderland flying boats were rising and falling quite perceptibly at their moorings. Even the waters in the harbour seemed to us quite choppy. The question at once arose: were the conditions safe enough for a heavily laden take-off?

* Air Historical Branch Draft Narrative: Malta (unpublished).

There was no doubt about Stan Turner's attitude. To Flight Lieutenant Dagg, the thoroughly competent and experienced captain of the aircraft, he expressed himself straightly: 'You're the captain of this aeroplane and it's up to you and your flying control masters – no one else – to make the decision. But if it's marginal, then let's get the hell out!' It was a characteristic stance.

'Getting the hell out' resulted in some pronounced buffeting and bumping as the flying boat's hull thumped against the waves while gathering speed for lift-off. The land-lubbers among us wondered whether the structure would stand up to the increasing strength of each impact. Relief showed all round (not least on Turner's face) as the captain coaxed the aircraft off the water and headed out over the English Channel. Having throttled back and settled down to a comfortable cruising speed, he set course confidently for a point well west of the Brest peninsula and well below the enemy's radar cover.

It was a curious fact of war that for a fighter pilot, accustomed to being alone in a small cockpit, doing everything busily for himself in the air, the role of passenger in a great hulk of an aircraft, with nothing whatever to do save sit, wait and listen, did not come easily. With Turner, the unease was manifested by a continuous vigil at one of the portholes on the port (enemy coast) side of the Sunderland. What good it would have done him – or anyone else – had he happened to see with his acute eyes a single or twin-engined enemy fighter was not explained. But it clearly tempered his uptight nervous system to be vigilant.

What Stan did say when he broke his long silences was that the dodgy period of the flight would stretch from about an hour and a half to two hours' flying time out, at a point roughly due west of Brest, and for another two or three hours or so as we pressed on southwards along the western extremity of the Bay of Biscay. Here operated, he said, and I sensed just a touch of apprehension in his mild transatlantic voice, the long-range fighter version of the Junkers 88, a very fine aircraft which the Luftwaffe was operating in strength from the Bordeaux area of south-west France. 'It has been causing Coastal Command and its anti-U-boat patrols one hell of a headache.'

Again, I wasn't quite sure how this intelligence was going to help us. There was nothing that he or we could do about it if the risk became a reality. Maybe it just helped him to get the information off his chest.

What these warnings did confirm to the observant follower (Raoul Daddo-Langlois noticed it, too) was that after the trials of France, Dunkirk, the Battle of Britain and the sweeps over enemy-occupied territory, all of which covered the best part of two pretty hectic operational years, Stan's nerve-ends were raw and exposed. It was a little difficult to understand what the forthcoming Malta experience was going to do for this condition save exacerbate it. After all the fighting, Stan was strung up so tight you almost felt you could 'ping' him.

Thankfully, none of the Squadron Leader's worst fears was fulfilled and soon we were out of the tricky Bay of Biscay area and pressing on southwards, well west of the Portuguese coast, past Cape St Vincent, before turning sharply south-east for Gib, where Flight Lieutenant Dagg's touchdown on the water west of the Rock was immaculate.

We had been airborne for $9\frac{1}{2}$ hours; it seemed like double the time.

The bright lights of Gibraltar and, across the Spanish frontier, Algeçiras made a striking contrast with the impenetrable blackout we had left behind. Well-stocked shops and bazaars, and food apparently in plenty, compounded the unreality of it all. It was a safe haven before the storm.

In the bar of the Bristol, Turner confided (looking round to ensure there were no eavesdroppers because the place was said to abound with spies) that we would be staying the night and all of the following day. Then, weather permitting down the 1000 miles or so of Mediterranean, we would take off in darkness and fly through the night, so timing things to touch down in Kalafrana Bay at first light on the morning of 16 February, on the third day after foregathering in Plymouth. The trip eastwards, along the French North African coast, past the enemy-held island of Pantelleria, and through the Narrows to Malta would take about 11 hours. (In fact, it took 11½ hours and, again, seemed like an eternity.)

When we went to bed that night in Gib, none of us had the slightest idea that this would be the last quiet night's sleep we should enjoy for weeks. Such was the bliss of ignorance.

The last leg down the Med, through one violent electric storm after another, was uncomfortable. There was nothing gallant about huddled figures trying to sleep on hard surfaces while the flying boat was bumping violently about in the turbulence. On our deck of the largely stripped-down aircraft, its portholes blacked out and its interior lighting dim, there were four Englishmen, an Australian and an American – a dark, sallow-skinned character, strong and upstanding, from Bobville, Texas. Hiram Aldine Putnam, with his languid southern accent, was called – inevitably – Tex. He had been numbered among those 244 selfless US volunteers who made up the three American Eagle Squadrons in the Royal Air Force – Nos 71, 121 and 133. Like several others among his compatriots in those squadrons, he had fancied the challenge of defending a small island in the sun and had volunteered for the privilege.

Companionable and agreeably relaxed – despite the circumstances – Tex made one pause and contemplated what it was that had motivated him to quit a good job in his native land, which wasn't then at war with Germany, and leave the comforts of a stable family home, to make our cause his. Like many of the other Eagle Squadron volunteers, Tex murmured something about having 'seen the curve coming' and wanting to be 'in there pitching, well ahead of the game'.

For Tex Putnam, a fine US citizen, the Malta game wasn't to last long. He was shot down and killed on 17 May while himself attacking and destroying a Junkers 88. From the silk of his damaged parachute, some of his friends had handkerchiefs made by a local Maltese seamstress. I retain one to this day, a reminder of one American's sacrifice.

In contrast to the worldly Putnam was Harry Fox, a small, dark-haired, good-looking young English pilot officer. Harry looked to me so young and fresh that I felt he must have fudged his age to get into the Service and volunteer for aircrew. He was quieter than the others in our little group, and seemingly a thinker; but his performance was later to belie first impressions. He turned out to be like a hunt terrier in the air, always searching about and sticking his aeroplane into any situation which attracted him. He was to make the most of this time in Malta. But his enthusiasm for the fight was cut short as quickly as it had blossomed. He fell – 'bumped' was then the word – on 19 March, barely a month after his arrival. We missed him.

The sixth member of our close-knit circle on the top deck (that is, besides Raoul Daddo-Langlois, Bob Sergeant, Tex Putnam, Harry Fox and myself) was an Australian sergeant with quick and confident reflexes. He was later to become a squadron leader with many enemy aircraft destroyed. Tim Goldsmith – Adrian Philip Goldsmith – was twenty and had married an English girl named Rosemary only two months before. He was a precocious twenty-year-old and was quite soon to take his place naturally and easily alongside his similarly gifted countrymen, Paul Brennan and Jack (Slim) Yarra. This trinity of talented Australians, all under twenty-two (but ages didn't seem to matter, one or two were nineteen, I was nearly twenty-seven, a few were older, we all felt much the same) would, between them, account for well over thirty enemy aircraft in combat over and around the Island before they were through. Of these three sparkling Aussies, only Tim Goldsmith would survive the war.

Here, then, was the variously assorted mix which formed part of the nucleus of reinforcing pilots who had been persuaded before they left England that the Spitfires would have reached Malta by the time they arrived – a myth which had already been exploded during our short sojourn at the Rock. Conned – and not for the first time in our service life – we were resigned, at any rate for a while, to having to stomach the Hurricane IIs against the Messerschmitt 109Fs with all the advantages which we recognized would still accrue to the Luftwaffe's fighter *staffeln* in Sicily.

We did not expect to see, with our own eyes, corroboration of Basil Embry's advice to the Air Staffs in Cairo and London so quickly. As the Sunderland flying boat touched gently down on the waters of Kalafrana Bay at the start of a perfect spring day, evidence of the deficiency of the Hurricane was provided almost at once. After twenty-one hours in the air from England, it wasn't a sight to gladden a tentative heart.

As the tender took us from the aircraft to the quayside, and we began to make our way to the nearby Mess for what would purport to be breakfast, the sirens began wailing out their warning of the Germans' first air raid of the day. Turner, who was in the van of the party, quickened his step and started scanning the brightening sky. Within moments, the sound of fighter aircraft, climbing at full bore, heralded a scene which was to issue ominous notice of events to come.

A strung-out, antiquated VIC of five Hurricanes, breathlessly clambering to gain height, was heading south-east out of the early morning haze in a palpably forlorn quest to achieve some sort of position from which to strike at the incoming raid.

High above, three sections of four Me 109s in open line-abreast formation were racing at will across the powdered sky, the 'blue note' of their slow-revving Daimler-Benz engines spelling out a message of unmistakable supremacy.

Stan Turner, empty pipe turned upside down in his mouth, gazed up, astonished, as the Hurricanes were soon lost in the haze. Stunned by what he had seen, he removed the pipe from between his teeth. 'Good God!' he muttered, and hurried on to the Mess.

# 5

## TRADITION IS SO OFTEN A SPUR

The impact of the scene we were now confronted with in Malta was overwhelming. But it wasn't just the endless air raid warnings, the crack and bark of gunfire, the scream of bombs or the extensive rubble which had once been sand-coloured stone buildings that made, for us, the impact. It wasn't only the lack of fuel and transport and, with it, the immobility, which often meant aircrew having to walk three miles from their billets. It wasn't solely the monotony of the food and the predictable diet of McConachie's stew or bully beef, local 'gharry grease' for margarine, hard biscuits, bitter 'half-cast' bread or the paucity of it all; nor was it, for that matter, the surprise at seeing the spare look of squadron pilots and the pinched, drawn faces of those who had been sweating it out on the Island for weeks and months, without rest or respite, in unequal combat with a superior enemy; nor, again, had it all to do with the diminishing aircraft strength and the absence of spare parts with which to maintain serviceability . . .

It was something much more comprehensive. It was, in fact, the primitiveness of everything and the governing lack of essentials in Malta by comparison with the well-endowed, orderly stations we had left behind so recently in Fighter Command, with their profusion of stores, supplies, equipment of all kinds and even aeroplanes. We realized that here, on this battered and isolated Island, on this piece of rock 17 miles long by 9 miles wide (no bigger than the Isle of Wight) set in a mainly hostile sea, everything had to be improvised. The do-it-yourself, make-do-and-mend, cobble-the-parts-of-three-damaged-aircraft-together-to-make-one-fly concept ruled everywhere. This was what over-whelmed us, and the remoteness of the place – 1000 miles or so from Gibraltar in the west and some 800 or 900 from Alexandria in the east, with the enemy controlling much of the coastline to the north and to the south. Once here, you were plainly here for keeps with invasion, as we were soon to discover, ever an imminent threat.

The weather was another additional adverse feature of life on this outpost. The Island was in the middle of a time of quite exceptional rainfall. Five-and-a-half inches – just double the normal average – were to fall in this the second month of the year. It played havoc with airfield and dis-persal surfaces, and surrounding roads. Mud and slush abounded. Nor were things helped, operationally, by a lack of tractors, which, like the petrol bowsers, had fallen victims to incendiaries or a simple absence of spares. Manhandling aeroplanes stuck in the mud, and drums and cans of aviation fuel (or building pens with sandbags to protect them from bombing), was not usually on a fighter pilot's slate.

But if the first impressions of a newly arrived bunch of Spitfire pilots, accustomed to being cosseted and spoon-fed on the permanent bases at home, were bleak, reflect for a moment upon the lot of the groundcrews whose job it was, in the face of privations and every known danger and discom-fort, to keep such aircraft as there were flying. Theirs was the unsung glory of the island battle. The job which they did was unsurpassed (the temptation is to write 'un-equalled') in any contest, in any theatre, of World War II.

The airframe and engine fitters, armourers, instrument and wireless repairers, signals technicians and others on the ground staff were a race apart, dedicated to a single, govern-ing aim – 'to keep the few bloody kites we've got flying'. In their struggles to accomplish this they had an advantage, one to which they would not necessarily subscribe. The senior non-commissioned officers (NCOs) who gave the lead, fashioned and held the ground effort together, were often peacetime-trained members of the Royal Air Force, frequently with extensive service behind them. They were possessed of a training and a discipline which would not entertain for an instant the possibility of packing it in under fire; and those of them who, later, became commissioned officers were steeped in knowledge and background which enabled them to spot every trick and dodge in the trade. If by cannibalizing three damaged aircraft they could conceivably bring one aircraft back on to a squadron's operational strength, nothing would be allowed to hinder the process.

The influence which the senior NCOs exerted and the astonishingly cheerful support which was spontaneously offered by the crews, made up one of the decisive factors in the Island's struggle for survival. It finds justifiable expression in one passage of the Air Historical Branch's unpublished Draft Narrative of the battle. Commenting critically upon Fighter Command's well-established habit of 'keeping their best pilots for themselves, and sending the "also rans" to the Island', the text is generous in giving praise where it was undoubtedly due:

Malta's pilots put up a superb performance in the face of great odds and difficulties which, in some ways, were greater than at the time of the most bitter air fighting in the Battle of Britain. Malta's fighter force had no defence in depth and could only operate from three bases which were frequently made unserviceable from the concentrated bombing, which resulted in the almost intolerable stresses under which air and ground crews were working. 'To defeat the enemy,' says an entry in HQ, Malta, Operations Record Book, 'we must maintain our present state of readiness. It is very hard on the men [the groundcrews] as they cannot leave their pens from 0530 each morning until 2030 hours. They are fed in their pens. We must accept these long hours. The men [the groundcrews] do so cheerfully.'

It was the journey by road north-westwards from Kalafrana,

and the airfield at Halfar, to Rabat and Mdina, standing on the high ground overlooking Takali, our aerodrome-to-be, which further lifted the lid on the developing Malta scene.

After breakfast, such as it was, we had expected to find some form of service transport waiting to take us the 8 or 10 miles past the principal airfield at Luqa and across Malta's flat, central expanse to our destination, lying roughly in the middle of the Island. 'No transport available,' they said when we inquired in the Mess. 'Haven't seen a serviceable truck here for days.'

Instead, a dirty and dilapidated civilian bus had been commissioned, driven by a splendidly high-spirited and garrulous Maltese, who would clearly have been at home in a Spitfire had we had one handy. Into this vehicle we piled with our luggage. 'Goddam this,' said Turner dismissively, as he clambered into a front seat beside me. It wasn't exactly clear to what or at whom his brief comment was directed. I assumed that it was intended to be all-embracing.

The driver was patently at pains to give himself, his vehicle and his passengers every chance of making the final pull up to the hilltop on which Rabat stands. After a couple of stops *en route* for necessary engine adjustments, he took a long run at it from the low, airfield level, and with every-thing vibrating, and the engine racing as he dropped to bottom gear, the bus finally made it to the top to a crescendo of ribaldry. Looking anxiously over the driver's shoulder from my front seat, I noticed the needle of the temperature gauge had gone off the clock. Steam was beginning to issue freely from the engine.

The Mess at Mdina, where some of us were to live happily (but on Spartan rations) for the next six turbulent months, was a fine old palace, an attractive example of fifteenth- and early sixteenth-century architecture which had been the residence of one Baron Chappelle in peacetime. As we spilled out of the bus on to the courtyard of the Xara Palace, the driver, to whom we had now become quite attached, gave us a valedictory salute. 'You'll be safe here,' he said confidently. 'Mdina is a holy city. The Holy Father will not let the Germans bomb it.' Turner gave the driver a wave, but made no comment. He was off to find Jack Satchell, the CO of Takali, whom he said he hadn't seen since Duxford and the Battle of Britain.

I sensed immediately that in this fine old walled city of Mdina, with its bastions and ramparts, and the sheer drop of a couple of hundred feet to the ground below, we were shaking hands with history. I was to find, in time, that the story of this ancient and entrancing citadel, one of the few remaining medieval and Renaissance fortified cities of Europe, with its Spanish and Siculo-Norman palaces and churches, fascinated me. In the long off-duty hours which the lack of aircraft inevitably produced, there was always something here to absorb one, some old building to see, some new facet of the city's 2000-year-old history to encounter.

Six hundred feet above sea level, with its commanding views north, east and south across the Island to the sea, Mdina – or Melita as it was called until the middle of the sixteenth century, when the Order of St John built Valletta – had been for centuries the seat of power and the natural capital of Malta.

Local history has it that perhaps 5000 years ago there was a neolithic village on the site, while there seems no doubt at all that the Phoenician adventurers founded a settlement on the obvious highpoint. However, it was the Romans, between 21 BC and AD 870, who took real advantage of the location and established a fortified city on this dominating ground.

It was at the Mdina Palace – now the site of the cathedral – that the great Paul of Tarsus, St Paul, accompanied by

St Luke ('our beloved Luke, the physician'), spent three days in AD 60, after his shipwreck, as the guest of Publius, 'the chief man of the Island'. Paul, having healed the governor's ailing father, converted Publius to Christianity, paving the way for his consecration as the first Bishop of Malta.

And it came to pass that the father of Publius lay sick of a fever and a bloody flux: to whom Paul entered in, and prayed, and laid his hands on him, and healed him. So when this was done others also which had diseases in the Island, came and were healed.*

I recalled the relevant passage because, eight years before, I had been obliged to memorize it – and much else in the Acts of the Holy Apostles – to satisfy the Cambridge examiners that I was a suitable candidate for admission to the university. How strange, I thought, that it should take a war for me to be able actually to see, at first hand, the scene of one of the Bible's stirring stories, and the site upon which was founded and built the world's first Christian church. Paul, the patron saint of Malta, had been on his way to Rome to stand trial before Caesar, a worthy harbinger of the church militant here on earth.

I learnt, too, from my on-the-spot researches, and my talks with the well-informed inhabitants, that the Arabs had succeeded the Romans and it was they, in AD 870, who had given the city its truly fortified strength, reducing its outer boundary, for security, to roughly the measure of today's periphery. Then it was the turn of the Normans, followed by the Spaniards and their religious orders – the Franciscans, Carmelites, Benedictines, Augustinians and Dominicans. (The Jesuit Order came much later, at the end of the sixteenth century.) Charles V of Aragon, overruling Alfonso V's earlier promise to unite Malta and its islands

* Acts 28:8–9.

33

'in perpetuity to the Spanish crown', took it upon himself in 1530 to make a gift of Malta and its northern island of Gozo to the Order of St John of Jerusalem to the end that they might 'perform the duties of their Religion and employ their forces and arms against the perfidious enemies of Holy Faith'.

Charles clearly knew his business, for the Knights of Malta – as the Order of St John became known – were a rugged and dedicated lot who would prove to be true to their remit. It was they and their followers who, against all the odds, saw off the Sultan of Turkey and his devilish, 40,000-strong invasion force in the first Great Siege of Malta in 1565 . . . A nice precedent, I felt, for the events which might follow in the spring and summer of 1942, rather less than 400 years later.

Napoleon and the French rather dented the legend by toppling the Knights off their perch in 1798, but their ascendency was short-lived, for no more than a couple of years later, at the turn of the century, the position was reversed. The arrogance and greed of the French in suppressing the Island's monasteries and confiscating much of the treasure in the cathedral at Mdina, was quite enough to stir the patriotic Maltese against the invader. Smart enough to encourage the British to their side, the Knights and the islanders used their new allies to force the capitulation of the French garrison. Thus were things to remain for the next 142 years until a bunch of Spitfire pilots, following the courageous exertions of their Hurricane counterparts, judged that, given the aeroplanes, the second Great Siege of Malta must stand a pretty good chance of going the way of the first.

All this seemed to me, when I had had time enough to absorb the background, to make a solid and justifiable base upon which to mount a spirited, modern defence against the Axis predator. And Mdina, our base, which, down the centuries and through all the ups and downs of history, had retained its ancient beauty, was well worth fighting for. We determined there would be a high price to pay for the Island's submission. And it seemed that Field Marshal Albert Kesselring, with the Me 109s, the Ju 87s and 88s of his Luftflotte 2, and, within it, of General Bruno Lörzer's Fliegerkorps II, sitting some 60 miles or so away across the Sicilian narrows, and supported without too much enthusiasm by the Regia Aeronautica, might be prepared to pick up the check.

# 6

## A MONTH OF HURRICANES

There may be trouble ahead . . .
Before they ask us to pay the bill
And while we still have the chance
Let's face the music and dance . . . Dance . . .
Let's face the music and dance.

*Irving Berlin*

It didn't take us twenty-four hours to realize that for the Island and for the Royal Air Force's three airfields – Takali, Luqa and Halfar (reading from north to south) – there would be trouble aplenty ahead. On 21 February, four days after our arrival at Takali, the Governor of Malta, Lieut.-General Sir William Dobbie, a serious man of stout religious faith, not much given to gaiety and laughter, and a declared protagonist of the ideals of the Plymouth Brethren, put the picture squarely to Sir Archibald Sinclair, the Secretary of State for Air, in a signal to the Air Ministry in London: 'The inferiority of our fighter aircraft to those of the enemy, in performance, has been a cause of marked depression . . .'

The discrepancy in performance between the Me 109F and the Service's old Hurricane IIs was certainly there, yet none could deny the fortitude and spirit of the pilots as they battled their antique flying machines against the dominance of the Luftwaffe.

Their record, achieved against all odds, had earned them the right to immortality. The names of the heroes were there for all to see: George Powell-Sheddon, Don Stones, James MacLachlan, Jack Satchell, Butch Barton, Bob Wells, Innes Westmacott, Mortie-Rose, Ragbags Rabagliati, Philip Wigley, Sonny Ormrod and others had, for weeks, been delivering the impossible. Nor was it the first time that some of them had done it. There were those among the select few who had been through the fire before – in France, over Dunkirk and in the Battle of Britain. No sooner was that over than they had been packed off to the Mediterranean, there to face the music in conditions even worse than those they had already experienced.

They were a dauntless, cavalier lot who made light of their trials. Unlike most of us who were now following after, many of them had had the special advantage of having learnt to fly in peacetime or as peace was slipping into war. The truth was that, until the second half of the war, by which time the amateurs among us were just about qualified to sign professional forms, their ability in the air was noticeably superior to ours. The training they had received so deliberately before the war made them 'blue chip' stock in the Royal Air Force's portfolio. Early on, they produced a more dependable yield than the somewhat speculative investments acquired in the rather volatile wartime market. They were the 'bankers' and their quality was undoubted.

However, since they had left England, the tactical flying of 11 Group and Fighter Command against the Luftwaffe's best in the sweeps over France, had undergone important changes. Gone were the old-fashioned VIC and line astern formations, reminiscent of France, Dunkirk and the Battle of Britain. 'Weavers', snaking about above a squadron formation to protect those at the back – the tail-end Charlies – and the stragglers against the attentions of Adolf Galland's aces in Jagdgeschwader 26 over Abbeville, St Omer and Lille, were now eschewed by the well-led units. In place had been substituted the basic principle of two aircraft flown hard and fast, in wide-open line abreast, with each pilot looking mostly inwards towards his mate, and covering the sky from twelve to six o'clock. That, and the loose 'finger fours', sections of four aircraft positioned like the tips of the fingers in an outstretched hand, had mostly come to stay.

Bader had developed this rudimentary formation during his leadership of the Tangmere Wing in 1941. Other leaders like Al Deere, Biggin Hill's brilliant New Zealander, and Bader's exceptional protégé, Johnnie Johnson, had been similarly minded when their chance came to command and lead. The blueprint for this modern style of fast, open and flexible flying was the product of the inventive genius of Werner Mölders, the Luftwaffe's master tactician. He had devised and flown it four or five years before in the Spanish Civil War. Now, Galland and his followers were employing it with aplomb and success over northern France. It had transformed the lot of the wretches who were positioned at the back; no longer did they feel so vulnerable or left out in the cold while those in front were cosy and secure.

The modern concept had not yet percolated the old Hurricane squadrons in Malta and this is where Percival Stanley Turner, who had flown the line-abreast, finger-four principle with such signal success with the Tangmere Wing, made his mark on the Island and at Takali in particular. In the introduction of his instant change of tactics I was a learner, a first-hand witness, an accomplice and an accessory after the fact. What Turner was to achieve against – let's face it – some initial, outmoded and deep-seated opposition in his first five or six weeks in Malta, during the critical transition from Hurricanes to Spitfires, deserves a place in the history of the Mediterranean war. It stamped the Canadian with Lloyd, the AOC, and the recently installed Group Captain A. B. Woodhall, who quickly became the Service's outstanding controller of the war, as a principal architect of victory in this gruelling contest.

From an operational standpoint, the circumstances which Stan Turner and his other newly arrived cohorts found at

Takali (and similarly at Luqa and Halfar) were lamentable and catastrophic. Counts made during February and early March revealed that, out of some sixty or seventy aircraft in varying states of damage and disrepair, there was a daily average of roundly a dozen serviceable Hurricane IIs on the Island against Kesselring's front-line strength of some 400 aircraft in Sicily supported by another 400 of Mussolini's Regia Aeronautica in Sicily, Sardinia and southern Italy.*

In terms of maintaining an effective concentration of fighter aircraft, upon which Malta's immediate future would inevitably depend, the picture was laughable – if one could see it that way. A dozen serviceable Hurricanes, out-performed and out-gunned by a mass of Me 109Fs, based with the Ju 87s and 88s little more than 60 miles away, represented a horrendous challenge. It was unrealistic to regard it other- wise. Yet the air and the groundcrews, to their eternal credit, stuck at the daily task with verve and courage.

On the personnel side, Lloyd's hand was also anything but strong. To service his 'base personnel offices, command wireless, major overhauls and all repairs to airframes and engines, the stores depots, staff of Command HQ, station filter and operations, etc.' the AOC had available '4000 other Royal Air Force ranks'. This complement, according to the Air Historical Branch's Narrative, was required to service and operate 'two bomber squadrons, one reconnais- sance squadron, five-and-a-half fighter squadrons, some fighter Blenheims and various other aircraft detachments'.

It made a blatant comparison with the abundance and plenty of the UK establishments. The Narrative offers the evidence. 'One station [in the UK],' it runs, 'with two bomber squadrons [based upon it] numbered 2000 men – with separately recruited airmen for defence.' The kick comes in the tail. 'In Malta, all airmen and soldiers worked

---

* Air Historical Branch Draft Narrative: Malta (unpublished).

a 12-hour day' on, it should be added, substandard rations.*

Another factor confronted Turner in his task of giving the Island's operational flying a collective refit. With the damage from remorseless attacks as well as from air combat, the resultant lowering of aircraft serviceability meant that there was now a heavy excess of pilots over aeroplanes to fly. Individual squadrons during this early spring period could often put up no more than a pair of Hurricanes apiece at any given moment. Thus for a squadron or flight commander, bent upon sharing out fairly the slender operational opportunities, this represented an unenviable hand to play.

To relieve the impasse, Turner, with Woodhall's support, began by creating a pool of serviceable aircraft and making it available, in turn, for nominated squadrons to draw on. Not only did this give a squadron commander a chance to put up one, two or even three sections of four serviceable aeroplanes; it also offered the opportunity for Stan to look at, assess and, where necessary, revitalize the operational characteristics of individual units. Even with this scanty force, a semblance of purpose and method began to be injected into this tenuous exercise.

It also resulted in the movement from squadron to squadron and station to station of several of the recent arrivals from England. It was a salutary and unsettling process. Random entries in my diary for our first weeks on the Island confirm starkly the extent of this game of musical chairs.

February     18     Takali: 249 Squadron.
             19     Takali: See AOC: posted to 185 Squadron
                    still at Takali.

*ibid.

| | 21 | Takali: Posted to 605 Squadron. |
| | 27 | 605 Squadron moves to Halfar/Kalafrana. |
| | 28 | Raoul (Daddo-Langlois) and I posted to 249 Squadron: Back to Takali from Halfar in a ration lorry. Cor, the bumps! |
| March | 1 | Turner says 249 is picked but not formed. Raoul and I are definitely in it. Goodo. Saw squadron billet with adjutant. |
| | 3 | All aircraft u/s: Went to Sliema with Raoul to order kit from Red Tailoring. Bombed while there. Superb bombing of Luqa by 88s. |
| | 4 | Posted (yet again) to 605 (temporarily). Flew Hurricane UP-N to Halfar. Air raid in progress. |
| | 5 | Readiness Halfar: Interception Patrol in UP-N, 1 hour 50 minutes. Bags of joy. Turner says come back to Takali. |
| | 6 | Back to Takali and 249. Thank God. |
| | 7 | Takali: No aircraft. Dispersal-pen building with Army. Sandbags galore. Beaufighters arrive Luqa. |
| | 9 | Harry Coldbeck (NZ, ex 66 Squadron, with us Perranporth, Cornwall) arrives in a PRU* Spitfire. Bless him, a splendid man. |
| | 10 | Two Interception Patrols in Spitfire VB GN-A, 50 minutes and 1 hour 05. What a party! Saw *I'm a Sweetheart* at the Rabat Plaza in evening. |

Against such a catalogue of change and counterchange, it is worth noting that, on arrival on the Island, Raoul Daddo-Langlois, Bob Sergeant, Ronnie West, Harry Fox and I from the United Kingdom, Stan Turner and Bud Connell from

*Photograph Reconnaissance Unit.

Canada, Jeff West from New Zealand, Zulu Buchanan from Rhodesia and Tiger Booth, Richard McHan and Tex Putnam, all from the United States, had been taken on the station strength at Takali. Thereafter, we had been allotted – 'posted' has much too permanent a connotation – to 249, the Gold Coast Squadron (motto: *Pugnis et Calcibus* – With Fists and Heels!) under Turner's overall command. And there, eventually, after all the interim vicissitudes, we would end up to develop a pride in the unit which could not have been surpassed elsewhere in the Royal Air Force. We began quickly to think we were the best and when, ultimately, the survivors came to take their leave and depart their separate ways, there wasn't a trace of a doubt in our minds that the original assessment was correct.

Much was owed, of course, to the lead which the Squadron's pioneers had given it. After its blooding late in World War I, and its subsequent disbandment, the unit had been reformed at Church Fenton, in Yorkshire, in May 1940 under the command of Squadron Leader John Grandy who, more than a quarter of a century later, would become Chief of the Air Staff and a Marshal of the Royal Air Force.

Grandy, whose orders were to get the Squadron operational within a month, and who was allotted two able flight commanders, Robert Alexander Barton and Ronald Gustave Kellett, to help him do it, led the unit for the greater part of the Battle of Britain. He was supported by first-class groundcrews and a strong mix of Cranwell-trained pilots who had graduated from the university air squadrons.

When, eventually, the future CAS was shot down over Kent towards the end of the battle, and wounded, command passed to the Canadian, 'Butch' Barton, the senior flight commander, who subsequently took the Squadron out to Malta in May 1941 and led it with signal distinction for the next seven months.

Meantime, Kellett had been posted early in the fighting

over south-east England to lead 303, the exceptional Polish Squadron, at Northolt. It was no coincidence that 303 and 249 became two of Fighter Command's most successful squadrons in the battle. By the time 249 arrived in Malta, with seventy-five enemy aircraft already destroyed, its pedigree had been established.

Years afterwards, the celebrated air-force historians Christopher Shores and Clive Williams were to write of 249, in the context of World War II, 'It was, without doubt, the highest scoring squadron of the British Commonwealth air forces . . .'* This may well have been so; in my judgement, it probably was so because the Squadron had tended always to be successful in the right place at the right time, i.e. when there was plenty of game to shoot at without too many high birds. But it should also be said that in my time in the House of Commons I once put down a question on the order paper to the Secretary of State for Air asking which was in fact, the top-scoring squadron and how many victories 249, in particular, had scored in World War II.

The minister's answer was that no such comparative records were available or kept and that therefore a conclusive answer could not be provided. In any case, the issue can only be of academic interest. What is important in this context is that Stan Turner's leadership of the unit in Malta's traumatic, early spring days of 1942 was to have a profound effect upon its subsequent record.

The Squadron, on the other hand, did something for Turner in return. Command of it gave him the base to conduct his crusade to modernize the Island's flying. It provided the platform he needed to discharge the responsibility which Lloyd and Woodhall had bestowed upon him and which he now set about tackling with unblinkered determination.

*

*Christopher Shores and Clive Williams, *Aces High*, Neville Spearman, London, 1966.

43

One morning – it was 24 February – Turner took me by the arm in the Mess at Mdina and led me out on to the balcony overlooking the airfield. I felt I had by now penetrated the shell which enclosed this unpredictable character. I had begun to feel comfortable with him and could understand the following he had established for himself in England. Although no one was about, he followed his usual ritual of looking round to ensure that he would not be overheard.

'Look here,' he said, 'you'll be one of the flight commanders in the Squadron and I shall look to you to help me with changing the flying pattern here. We can't have any more of these goddam VIC formations otherwise we'll all get bumped, that's for sure. I want you to learn this line-abreast stuff with me. And quickly.' He then removed the empty pipe from his mouth and with it started marking out on the dusty floor of the veranda all the line-abreast manœuvres, emphasizing the need to get the crossovers in the turns, as he put it, 'spot on'. 'This way,' he said, 'a couple of guys will never get bounced: attacked maybe, yes; but never surprised, no kidding.'

Reflective, yet impatient, he looked down at the airfield. 'They've got several serviceable aeroplanes down there this morning. If Ops have got nothing on the table* we'll grab a couple of aircraft and run the sequences through. If a raid develops while we're up, we'll get stuck into it.'

My log book shows that we were airborne for thirty-five minutes in our clapped-out Hurricane IIs. My recollection is that during that time it seemed that Stan had the throttle of his aircraft permanently 'through the gate'. It was all I could do to keep station. His taut nerves dictated his air speed. All the while, Woodhall, controlling from the 'hole' in Valletta, was in touch over the R/T, his deep, unhurried voice dispensing confidence.

*Plotting table in the Operations Room showing the incoming raids.

'Stan,' he said, rejecting the Squadron's 'Tiger' call sign, 'there are some little jobs [Me 109s] at angels 20 [20,000 feet – we were at about 8000] going south very fast. They may be working round up-sun behind you. Keep a good lookout.'

'OK, Woody,' said Stan, 'I can see them.' With that, he seemed to find a bit of extra boost and headed up towards the sun. 'We'll just have a swing round,' he said, over the R/T, 'and see if we can get at the bastards.' There wasn't a chance of it.

Nothing doing, we went back to Takali and landed having done few of the manoeuvres Stan had been talking about. We walked back to what had once been 249's dispersal hut from our aircraft in their sandbagged pens. The CO lit his pipe. 'That's it, then,' he said, 'that's all there is to it. Just remember to keep the speed up. It's no good floating about round here.'

I had seen nothing and, broadly, done nothing save fly a vibrating Hurricane flat out for half an hour, yet for some inexplicable reason I felt I had moved up into Division I of the Flying League. When he wanted to – and only when he wanted to – Stan Turner had the capacity for making a follower stand taller than he was. No kidding.

We flew those old Hurricanes for the best part of a month against the Me 109Fs before the Spitfires arrived. It was a taxing experience we could well have done without. But it taught us at first hand what the squadrons who had been wrestling with Kesselring's and Lörzer's fighters for the last two or three months, since the Luftwaffe had largely taken over from the Italians, had been up against. My good fortune was to have flown alongside Turner in the interceptions we had done together while he was still commanding the Squadron.

As a golfer, the experience reminded me of something I

had long since learnt in pre-war days. It is one of the game's truths that you cannot really tell how good a player is until you have actually played with or up against him. It's one thing to watch him on a course or a practice ground; it's another thing to match him shot for shot. So it wasn't until I had spent a fortnight with Henry Cotton at his club at Waterloo, near Brussels, three years before the war, practising with him for a couple of hours each morning and playing a round with him in the afternoon, that I came to understand how far he was ahead of his contemporary British and American rivals as a striker. He stood apart from the rest.

This analogy is applicable to Turner in the Maltese spring of 1942. In experience and all-round ability, he was on his own; but you couldn't recognize it until you had witnessed it at first hand.

Although we accepted the hazard at the time – indeed, there was nothing else for it but to lump it – the fact is that there was a terrible failure to supply Malta with up-to-date fighter aircraft commensurate with the challenge which, palpably, was going to confront the air defence. Strategically, it was an inexcusable and surprising oversight on the part of the Chiefs of Staff and the Air Staff at the Air Ministry.

Written, admittedly, years after the event, with all the advantage of hindsight, the historians of the Royal Air Force's Air Historical Branch have seized on this failure to anticipate the Island's needs. The case is unanswerable:

During the first three months of 1942, only 151 daylight enemy sorties were flown over the UK and a substantial proportion of these were sole reconnaissance flights. At the height of the Luftwaffe's assault against Malta, between February and April, the number of sorties flown against the Island amounted to more than 17,000. Malta's fighter defence consisted of three squadrons of

Hurricanes (83 aircraft of which 26 were serviceable [at peak strength]). Fighter Command disposed of 102 Squadrons comprising 2,395 aircraft of which 58 squadrons, or 1370 aircraft, were Spitfires. In squadrons, serviceable, they had 1,478 fighters, 886 of them Spitfires.

The importance of the security of the home base in the UK needs no elaboration. Nevertheless, this grave lack of balance in the Royal Air Force, at a time when the force in Malta was about to be subjected to such a severe ordeal can find no reasonable justification.*

There were other considerations which now weighed heavily with us. Apart from the aircraft position, the lack of supplies and stores had become the paramount concern. The February convoy from Alexandria, consisting of three merchant ships and a heavy naval escort of three cruisers and sixteen destroyers, was a failure. Two of the merchant vessels, the *Rowallan Castle* and the *Clan Chattan*, were sunk while the third, the *Clan Campbell*, was severely damaged and had to return to Egypt. Thus was succour, upon which we were anxiously depending, denied to us. The denial struck hard at the squadrons, but harder still at the gallant Maltese people.

This reverse came just before Turner, blunt and frank as ever, offered a categorical warning to the AOC and Woodhall together. It came at the end of his first fortnight on the Island by which time he had been able to make his own assessment of the defence. 'Either, sir,' he said to Lloyd, 'we get the Spitfires here within days, not weeks, or we're done. That's it.' There was no mistaking his purpose.

Turner's ultimatum, for that is what it amounted to, coincided with a signal, sent on 28 February, by the Chiefs of Staff in London to the Commanders-in-Chief in Cairo.

---

* Air Historical Branch, Draft Narrative: Malta (unpublished).

It left no doubt whatever about the significance which was now attached to the Island's strategic position:

Our view is that Malta is of such importance both as an air staging post and as an impediment to enemy reinforcement route that the most drastic steps are justifiable to sustain it. Even if Axis maintain their present scale of attack on Malta, thus reducing value, it will continue to be of great importance to war as a whole by containing important enemy forces during critical months.

The statement prompts an obvious query: if that was the view of the Chiefs of Staff, why was not more done earlier to redress the imbalance of the Island's fighter force with that of the enemy, standing only 60 miles away?

It came back to the CO of 249 Squadron's point. The key – indeed, the only key – to whatever chance Malta might now have of halting the slide to disaster lay in the urgent supply of Spitfires, which could only be provided from the aircraft carriers standing off some 600 or 700 miles west of the Island and sustained by an all-out effort from elements of the Royal Navy's Mediterranean fleet.

If any had thought that reinforcements of more Hurricanes from the Middle East could apply even a temporary tourniquet to the fatal haemorrhage which was now developing, the fate of 229 Squadron soon changed their minds. Its twenty-four Hurricane IIs, fitted with long-range tanks, were dispatched from Gambut to Takali and thence to Halfar. The reinforcement was completed in three separate operations embracing ten, eight and six aircraft, and covering a period of little more than a fortnight.

Within a month the Squadron was declared non-operational, thus unnecessarily underscoring the uselessness of pitting these aeroplanes against the superior machines of Kesselring's fighter force in Sicily. The Squadron, claiming no enemy aircraft destroyed during its short tenure, lost nearly half its operational pilots, either killed or wounded (four killed and five wounded), while the elimination of two-thirds of its aircraft (nine destroyed and seven damaged) reduced its operational strength to eight aeroplanes. In the circumstances, there was nothing for it save to take the Squadron out of the line.

It took until 3 August to re-equip 229 with Spitfires.

While urgent, serious problems were pressing in Gibraltar, 1000 miles away to the west, in Takali's Operations Record Book an ominous little entry appeared: 'Sale of bread and sandwiches in EFI canteens to be discontinued until further notice owing to shortage of supplies.'* Malta's darkest hour still had sixty minutes to run. It was one thing to have to fight an enemy vastly superior in numbers and equipment while always feeling hungry, it was quite another to do it with the spectre of starvation at one's elbow.

---

*This was the only source, other than outside the camp, that an airman could tap to supplement his already dwindling rations.

# 7

## INCOMPETENCE

No man's knowledge here can go beyond his experience.
*John Locke*

All now hung on the Allies' ability to feed the Spitfire Vs to the fighter squadrons in Malta – and maintain the flow in the weeks ahead. Hugh Pughe Lloyd, for whom the next couple of months would prove to be the most tortuous of his command, could see how much depended upon the success or failure of the reinforcing operations which were now about to open. The supremacy of Herr Willi Messerschmitt's Me 109F had to be met and neutralized, at least, or deafeated, at best.

There were no two ways about it. 'Operation Spotter', the code name for the Mediterranean adventure to which the Royal Navy and the Royal Air Force had now jointly set their hand, had to succeed. To this end, the aircraft carriers *Eagle* and *Argus*, supported by strong elements of the Fleet, were to be commissioned for the task.

The fly-off was planned to take place some 650 to 700 miles west of Malta and 50 miles north-east of Algiers. There was great concern about the take-off. It would be the first time that any of the pilots had flown off a carrier and *Eagle*'s flight deck was only 667 feet long. Moreover each aircraft would have to carry an extra 90 gallons of fuel – quite an additional load.

The timing had become critical. With the total failure of the February convoy from Alexandria, another attempt would surely have to be made without delay from Egypt to run the gauntlet of 'Bomb Alley' – that hazardous stretch of sea between Crete and the Benghazi blister – to replenish Malta's fast-dwindling stocks of food, fuel, ammunition and medical supplies. Only Spitfires, operating within the extremity of their range, stood a chance of providing even the minimum cover which the merchant vessels and their escort would hope for on the final run-in to Grand Harbour. No one underestimated the strength of the anticipated onslaught from the Ju 87s and 88s, and the Me 109s, of Field Marshal Kesselring's Luftflotte II and General Lörzer's Fliegerkorps II (soon to be strengthened with elements of General Hans Geisler's Fliegerkorps X from Crete and North Africa), as the ships neared the Island.

Such had been the pressures exerted by Air Marshal Tedder in Cairo, and General Dobbie and Air Vice-Marshal Lloyd in Malta, upon the Secretary of State and the Air Staff in London that the Prime Minister, the War Cabinet, Defence Committee and Chiefs of Staff could have been left in no doubt of the necessity of pressing with all urgency this major reinforcing operation.

We who awaited the arrival of the aircraft at Takali recognized fully what was now at stake. Malta is a tiny island. Word passed quickly and there were few secrets which could be withheld from us. Evidence of the people's – and the squadrons' – plight was daily before us. Even across the passage of half a century, I can still sense the ethos which enveloped us during those anxious days. Fact and rumour mingled indiscriminately with agonies and hope to charge the atmosphere.

Stan Turner, never one for soft-pedalling an issue, was as forthright with us as he had been with Lloyd and Woodhall over the Spitfire replacements. The colloquial transatlantic idiom is always effective in maximizing effect. 'You guys may as well face it. The chips are down on the table.

This goddam operation has just got to succeed. If it doesn't, God help us, no kidding.'

On my arrival in Malta I found a close friend from whom I was able to learn at first hand the ground forces' picture. Nick Harrison of the Royal Artillery, an officer of special worth, had been a contemporary of mine for three happy years at Cambridge where friendships tended to be made for life. He and I and his several Harrovian friends in Pembroke and Trinity had lived together in agreeable accord in the mid 1930s, enjoying the privileges of undergraduate life, impervious to the clouds which were then gathering over Europe.

A major now, and always immaculately turned out (but somewhat thinner than I remembered him from our well-endowed university days), Nick carried Service responsibility for the important local area bounded by Birkirkara, Mosta and Takali to the east, Dingli, Rabat and Mdina to the south-west and M'tarfa to the north. The evenings when he came to dine in our Mess or one or two of us were invited to dine with him were boisterous, convivial affairs, a blessed, if short-lived respite from the tensions of the day. Food was scanty and alcoholic sustenance hardly compatible with the table Nick had habitually kept in halcyon times at home. With him, laughter – loud guffaws of it – was never far away. He was a tonic for any flagging soul.

One morning, in this period of waiting, while 249 Squadron was still operating its old Hurricanes, I was at readiness at Takali with my 'A' Flight. We had been down on the airfield since first light and were tired as we neared the end of our half-day's stint. 'B' Flight were due to take over from us at 1300 hours.

It had been an active time, with one quite long and eventful interception with a strong enemy presence. At the end of it, a final sweep of Me 109s, ranging at will high overhead, had showed the Luftwaffe's characteristic aggression by diving from altitude in pairs in fast passing attempts to pick off our aircraft as they joined the circuit, out of ammunition and with tanks almost dry, and prepared to land. The Army's gunners, who manned the Bofors sites ringing the airfield, had been engaged in some intense and accurate shooting in our support, giving these low-flying marauders some particularly uncomfortable moments and forcing them to leave their prey and pull hard back on the stick to climb sharply away and head back northwards for Sicily and home.

The gunners were a buoyant, resolute lot who stood to their posts when the bombs were falling all about. They never flinched and on these nasty, nervy occasions, they erected a canopy of steel over the airfield under which the Squadron could slip in and land. We admired their discipline under fire. I believe our admiration was returned as we fought our corner with them.

As we came off readiness and prepared for the long slog up the dusty road to Mdina, lying amid the bastions at the hilltop, Nick appeared from the back of our broken-down dispersal hut. Threading his way through the bombed rubble, he made for a posse of pilots; he knew most of them for he was a welcome and familiar visitor during spells of readiness at Takali. Smart as ever in clean, freshly pressed fawn trousers and open-necked khaki shirt, socks properly pulled up and secured, well-tailored hat poised at a jaunty angle, highly polished brown shoes which the airfield dust couldn't dull, cane tucked firmly under his left arm, he turned towards me. A friendly yet respectful salute for a junior flight lieutenant exposed his perennial good manners.

'Laddie,' he said, 'if you're walking up to Mdina, could we go up together?' I sensed at once he had something he wanted to say.

Looking thoroughly scruffy after a morning's readiness, Mae West still draped over my shoulders, shirt drying off after its soaking during combat, hair all over the place, I was no sartorial match for my old and now more senior friend. 'Of course, Nick,' I said, 'but let's take it easy going up the hill.' I knew his brisk step so well from other days. We let the rest of the Flight go on ahead.

'A rough morning,' he began. 'How did you chaps get on? We reckoned there were sixty-plus fighters with the 88s.'

I turned the conversation away from the interception. 'Those fellows on the Bofors sites were marvellous this morning. They certainly saved one or two of the Squadron as the 109s came down to pick them off in the circuit as they were about to land.'

'Good,' said Nick, 'but I don't know how much longer they'll able to keep that up.' This led him to what he had come to say.

'Ammo is now being heavily rationed again. New orders have been issued. We really are now pretty short – not so much the light ack-ack as the heavier stuff. I'm afraid it's going to get worse if we can't get another convoy in soon. There's a limit to what the submarines and *Welshman** can bring with all the other essentials. I reckon there's enough ammo for five to six weeks, perhaps not as much. But you'll get priority here at Takali as the fighter base.'

He paused before going on. 'I gather the Spitfires are expected here in a couple of days. The hell of a lot is going to turn on them. Will they come to you in 249? The Hun is bound to monitor their progress down the Med and make a dead set at Takali after they've touched down.'

This proved to be a prophetic comment, but Nick wasn't done yet.

'We're getting anxious now about the invasion threat. The Hun will know that stocks here are getting low without

*Royal Navy's fast mine-laying cruiser.

a convoy for weeks. He and the Eyetyes might reckon that it was worth having a go for it in the next couple of months. The general* was on about it yesterday. The build-up of aircraft in Sicily is going on all the time. We wonder whether it can only be for the bombing of Malta. I believe PRU† at Luqa are stepping up their coverage of the Sicilian airfields and the areas close to where gliders and airborne forces would have to gather.'

We had got to the top of the hill and were about to turn right for Rabat and Mdina before Nick had finished. Then he broke away to continue his rounds. 'Come and dine tonight if you're doing nothing.' The invitation was his parting shot. 'Bring a couple more of your chaps if you'd like to.'

The exchanges with Nick fastened my mind upon imminent events and the proximity of the Spitfire delivery. His realism was not particularly comforting, and yet I am quite sure that at that finely balanced moment neither he nor I nor any of the members of 249 Squadron really gave serious thought to the possibility of invasion, surrender and defeat. Such was the confidence we had in our destiny.

Stan Turner was just getting up from the table as I walked into the dining room of the Xara Palace for lunch. He spoke briefly. 'I'd like to have a word when you've finished your food. There's some background you ought to know. I've seen the AOC and Woody this morning. Come out on to the balcony when you've finished.'

Two slices of bully beef later, I joined Stan on the veranda; he was by himself, gazing pensively out across the airfield and Malta's flat central plain to Grand Harbour and the sea. 'Look,' he said, 'there's some goddam cock-up

---

*Major-General C. T. Beckett.
†Photographic Reconnaissance Unit.

with the Spits in Gibraltar. Woody and the AOC are livid about it. They didn't go into a lot of detail, but I gather some modifications have got to be made to the aircraft before they can take off from the carriers. Something to do with the overload tanks, I believe. It's the hell of a nuisance. They won't be here for two days, possibly more. We'll be told the zero hour for arrival.'

The 'goddam cock-up' in Gibraltar was an understatement. What had occurred was, in such an emergency, almost incomprehensible.

The reinforcing operation had originally been scheduled for 1 February. There had been nine long, tedious months of discussion between the Admiralty and the Air Ministry when it was accepted that only by aircraft carrier could Malta be supplied with Spitfires. And this wouldn't be easy. To avoid unnecessary hazards, the fly-off should take place no more than 300 nautical miles or so east of Gibraltar; even that would subject the Fleet to submarine exposure. Further on, the Luftwaffe could come into play with its bases in North Africa and Sardinia. However, with the large, 90-gallon drop tanks slung under the belly the Spitfires could fly the 650–700 miles to the Island.

Other problems had loomed. It was found that only the carriers *Eagle*, *Argus*, *Hermes*, *Furious* and *Indomitable* were technically capable of accommodating the Spitfires. On other carriers the aircraft would have to be dismantled as the lifts weren't wide enough to take them in their assembled state. It took thirty man-hours to dismantle a Spitfire and thirty-five to reassemble it – hardly an acceptable exercise for a Naval captain bent upon proceeding to an advanced fly-off point, completing the dispatch and returning to port, all the while being exposed to varying dangers of attack. Few of the suitable carriers were readily available. The Royal Navy's commitments in the Atlantic, the Indian

Ocean, the Mediterranean itself and home waters were stretching their resources to the limit.

The first attempted fly-off from *Eagle* in the early morning of 28 February 1942 had been a fiasco due to what was loosely described as 'petrol supply difficulties with the extra tanks' which the fighters were carrying. The fault – a comparatively simple one – was causing an airlock between the spring-loaded joint on the aircraft and a rubber ring on the outlet supply pipe on the long-range drop tank. The embarrassment for the Royal Air Force was acute, the annoyance of the Royal Navy understandable.

The fault was one thing; it was when it was found that none of the long-range tanks had been tested before leaving the United Kingdom that irritation turned to fury. Further, when the armourers inspected the Spitfires' cannons, it was found that they required important adjustments before they could be fired. They hadn't been air-tested before leaving the United Kingdom.

If this wasn't enough, when the fitters and riggers came to look for spares for the aircraft they were found to be missing. This, in turn, meant that one precious aeroplane from the delivery complement had to be taken out and cannibalized to provide the parts which were needed. It represented a catalogue of omission, oversight and inefficiency which, to be fair, was totally out of character with the normal, organized supervision which the operational squadrons of the Royal Air Force usually enjoyed.

When the details of this sad business reached the Air Ministry in London, it provoked a justifiably critical minute from Air Chief Marshal Sir Wilfrid Freeman, the estimable Vice-Chief of the Air Staff, to the Deputy Air Member for Supply and Organization:

The CAS had great difficulty in obtaining the use of a carrier for this operation. These failures are unfortunate, put CAS in an impossible position and bring discredit to the Service. Apart from this, it is clearly wrong to expect pilots to take off on a hazardous flight, under abnormal conditions, with an untested petrol system and unsatisfactory armament.*

Once the trouble with the fuel supply system in the long-range tanks had been uncovered, tests were immediately undertaken in England, with Vickers' Chief Designer present. A modification was at once devised and the details rushed to the senior engineer officer in Gibraltar.

The old adage 'It never rains but it pours' was now finding practical – almost ludicrous – testimony. On the eve of the second attempted fly-off another major, and equally unexpected, reverse arose. So apprehensive were the planners in the United Kingdom about the Spitfire leaders' ability to navigate their way to Malta down nearly 700 miles of the Mediterranean that it was concluded to be essential to provide Blenheims, with trained crews, to act as navigators.

Although experience with able Spitfire leaders eventually showed this to be quite unnecessary, the decision was understandable. While the losses from these reinforcing operations both before and after 'Spotter' worked out at rather less than 5 per cent, there had been one appalling mix-up on 17 November 1940, in the earliest days of these supply missions. Then, eight out of twelve Hurricanes bound for Malta were lost after flying off the carrier *Argus*. None perished as a result of enemy action; all ran out of fuel while short of the Island, the result of inept and slapdash planning on the part of the two Services which were responsible for the operation.

Eight Blenheims were, therefore, flown down to Gibraltar from Portreath in Cornwall. Their remit would be to rendez-vous with the Fleet at first light at the fly-off point, pick up

* Air Historical Branch Draft Narrative: Malta (unpublished).

the Spitfires as they set course for Malta and take them on safely to the Island.

The rest of the story hardly bears telling. On arrival at Gibraltar, all, repeat all, the eight Blenheims were found on inspection to be in what was charitably described as 'poor condition'. The fitters and riggers on the Rock called them 'bloody ropey'. One crashed due to engine failure, another on account of trouble with its hydraulics. Nor was that the end of it. Of the eight crews sent out from England for this vital operation, four were found to have insufficient experience to take off from Gibraltar at night, fly through two or three hours of darkness and make a precisely timed, pinpoint rendezvous with the Fleet at first light. Accurate co-ordination and timing were essential to allow the Spitfires to take off at the designated hour and so control the timing of their arrival in Malta where a planned reception would be laid on.

Only one genuinely experienced navigator was found among the crews. The others were mostly fresh out of an operational training unit with virtually no operational experience in their log books. Moreover, the two navigators who were alleged to have been 'specially selected' for this operation by 2 Group of Bomber Command – the famous Blenheim Group of 1940 and '41 – turned out to be, when tested, 'much below average'.

It was a pitiful tale, the consequences of which could have proved disastrous to the Island's cause. For sheer incompetence it would have taken some beating. The truth was, of course, that when squadrons or other units in England were asked to detail pilots or crews for overseas service up to around the middle of World War II, they usually got rid of the people (and aircraft) they least wanted to keep. We ultimately got this changed in Malta as a result of strenuous representations, but it took some time for the message to get through and be implemented.

*

When Operation Spotter did eventually get under way, the Axis powers, through their various sources and agencies, were well aware of the Allies' intentions and timings. *Eagle* and the rest of the Fleet were shadowed for nine consecutive hours as the great concourse of ships sailed eastwards down the Mediterranean to the dispatch point. Predictably, the time-keeping of the Blenheim crews in rendezvousing with the carrier left much to be desired, and all the while the operation was being accurately monitored by the enemy. An announcement by Rome radio, courtesy of the Royal Air Force, let the Italian people into the well-kept secret that a reinforcing operation involving Spitfires for Malta was in progress, with all relevant details being freely given.

General Lörzer's Fliegerkorps II in Sicily had thus obtained all the advance notice it required to ensure a lively reception for the new arrivals after touchdown. The marvel was that all fifteen Spitfires and their escorting Blenheims reached the Island safely.

In the post-mortem which followed, the senior officer of the Royal Navy's 'H' Force, the means by which the first fly-off had miraculously succeeded, provided the Lords of the Admiralty with a scathing signal the contents of which would serve as convenient ammunition for passing to the junior Service in London:

Connecting up of Blenheims [from Gibraltar] with Spitfires was always giving cause for anxiety despite excellent visibility. Inability of Blenheim crews to take off from Gib in dark, irregularity of their time-keeping . . . and *Eagle*'s inability to communicate with them, and their small margin of endurance, created difficulties any of which might have jeopardised the operation.*

The implied criticism was wholly justified.

A final, depressing postscript to this discreditable saga

*Air Historical Branch Draft Narrative: Malta (unpublished).

had yet to be written. The difficulties and delays which had arisen over the initial dispatch meant that the delivery of the balance of the Spitfires in this consignment required *Eagle* and its supporting escort to make two further sorties down the Med – on 21 March and again on the 29th. The Royal Navy wasn't exactly having a ball in Gibraltar at the prospect.

True to form, trouble recurred with the Blenheims and their crews. Serviceability at Gib once more fell below the level of events. When the aircraft were made operational, there then followed an abysmal performance on the part of the crews. Their failure to rendezvous with 'H' Force at the correct time and in the prescribed manner, set off an unfortunate chain reaction.

Again, that wasn't the end of it. The gremlins which had bewitched the operation from the start still had a last hand to play. The Air Historical Branch's Narrative puts it bluntly: 'Due to an unwarrantable error of judgement [the pilot of the leading Blenheim] considered the head wind [to be] too strong to permit safe passage to Malta . . .' Whether it was truly 'an unwarrantable error of judgement' or a lack of something else far more heinous is no doubt arguable. What is not open to debate is that only nine of the sixteen Spitfires could make the journey on 21 March, the remaining seven having to follow on the 29th – and then only after two of the navigating Blenheims, for reason or reasons unknown, had run into further difficulties and had had to return to Gibraltar.

No wonder the Chief of the Air Staff felt constrained to put a brief minute on the appropriate file: 'It's quicker by rail.'*

* ibid.

# 8

## QUALITY NOT QUANTITY

This is not the end. It is not even the beginning of the
end. But it is, perhaps, the end of the beginning.
*Winston S. Churchill, Mansion House,
City of London, 10 November 1942*

The sight of the first Spitfires landing at Takali acted as a
fillip for the pilots who had been waiting for weeks, with
increasing exasperation, for their arrival. Like small boys
delving excitedly into their stockings at dawn on Christmas
Day, so we rushed down the hill from Mdina to the airfield
to touch and stroke our new toys. No Christmas or birthday
morning in our short lives had ever produced such genuinely
longed-for presents. Nor was Stan Turner slow in exerting
his substantial influence to acquire the new aircraft for the
Squadron. 'If it's the last goddam thing that I do, I'm going
to see that 249 is re-equipped with these airplanes first.'

Stan was true to his word, but the trouble was there were
too few to go round. The reinforcing delays in Gibraltar
had denied us the impact which would have accrued had
the second batch of sixteen Spitfires, out of the total consignment, been delivered to the Island within a few days of the
first, the original intention. For the time being, therefore,
the earlier plan of pooling the resources of serviceable aircraft and allowing squadrons to draw on them according to
their state of readiness, had to remain in force. It took some
of the shine off the operation.

For the most part, 249 found itself sharing living quarters
in the Mess, and aircraft on the airfield, with 126 Squadron,
a fine lot, with an engaging US Eagle Squadron influence
among its members. Such was the natural discipline of the

two units, and the customary give-and-take of the air, that the small injustices, when they arose, were accepted with an uncomplaining grace. Much more troublesome was the daily reduction of these beautiful new aeroplanes as the accurate German onslaught and regular combat damage combined to take their toll.

The Luftwaffe's determination to press its attack on Takali and against the Spitfires in their dispersed, sand-bagged pens meant that the airfield was frequently unserviceable despite the heroics of the Army's repairers. Thus we had to move across to Luqa, and its larger confines, only to be followed by Bruno Lörzer's dashing minions, creeping up behind us like some progressive bush fire.

Even so, the fact that we had got our hands at last on a small number of what the connoisseurs called 'the greatest defensive fighter aeroplane of the War', was enough to maintain our buoyant spirits. With 249's finely drilled flying, and the good conceit we had already developed in our ability, we felt we were at least back in business. Woodhall's brilliant controlling from the Operations Room underground in Valletta added to the new-found confidence.

The numerical odds might be stacked heavily against us, but mount for mount and man for man we knew we had an unmistakable edge over our opponents. For the past weeks it had been like having to sit in the cockpit with one arm strapped to one's side. Up to a point, it is quality in the air, not quantity, which scores. We sensed, then, that at last this was the end of a thoroughly unequal beginning.

The Luftwaffe's answer to the arrival of the Spitfires was immediate and positive. Apart from increasing the weight of his bombing attacks, Lörzer simply stepped up the strength of the fighter escorts. The adverse odds once more rose sharply.

Fresh complexities accompanied this new phase in the

fighting. They sprung principally from the heavy excess of pilots over serviceable aircraft to fly which was now building up. Had the morale of the Squadron not been on a high and rock-solid level it could have had serious and damaging consequences. As a flight commander, it was my job to ensure, as far as I could, that the opportunities for getting to grips with the enemy were fairly shared. With the current aircraft losses, this was by no means easy.

My own case makes a good example of the problem we faced. Allowing for the fact that I, obviously, had to set an example of selflessness, I reckoned I was myself lucky to be able to record eleven hours and ten minutes of combat flying in my log book between 9 March, the date of my first Spitfire sortie, and the end of the month. This was about a third of the amount of operational flying – perhaps rather less – than I would normally have expected to get with a fighter squadron in south-east England. However, in terms of close, hand-to-hand combat, it was probably something like six times as much as I would have anticipated experiencing in the fighter sweeps and circuses with the medium bombers over northern France. Such was the practical difference between operating over enemy-occupied Europe at this time and the daily fare we had grown accustomed to expect over and around the Island.

The discrepancy at once exposes the reason why it was an act of criminal negligence for a group, sector or squadron in Fighter Command in the United Kingdom to post a fighter pilot without combat or at least genuine operational experience to Malta purely for the ungallant purpose of getting rid of an officer or NCO who was not worth his salt in the air or didn't fit in with the unit. The unfortunate victims of this frequent practice seldom survived more than a fortnight in the Mediterranean cauldron. Very often it was less than a week.

*

It was an operational truism in the squadrons of the Royal Air Force that the more a pilot flew the more, generally, he would want to fly. The converse was also largely true. Inactivity numbed the enthusiasm and, with a certain type of character, promoted apprehension. A good leader would always work a squadron or a wing hard. In Malta this wasn't possible in the rough spring of 1942. Admittedly, the work was intense and hazardous while we were in the air, but its volume, by comparison with the pattern of western Europe, was diminutive. It made for enforced idleness and this affected pilots in different ways, most of them adversely. Principal among them was the time which it offered to think and to brood over the odds facing us, the chances of survival, the enemy's intentions about invasion and, on a different tack, what might be going on at home. Mail was infrequent and London newspapers, when we got them, were often a month old.

We lived a life far removed from the habitat for which virile young men customarily yearn. 'If you aren't doing it, you're talking about it. If you aren't talking about it, you're thinking about it. You're all the same, you lot.' The WAAF's* celebrated taunt after seeing off her frustrated pilot pursuer wasn't heard in Malta in those spartan days. And what's more we lived our life on an island the size of a pocket handkerchief from 25,000 feet, which seemed to get smaller the longer one stayed on it. The constant bombing and the alerts, the siege conditions from which there was no realistic means of escape, the ever-present threat of airborne attack (Crete had set a well-cited precedent a year before), made for an unsettling, claustrophobic existence which wasn't helped by having time to ponder.

For the Maltese, of course, it was far worse. Mostly, they were gathered – herded is a better word – in Valletta and its

*Women's Auxiliary Air Force.

close-knit suburbs, bombed, literally, to death, with food and water short and getting shorter; hygiene a travesty; days and nights spent in caves and shelters; fresh air losing the contest with the strengthening stench of bad drains and sewage; endless houses lost and homelessness rampant . . . And, unlike us, they had nothing to hit back with save their spirit and their unwavering faith.

There was a stoic courage and buoyancy in the East End of London during the worst of the Blitz which had never been exceeded at any time elsewhere in the world. It was matched, mother for mother, child for child, family for family, ruin for ruin in Malta in those terrible months of March and April 1942. Bravery of that quality has to be seen at first hand; it cannot be imagined. It was this little island's 'finest hour', but I doubt whether its people realized it – not, perhaps, until King George VI, himself a monarch of unyielding resolve, awarded them, in an act of genius, the George Cross. It made them realize they were special.

It was the lack of commonplace comforts and facilities in this unnatural environment which made life so difficult for the squadrons and their commanders. To pick out a few now is to underscore their reality.

The absence of transport for anything save the most essential operational purpose (and even then there was little of it) proved, for me, the most frustrating constraint. The inability to ring up the Motor Transport (MT) Section (such as it was) and get a car, a jeep or a truck to take members of one's Flight into Valletta to see a movie (usually stopped half a dozen times for air raids or alerts in a full-length film) or go to a bar, club or restaurant for a drink or a meal, was profoundly inhibiting.

Movement had generally to be on foot. Reliable bicycles, with decent tyres, capable of being ridden any distance were in short supply and, in any case, impossible to keep.

Local animal-drawn vehicles – karozzas, gharries and the like – had distance limitations. Hitchhiking offered few fruits and for those who lived in Mdina or Rabat any premeditated excursion had to end with the unavoidable pull up the hill, rendered less attractive as spring turned into summer and the heat of the noonday sun beat down upon the arid and dusty land.

My dominant recollection of attempts to mitigate the boredom of long off-duty hours is of walks – endless walks with Raoul Daddo-Langlois and Norman MacQueen, a native of Rhyl, in north Wales, one of the stars in 249's firmament, a modest and transparently honest, fair and curly-haired young flight lieutenant, with attractive good looks and a personality to match. We used to walk the few miles (occasionally we could rake up three serviceable bicycles) along the rough, stony roads to Luqa to see Harry Coldbeck, the New Zealand ,fighter-turned-photographic-reconnaissance-pilot who used to be airborne three or four days a week in his unarmed, blue Spitfire taking pictures of the Sicilian airfields and the harbours on the Italian mainland right up to Naples and beyond. His was an exacting and excessively demanding role which required a durable courage.

Harry, one of the most dependable of Commonwealth citizens – as we had learnt earlier in 66 Squadron in England – was usually up to date with news of the enemy. I felt he ought to have been writing the Stop Press column – the 'fudge', we called it in Fleet Street – for an island evening newspaper. He was invariably well-informed and his first-hand sightings were always tempered with a sound and discerning judgement. He would have made a good bishop, and his flock would have trusted him and respected him for his principles. The nature of his job meant that he had to be selective in his choice of friends – and of his audience. Raoul, Norman and I were happily numbered within his tightly circumscribed and privileged circle. Ours became an 'impregnable quadrilateral', built on trust and fashioned out of respect and friendship. We met frequently at Luqa or Takali.

With the aircrews' lively and impatient minds, it was the absence of anything but the very minimal degree of entertainment and recreation to fill the idle hours which so irked us. By the late spring of 1942, when Malta was being 'pressed to its last gasp', the social life of the Island had largely fallen away. This was in contrast to the conditions of 1941 when the Regia Aeronautica, rather than the Luftwaffe, was keeping the Garrison at bay.

There were, of course, still the socially conscious and well-regarded Maltese families who gave sanctuary and, indeed, hospitality to the chosen few. How they were able, with all the known privations, to dispense such kindness and consideration was something at which we could only marvel. However, they took few chances with their daughters who were kept on a relatively tight and well-chaperoned rein. Even so, for Nick Harrison, who had already played out a long innings on the Island and made his distinctive mark upon what remained of Malta's social scene, this never seemed to be much of an impediment. As one might have expected, such was his accomplished technique that he remained a trusted, eligible and sought-after guest.

For me, Nick became an ally, contriving discreetly, whenever there was a chance, of manoeuvring me on to some small and select guest list. I felt the Army had a head start in this rarefied field. Maybe it was because their representatives were a more constant lot. They had arrived earlier and were known to be staying longer. The Royal Air Force clearly tended to be regarded as more inflammable – and more transient – material. Moreover, Nick, through his mysterious Army sources and regimental messing responsibilities, appeared to be able to conjure transport out of a vacuum in a way which no one else I came across in Malta could even attempt to equal. He played his winning, social card with taste and good manners, always remembering to show extrovert admiration for his hostess's efforts and attractions. He was of that rare Service species which seemed to be *persona grata* in the higher reaches of the Island's social life. The times when he enabled me to benefit from his carefully conceived groundwork were happy interludes in an otherwise humdrum and barren scene.

The fact was that at this nadir in Malta's fortunes, the other sex – apart, of course, from the hard-working professionals readily available in the clip-joints, nightclubs and sleazy bars along Valletta's Street called Straight, in the area known to seafarers as The Gut, was largely out of reach for the majority of those who flew the Spitfires. Certainly, it was in much shorter supply than is deemed to be healthy or natural for sex-denied young men. Aircrew, daily facing the extreme pressures of operational work, needed the mitigating company of women to preserve a balance in their testing lives.

Be that as it may, there were welcoming havens from the fire of battle and from their rather special owners who took the Royal Air Force to their hearts. Memorable among them was the Scicluna family, who, at Naxxar, offered the Service their Parisio Palace with one of the finest high-walled gardens in all the Mediterranean theatre. Here, the Marquis and Marchioness gave refuge to families and, later, to aircrew for lodging and a Mess. Beyond this, there were invitations to the family's Dragonara Palace beside St George's Bay, on the Island's east coast. Tennis, swimming and tea were on offer when operations allowed, a blessed change from Takali's dust and heat.

For 249 Squadron too, the Pullicino family, whose head, Sir Philip Pullicino, was Malta's Attorney-General and Legal Adviser to the Forces, held out a welcoming hand at the Bastions in Mdina to our broad Commonwealth and UK mix. Here, again, was another enchanting period house and garden situated at the northern end of the old city with its views from the ramparts across the valley to Imtarfa and north-eastwards to St Paul's Bay and the Sicilian Narrows beyond.

Johnny Plagis, our formidable Greek-ancestored Rhodesian, who became the Squadron's stand-out in the pre-George Beurling era, surrendered his heart to Anne Pullicino and, in the process, left other contenders trailing. It was understandable for here was a girl with arresting ways and a habit (I suspected it was artfully contrived) of picking up Service jargon and then giving it an unfamiliar twist.

For Donald McLeod of 126 Squadron, an American from Norwich, Connecticut, an ex-121 (Eagle) Squadron character, with no noticeable inhibitions, she coined a catching epithet. Mac's flow of transatlantic conversation coloured events and brought individuals graphically to life. In speech, he was the antithesis of the reserved Englishman. Anne Pullicino thought Mac was a card and felt she had read him aright. 'Mac,' she said one day, in the hearing of a few of us, 'is a great shoot-liner.'

Few, thereafter, escaped the appellation.

There was a third friendly port of call during the Island's storms to which Nick Harrison and I, and many others, were fortunate in being able to have recourse. Mabel Strickland, whose name and family were synonymous with *The Times of Malta*, cared about the armed forces, and her Villa Bologna at Attard reflected that warmth. My pre-war journalistic career with Beaverbrook Newspapers in London made common ground between us, and gave me the chance, now and then, to banish off-duty boredom by visiting the newspaper's premises in St Paul's Street, Valletta. There I sensed again the nostalgic smell of newsprint and printer's ink. Mabel Strickland's deputy, Mr J. Olivieri Monroe, was

always ready with a welcome, recognizing a young newspaperman's interest. He encouraged my visits.

Fleet Street's production of newspapers at the peak of
the London Blitz, like the courage of its East End readers,
mark a remarkable chapter in the story of British journalism.
But no newspaper in Fleet Street could surpass the production record of *The Times of Malta* in the eventful days and
nights of 1942 when its offices lay so close to the centre of
the Luftwaffe's targets. Never once in all those times did
the paper fail to appear. How the staff did it was another of
Malta's wartime wonders. Whenever I saw them at work in
such conditions I felt reflected pride in knowing that these
representatives of my peacetime profession were writing a
lead story in world history. Mabel Strickland's OBE,
awarded in 1944, a year after the lifting of the siege, was
a symbol of her own – and the newspaper's – dedicated
courage.

Considering all these extensive periods of inactivity and
boredom interspersed with moments of hectic endeavour, it
was perhaps surprising that boozing among aircrew was at a
low level. It was certainly much less than was the case with
a number of the day fighter squadrons in England. True,
there were the occasional squadron 'blinds' in the Mess, in
Godfrey Caruana's bar in the Strada Reale, Valletta's main
thoroughfare, the Union Club or in some other desirable
watering-place in the capital. These were normally to cel-
ebrate the award of a squadron 'gong', a farewell, a promotion or a particularly good enemy 'bag' for the day. They
gave the pilots a temporary release from the tensions and
pressures which were preying on their minds. With a bunch
of exuberant fighter pilots, living that kind of knife-edged
life, it would have been unnatural indeed had this not been
so.

However, the steady (but pretty innocuous) intake of

alcohol reminiscent of some of the squadrons at home, wasn't there. It was not through a lack of the 'hard stuff'. Whisky and gin, unlike other necessities, were relatively plentiful. So were reasonably acceptable wines although the beer was largely undrinkable. It was quite simply because pilots who had survived a fortnight or so on the Island knew instinctively that to compete in that lethal arena, with the odds stacked so heavily against the defence, demanded a sharpness of mind and eye which an excess of alcohol was unlikely to assist. Nor in that kind of class was the age-old, morning-after remedy of sitting for 10 minutes in the cockpit of a Spitfire with a mask on and the oxygen turned up to full bore the panacea it was held to be for all overindulgent ills. Malta was not such a civilized ball game. It was a rough and ruthless, swift-moving business which required something rather better than 100 per cent efficiency. Booze, most realized, couldn't provide it.

So much, then, for the habits of the fighter pilots in the Mediterranean spring and summer of 1942. For the groundcrews, whose aim from dawn to dusk – and often in the workshops through the night – was to keep the 'effing kites flying', cannibalizing one to maintain the serviceability of another, it was an unrelenting struggle with adversity. Bombed at work (but still carrying on), largely denied transport, often undernourished and always short of spares and sometimes tools, it was a dispiriting existence. Yet never did they openly show it. Their morale, despite the usual vociferous protests, matched that of the pilots whom they sustained. They were manifestly so much a part of the joint effort that they felt – and the pilots encouraged it – that they were playing in the same team, in the same colours and in their rightful place on the field.

While their job might, perforce, keep them working in the dispersal pens or in caves cut into the hillside, their intimate involvement in the daily battle raging thousands of feet above was recognized by all. In a sense, the Squadron might have been standing proxy for them in the daily cut and thrust of combat.

If the pilots knew that their tour of duty on the Island would be limited to six months (it was reduced to nearer three as the pressures escalated), the groundcrews' expectation of service was measured in years. Some had come out to the Island in 1940, but far more had arrived early in 1941. If they survived – and Malta remained free from invasion – they knew they were there ostensibly for keeps. It was scarcely an uplifting prospect.

Of these dependable and long-serving characters, 249 Squadron's Jim Somerville – Corporal James Somerville, a redoubtable Scot from West Lothian and an airframe fitter at that – makes as good an example as any. He was on the Island for three straight years, from April 1941 to March 1944, most of the time being spent at Takali throughout the mounting crescendo of attacks on the base.

Jim, off duty at the time, had the distinction of being an eyewitness to the incident, now highly embellished, when, at 1640 hours on 9 April 1942, during a Luftwaffe attack on Takali, a 'sprayed' German bomb penetrated the famous unsupported dome of the adjacent Mosta church, fell to the floor, yet failed to explode. Those who were gathered in the church at the time may well have felt that the hand of the Lord was resting upon their collective shoulder.

The dome, the third largest in the world, although pierced, astonishingly remained intact, giving credence to Somerville's belief that the bomb, variously estimated since to have weighed anything from 500 to 2000 kg, was in fact one of 50 kg, the type used frequently by the Luftwaffe in its attacks against airfield targets. Jim, who, at the time, was billeted with others among 249's groundcrews in Mosta village, little more than 100 yards from the church, gave 'thirty to forty' as his estimate of the number inside the church when the incident occurred, suggesting that a congregation of 300, which has since come to be regarded as something of an authoritative guesstimate, may well have been wide of the mark.

Whatever the circumstances – and certainly those then present were dead lucky – the event made a diversionary talking point around the dispersal pens at Takali the next day.

The groundcrews who, under their officers and NCOs, supported the operational commands of the Royal Air Force at home and overseas in World War II, performed a prodigious service and got precious little for it. But I doubt whether there was another theatre where, taking account of all factors – the concentration and duration of the bombing, and the ever-present threat of invasion with the lack of practical means of escape – their contribution to the Allied cause ranked higher.

A brief, staccato entry in Takali's Operations Record Book about this time gave a reality to the airmen's lot: 'Cut in rations ... Difficult [now] to feed men adequately ... Men suffering from trouble with their feet owing to lack of boots and shoes ...' As a 'feeling' flight commander, I found it difficult in such conditions to come down to the airfield for dawn readiness of a morning and ask the flight sergeant in charge: 'Flight, how many serviceable aircraft have we got on the strength today?' And if the answer was, say, five, then to add the rider: 'Do you expect any more within a couple of hours?'

I knew the airmen were giving more than their best. Yet there was nothing further we could do in return to make their life better ... Characteristically, they accepted it without moaning and just stayed stuck in ...

# PART TWO

# 'PRESSED TO THE LAST GASP'

# 9

## THE WINDS OF MARCH

O! I have suffer'd
With those that I saw suffer: a brave vessel,
Who had, no doubt, some noble creatures in her,
Dash'd all to pieces.
*William Shakespeare*, The Tempest, *Act 1 Scene ii*

I do not recall, in all the ups and downs of the Malta battle, ever succumbing to pessimism about our future. Nor, frankly, do I believe there was a member of my Flight or, indeed, the Squadron, who was overtaken by forebodings about the likely outcome of events. True, there was concern over the extent of our plight. It had quickly become obvious to us that a few Spitfires, flown well and aggressively, were not going to make much impact on the Island's worsening position. Far greater numbers of fighters would be needed before there could be a genuine prospect of an upturn. But hope springs eternal and fresh rumours of further reinforcements from the carriers kept our spirits bubbling. We just didn't think that we could lose. Absurd, of course, but there it was . . .

Nevertheless, March wasn't turning out as we had expected. The deterioration in the serviceability of our aircraft from the heavier bombing and increasing combat was beginning to be manifested in various, and sometimes curious, ways.

Young Maltese boys, seeing us walking about the streets of Valletta between raids and alerts, apparently with nothing else to do, would point at us provocatively. 'Peelots, peelots,' they would cry and there was a touch of ridicule in their high and penetrating voices. Children cannot hide their thoughts for long and these young lands could not comprehend why we were on the streets instead of mixing it with an enemy who was daily invading Malta's air space and causing havoc with their homes and families. It was understandable, yet the implied jeers did not endear these boys to the less patient among our Commonwealth 'peelots'. They were surprisingly sensitive about being made the butt of ignorant jibes albeit out of the mouths of juveniles.

The children's parents knew better. What they realized was that, after the débâcle of the February convoy, another attempt at running three or four merchant vessels through to Grand Harbour must very soon be made if Malta was to have a future in Allied hands. It was no secret that famine would quickly become the menace if relief was not forthcoming.

The anticipated effort came towards the end of the month. 'Operation MW 10', the March convoy's code name, was launched from Alexandria on 20 March with four motor vessels – Breconshire (10,000 tons and a top speed of some 17 knots), Clan Campbell (7500 tons and 14½ knots), Talabot (7000 tons and 14½ knots) and Pampas (5500 tons and 15 knots), all carrying vital supplies and supported by five cruisers, with Rear Admiral Philip Vian in command, flying his flag in Cleopatra. Sixteen destroyers made up the complement.

Two days out from Alex, the Luftwaffe began its attacks, and then to the north, as the ships were spilling out into the Ionian Sea, elements of the Italian Fleet began grouping for an assault. But their commander, Admiral Iachino, sailing in the battleship Littorio, prize of the Supermarino, reckoned without 'Vian of the Cossack'.

Faced eventually by Littorio, with its two supporting cruisers and ten destroyers, the British admiral, although vastly outgunned, decided to face the Italians and take his force in. Fortune usually favours the brave, and in one of the classic naval engagements of World War II, with the Luftwaffe continually intervening, the Royal Navy compelled the enemy to withdraw ignominiously to safer waters while the rest of the convoy, covered by smoke and unmolested, moved well away to the south-west. There, it prepared for the last critical lap of the voyage which would take it to the Island's approaches and the start of the final run-in to Grand Harbour.

Then, under cover of such serviceable fighters as we could muster, it would brace itself to meet a maximum effort from General Lörzer's Fliegerkorps II, marshalling for the attack in Sicily. Neither side had any illusions about the size of the stakes which were being played for. Certainly we didn't in the fighter squadrons. The stage was, therefore, set for the battle which would determine the defending Garrison's ability to stand its ground and fight until fresh Spitfires could be flown in from the carriers. With them would come a real prospect of another, larger convoy being run through from east or west in the late spring or early summer.

As tension mounted on the Island's airfields, I remember thinking how stirring it was to be playing a part in the final stage of the drama which was now unfolding. The needle was there, but so, too, rightly or wrongly, was the confidence.

I felt we were aided notably at this moment by our close relationship with the Royal Navy in Malta, with its brave submariners and with its Fleet Air Arm squadrons of Swordfish and Albacores, based at Halfar. From our Air Marshal and his opposite Naval number, Admiral Ford, right down to squadron and flight commander level, we worked together in easy accord. So when the tests came, as they were coming now, we were prepared to go to the stake for the senior Service and for the Merchant Navy which it succoured.

\*

The German Air Force, while monitoring methodically the progress of Operation MW 10, had already staged a dress rehearsal of the show to come. Pulverizing attacks on Takali, which had left the airfield largely unserviceable, and in the hands of some of the Army's 2000-strong aerodrome repair force, meant that we had to move over to Luqa, there to join 126 Squadron and be in place when the ships came within range of the Spitfires.

At much the same time, there had been a change in command of 249. Stan Turner, utterly spent after two years of almost continuous operational flying, had relinquished the job and been promoted to Wing Commander Flying at Takali. It was a nominal, holding appointment, simply designed as a stepping-stone to joining the operations staff at HQ in Valletta under Woodhall whom Stan revered. He had played out a magnificent innings and now stood tall, and apart, in the eyes of the squadrons in Malta. As for me, I would remain for ever in his debt. In those three or four initial weeks on the Island, flying the old Hurricane IIs, he had offered me a crammer's course in the art of leading and tactical flying in preparation for the scholarship examination which was soon to open. Stan wouldn't allow his pupils to fail.

Turner's place at the head of the Squadron was taken by another Stan – Stanley Bernard Grant, an English officer of stature, looks and impressive credentials. Charterhouse and Cranwell-educated, Stan Grant fastened an easy, yet assertive, grip on 249 the moment he took over. He knew what he wanted from the unit and what he expected from his subordinate flight commanders.

They used to say in the Royal Air Force 'never follow an outstanding CO', but Grant suffered nothing from succeeding Turner. Eventually to finish as an Air Vice-Marshal with the CB and a pair of DFCs, he was cast unmistakably in the Cranwell mould. After my first half-hour's talk with him, I was certain we would hit it off in the exceptional circumstances which, we both knew, weren't easy. He was efficient, liked things to be buttoned up and expected his flight commanders to get on with the job without being told. He didn't interfere – provided we delivered the goods. He stood back until it was necessary to intervene. He let me have my head, which I much preferred.

In March and April, with our low serviceability and few aircraft, we seldom operated as a squadron, but rather as separate flights, one coming to readiness at first light and the other relieving it at 1300 until dusk. Stan seldom flew with my Flight. I never asked him why, for one thing it wasn't my business whom he flew with. But I got the feeling he thought I was better left alone with my versatile, rugged Commonwealth mix. On the few occasions when he did come and fly with us, I could see at once he was a good general in the air, never selfish or individualistic, but always with a comprehensive grip of what was going on. He seemed to be thinking of his clutch, but that didn't stop him going hard for an opening himself if he saw one. When he could, he got in close to the enemy and wouldn't let go. He flew precisely and accurately and this made his aircraft a good gun platform. From what I saw of him, he didn't waste ammunition on unpromising targets; he shot when he reckoned he was in with a worthwhile chance to score. This wasn't always a common habit. I judged him to be a high-class all-rounder.

Stable and friendly, I sensed that Stan Grant was glad to be taking over at a moment of crisis. It seemed to appeal to his natural authority. He was undoubtedly at his best when under the whip, and the enemy was certainly getting it out now.

It was the morning of 23 March when the merchant ships first came within range of our aircraft. My Flight was at readiness. From then on until 26 March, the squadrons at Luqa and Halfar used every hour of daylight to keep up, as best they could, some sort of vigil around the ships. We started with fourteen Spitfires and eleven Hurricanes serviceable – twenty-five fighters in all on the Island, a total only achieved by careful husbandry in the week or so before, and by the Herculean efforts of the groundcrews who drove themselves to the limit to give us the best chance. This was the high point. There were times when, at the end of a day's cover, the squadrons could put no more than six aeroplanes within touch of the ships.

Sixty miles away, across the Narrows, *Oberbefehlshaber Sud* – C-in-C, South – to accord Kesselring his full trappings, now had a front-line strength of some 500–600 aircraft – Ju 87s, 88s and Me 109Fs with the Gs yet to come. The Regia Aeronautica's additional 350 were, for the moment, being held very much in reserve. We faced a formidable arsenal.

The weather for the first day's cover was, I recall, thoroughly incompatible with our defence of the ships. A stiff onshore wind, rising at times to gale force – the Sirocco, they called it – was blowing out of the south-east, bringing with it a damp mist off the heavy seas which were running. It wasn't cold, but a thick covering of ten-tenths cloud from a base of 1000 to 1500 feet up to.5000 or 6000 made a convenient hiding-place for harassed attackers.

Beneath the overcast, the variable visibility was often down to one or two miles, ideal for the sneak raiders making judicious use of cloud cover to launch their opportunist attacks on the ships, but little use for the defenders who, as likely as not, would see their quarry escape into cloud before an engagement could be joined. I had often seen conditions like this golfing, in peacetime, on the east coast of Scotland – at Muirfield, St Andrews, Carnoustie or, further up the coast, at the courses along the shores of the

Moray Firth. Now they made it difficult to identify aircraft quickly and maintain a good tactical position from which to defend the vessels battling their gallant way to harbour.

Bad news hit first. From Operations in Valletta, we learnt that the merchantman *Clan Campbell* had been sunk 20 miles or so to the south-east before fighter cover could become effective. A Ju 88, pressing a resolute attack (and let's be clear about it, the Luftwaffe in Sicily were a ruthless and determined lot), had dropped a bomb on the ship from no more than 50 feet. It was the harbinger of things to come. Soon it was the turn of *Breconshire* to feel the heat. An old friend of the Maltese, this trusty vessel had, in the past, brought priceless oil cargoes to the Island. Now, some 8 miles south-east of Malta, and making good way, she received a direct hit in the engine room, stopping her almost at once in her tracks. The irony of it was that it was a single bomb of some 250 lbs, dropped by a fighter making a fast pass over the ship, which did the damage. A lucky hit it may have been (fortunately there was no fire), but the damage had been done.

With the seas which were running, there was no hope of throwing her a tow and taking her the last few tortuous miles to Grand Harbour. Instead, she anchored where she was, trusting her fate to three destroyers, busying around her like wild ducklings circling the old hen bird. Looking down from the air, it was tantalizing to see her riding the waves, apparently otherwise undamaged, with her cargo of fuel oil which, we knew, the authorities in Malta – and the waiting people – would have given their soul to secure.

If hopes were dashed over *Breconshire*, they rose again sharply as *Pampas* (hit by two bombs which providentially didn't explode) and *Talabot*, looking quite undamaged and seaworthy, ploughed on through the heavy seas to cover the last mile or two to the harbour entrance, after miraculously avoiding the worst that the enemy could dispatch.

Meanwhile 249 and 126 Squadrons, operating in pairs and relays from Luqa, kept up a series of running skirmishes with the 88s, with the 109s in attendance, as they tried to penetrate their way to the ships. It was a relentless and unequal struggle.

The nights brought comparative quiet. But then on 26 March, with the weather clearing, the wind easing, and the sea moderating, with *Pampas* and *Talabot* in Grand Harbour and *Breconshire* towed into Marsaxlokk Bay in the southeast, the Luftwaffe let drive a series of devastating raids, embracing over 300 aircraft, designed to dispatch the merchantmen once and for all. Against such an onslaught, neither the fighters, reinforced on 21 March by a further nine Spitfires flown in from *Eagle*, or the Grand Harbour barrage, could save the two ships. Both were hit and sunk under the noses of the Maltese, together with the destroyer *Legion*. The next day, in the bay hard by Kalafrana, *Breconshire* met a similar fate.

I found the loss of *Breconshire* personally dispiriting. Apart from the wider, and much more important reasons, I felt an involvement having, with others, been privy to her traumas as she lay, totally disabled, riding the waves on that first day of our cover. I and my No. 2, G. A. F. 'Zulu' Buchanan, the bronzed and upright Rhodesian policeman, one of our very best pilots, had joined up with another pair from 126 Squadron, led by the CO, Jumbo Gracie, a thoroughly capable and experienced character, who offset surprisingly poor eyesight with the heart of two lions. Jumbo was to play a king-size part in the Island's crisis and its eventual deliverance as the Station Commander at Takali.

The four of us had, on one sortie, fought around the merchantman for the best part of twenty minutes a no-holds-barred, all-or-nothing contest with some 88s and 109s darting about in and out of cloud and trying to dodge a way through to the stricken vessel. With the three destroyers coming fully into play, we had held off all comers, shooting down nothing that we felt we could properly claim, but seeing to it that no bomb wrecked our prize. 126 and 249 had joined hands that day in a noble cause; but now the reason for it had been lost.

Out of the 26,000 tons of vital cargoes which had left Alexandria a week before, only some 5000 had been salvaged from the ships with a small bonus of fuel oil from *Breconshire*. Still, so finely balanced were the Island's stocks at the time that the recovery of even a shade over a fifth of the original tonnage was enough to prolong, by a few blessed weeks, Malta's ability to survive.

As for the squadrons, our fighter strength at the end of the four days' intensive skirmishing was down to no more than five serviceable aircraft. To these we could add, two days later, a further seven Spitfires, the outstanding balance remaining from the second reinforcing operation from *Eagle*.

Well might Tedder, C-in-C, Middle East, describe the fighter supply policy as a case of 'too little and too late'.* At this cruel juncture, General Dobbie, the Governor, having seen with his own eyes the disastrous outcome of the Alexandria convoy, made a signal to the Chief of the Air Staff in London. His message, a personal one to Peter Portal,† was a model of balance and clarity. It was the more effective for its simplicity. Dobbie went to the root of the issue:

Malta can only continue to be useful if we are able to protect the ships and aircraft which operate from here. Moreover, Malta can only be held if we protect ships unloading vital supplies and thus ensure replenishment of our stocks. Our experiences of the last few days have made it clear that with our present resources, [and]

* Air Historical Branch Draft Narrative: Malta (unpublished).
† Air Chief Marshal Sir Charles Portal, later Marshal of the Royal Air Force, Viscount Portal of Hungerford.

in view of the great enemy strength in Sicily, we cannot do this. The situation thus disclosed is extremely serious and must *at all costs* [author's italics] be remedied.*

The balance sheet was not, however, weighted wholly against us. The Luftwaffe had been made to pay a heavy premium to insure against the effect of the Spitfires' arrival, and to maintain its continued supremacy. In March, roundly 20 per cent of its Ju 88 strength in Sicily had been lost, 14 per cent of it over Malta. Me 109 losses were 5 per cent less, but they still amounted to some 15 per cent of the fighters' operational strength. Put another way, in the first of these two critical months, when all hung in the balance, Kesselring had lost around 40 per cent of his serviceable bombers and some 20 per cent of the fighters' operational strength.†

We had certainly suffered a reverse with the March convoy, and others would, no doubt, follow. But in the fighter squadrons we were still convinced that, given enough tools, we could certainly finish the job.

* AHB, op. cit.     † ibid.

'Nothing that I personally saw in wartime matched the courage of those [Naval] Albacore crews on that Mediterranean morning in June, 1942'

*Left:* The Air Force and Royal Navy played it as one. Air Vice-Marshal Hugh Pughe Lloyd *(left)*, our AOC, with his then 'oppo' Vice-Admiral Sir Wilbraham Ford

*Below:* A master in the air – the brilliant Percival Stanley Turner, Canadian marvel

*Below:* The obsolete Hurricane IIs held the line miraculously against the Me 109Fs until the Spitfires arrived

*Above:* Building aircraft blast pens at dispersal; the pilots loathed the job

*Right:* Petrol bowsers had long since 'had it'. Spitfire tanks had to be filled by hand

*Below:* Groundcrews stood valiantly to their posts and sweated it out under the noonday sun

*Below:* Immaculate Major ... his gun crews saved us at Takali. The author's Cambridge contemporary and lifelong friend, Nick Harrison (*Laddie Lucas*)

*Above:* United States' Malta stalwart, Hiram Aldine 'Tex' Putnam from Bobville, Texas: killed in action (*Laddie Lucas*)

*Below:* Rugged Rhodesian policeman – 249's G.A.F. 'Zulu' Buchanan (*Laddie Lucas*)

*Right:* Linchpins of the squadron – Ozzie Linton (*left*) from Ottawa with Les Watts of Birmingham, England (*Laddie Lucas*)

*Below right:* Immortal trinity – E.J. 'Jumbo' Gracie, station commander, Takali, with Commonwealth stars, Australian Paul Brennan (*left*) and New Zealand's Ray Hesslyn (*Laddie Lucas*)

*Above:* Great World War II fighter pilot, 249's Johnny Plagis from Salisbury, Rhodesia (*Laddie Lucas*)

*Above:* Piece of New Zealand granite – PRU's exceptional Harry Coldbeck (*Laddie Lucas*)

*Right:* Not much of this about in impoverished Malta – the Island's Whizz Bangs

*Below right:* Adrian Warburton, reconnaissance legend, wrote his own ticket. It included his lover, attractive Christina Ratcliffe, and her Floriana flat

*Below:* Canadian quality in 249: Gerry de Nancrede (*right*) with compatriot, Basil (Mickey) Butler, a cast-iron pair (*C. S. G. de Nancrede*)

*Above:* 'A natural goodness adorned his mind.' Norman MacQueen (*left*), 249 pin-up, so soon to be killed, here seen with Raoul Daddo-Langlois (*Laddie Lucas*)

*Right:* Paul of Tarsus, patron saint of Malta: the island statue commemorates the scene of his shipwreck, AD 60 (*Laddie Lucas*)

*Below:* To St Paul's Island for 249 picnic. Scotland's Ronnie West takes the strain while robust Canadians, Bud Connell and Buck McNair, rock the boat (*Laddie Lucas*)

*Left:* Tragedy in Rabat. The Point de Vue takes a packet, and five squadron pilots, and a sixth officer, are killed in their Mess (*Laddie Lucas*)

*Below:* End of a mission. Italian Macchi 202 forcelobs on Gozo

*Bottom:* As the Royal Navy enters Grand Harbour, the Royal Artillery stands guard

*Above:* Genial Bavarian aristocrat and professional soldier-turned-airman, *Generalfeldmarschall* Albert Kesselring (with baton raised), C-in-C South. He saw Hitler's failure to invade Malta as fatal to Rommel's North African campaign
*Right:* Ready for Malta: the Regia Aeronautica's Mc 202s of 360 Squadriglia and 51 Stormo CT at readiness at Gela, south-west Sicily
*Below:* Scourge of Malta, and one of World War II's outstanding aircraft, the Luftwaffe's versatile Ju 88

## OFFSIDE

Accidents and reverses seemed to come in threes in wartime
– and come quickly. They did in Malta in the third week of
March 1942.

Prime among the set-backs was, of course, the convoy;
and a crippling blow it was. But two shocks which immediately preceded it compounded the hurt and the anger. On
21 March, two days before the convoy had been due to
dock, the Luftwaffe had delivered a damaging onslaught on
Takali. To the customary north-east to south-west or
south-east to north-west lines of attack, there was added
another. This was aimed at the airfield from west to east,
from the direction of Dingli Cliffs on the western coast.
Moreover, the pattern of this attack was different. The
bombers did not dive on the target, as was their habit, from
17,000 feet or so down to 5000 or 6000, releasing their
bomb load near the low point of the dive. This was the
tactic which had always given such accuracy against pinpoint
targets, and which had knocked out so many of our aircraft
on the ground.

With this new westerly approach, the Ju 88s maintained
their height, letting their load go in straight and level flight
from 15,000 or 16,000 feet. There was a bit of spraying.
Some bombs overshot the airfield and landed in the vicinity
of Mosta, but one, of substantial size, undershot and scored
a direct hit on the Point de Vue, a hotel in Rabat which
had been requisitioned by the Royal Air Force as a billet
for officers stationed at Takali.

Five pilots died in the attack; two of them – Pilot Officers
Booth and Guerin, the latter an Australian – were from 249

Squadron. Edwin ('Junior') Streets, a worthy representative of the Island's strong US contingent, was another who perished. A sixth officer, Flight Lieutenant Waterfield, one of our well-regarded station intelligence officers, was also lost in the blast. Coming on the eve of the arrival of the convoy, it was a numbing blow. Losing people in combat was one thing, but to have half a dozen wiped out at a stroke on the ground was cruel not least because it was exceptional.

But, as with all such disasters, it might well have been worse, providence alone intervening to save three more members of the Squadron – Buck McNair, Bud Connell and Ronnie West – from a premature death. Having just left an interrupted movie in Rabat, they had wandered slowly back to the Mess, hiding in doorways along the way, as the attack developed.

For Robert Wendell McNair, my opposite number in command of 249's 'B' Flight, with whom I had already established such an easy working accord, and who would achieve greatness as a fighter leader before the war's end, it was a deranging experience. Its scars were, I believe, to live with him for the rest of his life.

Buck was inside the building when the 2000-pounder fell at the hotel entrance. With hindsight, he later recorded, in graphic terms, the terrible scene after the Luftwaffe had struck.

When I came to, I didn't know where I was. I didn't feel I was dead, but I didn't feel whole. My eyes were open, but my jaws and chest didn't seem to be there. There was no pain, I just didn't seem to have jaws or chest. I felt for my tin hat, then I started to be able to see just as if the sun was coming up after a great darkness. I tested myself. I felt carefully with my fingers and found that I had a face and a chest, so I felt better . . .

It started to get light – the darkness had been due to the showers of dust from the stone building. I felt for my revolver, the one which Stan Turner had given me at Hornchurch, back in England. I mucked around and found it, knocking the dust off it and checking to make sure it was loaded . . .

As I became more conscious, I found I was upstairs; but I knew I shouldn't be upstairs. I should be downstairs. Then I realized I had been blown upstairs either through a door or through an opening at the turn of the staircase. I'd been thrown up 20 or 30 feet . . .

I went out on to the roof and back down the main staircase which was barely hanging in place. I saw the bodies lying at the foot of it. They were in a heap. There was no blood. The raid was still on – the All Clear hadn't sounded. But everything seemed very quiet. Heavy dust covered the bodies. I looked at them – studied them. One was headless, the head had been cut cleanly away from the top of the shoulders. I didn't see the head, but I could recognize the man by his very broad shoulders . . .

I heard a moan, so I put my hand gently on the bodies to feel which of them was alive. One of them I noticed had a hole, more than a foot wide, right through the abdomen. Another's head was split wide open into two halves, from back to front, by a piece of shrapnel. The face had expanded to twice its size. How the man managed still to be alive I didn't know. I thought of shooting him with my revolver. As I felt for it, I heard Bud Connell's voice behind me. 'Look at this mess!'

I put my hand against the wall, but it slithered down it. It had seemed dry with all the dust, but when I took my hand away I found it was covered with blood with bits of meat stuck to it – like at the butcher's when they're chopping up meat and cleaning up a joint. I turned to Bud. 'For God's sake,' I said, 'don't come in here.' Then I noticed that my battledress and trousers were torn and ripped . . .

Ronnie West appeared. It seemed natural to see him. He had been in the building with us, but he didn't say anything about me being there. He didn't seem to want to talk . . .

Now an ambulance and a doctor arrived. The doc asked me to help him with the bodies. I said 'Get someone else, I've seen enough.' But I did get one chappie on to a stretcher. He was still alive, but I couldn't recognize him. I put a cloth over his face and then a stupid orderly took it off. It was the most horrible sight I've ever seen and I've seen chappies with heads off and gaping wounds and horrible burns . . .

The realization of what had happened began to dawn very slowly . . . My left arm had gone out of joint when I was blown upstairs by the bomb, but I had shoved it back in place . . .

Ronnie and I sat on the kerbside and talked about it. As we discussed it we began to understand the awfulness of it all. Then we started cursing the bloody Huns; it was maddening that all we could do to them was curse. We were inwardly sick, sick at heart . . .

We decided to get drunk. When we got over to the Mess, the orderly refused us anything to drink and wouldn't open the bar. We broke our way in and each took a bottle of White Horse. We drank gulps of it straight. We decided to take another bottle each as we were leaving. We were both feeling mad, but the whisky was helping to relieve the tension.

Buck McNair was very tough. By sheer will power, he forced this incident into the background and drove himself back on to flying and the running of his flight as before. He kept it up for another two months much as if this dreadful episode had never happened. It was the measure of his courage. But underneath it all, I, who knew him so well and was so fond of him, felt the experience had changed him. The brash, complaining exterior was still there, but, behind it, there was a quieter, gentler man. But then the Malta experience changed many people. Most who survived it felt differently afterwards – as if an overwhelming effort, which had sapped the resources, was behind.

The impact of this mortal attack on the Point de Vue was the harder for us to absorb because, on the previous day, 20 March, an abhorrent fate had befallen another of our pilots. The Squadron had been ordered by the Controller to put up two separate sections of four aircraft, splitting up into pairs, to meet one of Fliegerkorps II's usual runs across the

Island. This time, the raid was divided into two thrusts, each going for a different target. McNair was leading one section and I the other. Duggie Leggo, one of the three Rhodesians in 249, was flying with us that day.

When the two sides clashed high up at 24,000 or 25,000 feet, there was the customary mêlée, with aircraft firing and spreadeagling all over the sky. Then, just as suddenly, all was quiet without a fighter apparently anywhere to be seen. Meanwhile, after combat and separation, pilots were looking for another to join up with in line abreast. The drill was now automatic. It was the best recipe for survival, given the odds stacked against us.

In my section, we spotted, far away to port, a single Spitfire obviously looking for a mate. As we turned to go to his aid, a lone 109, diving steeply and very fast out of the sun, pulled up, unseen, under the Spitfire. From dead astern, the pilot, who plainly knew his business, delivered a short, determined closing burst of cannon- and machine-gun fire, sending his victim rolling on to his back and spiralling down to earth or sea. It was a clinical operation. Relieved, we saw a parachute open.

As we watched the silk canopy floating down in the distance, with the pilot swinging on its end, another single 109, diving down out of broken cloud, made a run at the 'chute, squirting at it as he went and collapsing it with his slipstream as he passed by. The canopy streamed, leaving the pilot without a chance. The next thing we knew, the 109 was diving away for Sicily with never a hope of catching it.

When we landed back at base, we found it was Duggie Leggo who had 'bought it'. When Johnny Plagis, Duggie's countryman and inseparable friend, was told the story he couldn't credit it. Then the reality of it seemed to overwhelm him. For two or three days, he was morose and uncharacteristically silent and brooding. But the killer streak, which we knew so well, was palpably surging within.

There had been rumours of other similar action over the Island (which I had doubted), but here, after all the weeks of clean, hard fighting, was an example of it, confirmed at first hand. Sickened by it all, I wondered whether I could ever have brought myself to repeat the act had the positions been reversed, and the provocation been sufficiently strong. I concluded that, almost certainly, I couldn't, such were the unwritten rules of chivalry which we expected to honour – and see honoured. But the fact was that, for a few, no discipline, no matter how strict, could contain the blind fury which was aroused by knowing that such treatment had been meted out to a comrade, particularly one who was so well respected. In war, one bad turn will always beget another and I felt it could only be a matter of time and opportunity before some form of reprisal followed to level the score.

It came within days when a few of us saw a Canadian pilot, in a gesture of calculated revenge, dive on the dinghy of a ditched Ju 88 crew as it bobbed up and down on the waves, 6 or 8 miles south-west of Delimara Point at the southern end of the Island. The three occupants must obviously have reckoned they had a good chance of being picked up by air-sea rescue. A short, ruthless burst of fire and their hopes were at an end.

None of us who saw the first act forgot it, but those of us who witnessed the second set our faces against it, and said no more.

# BAD DREAM

Man does not live by bread alone, but by faith, by
admiration, by sympathy.

*Ralph Waldo Emerson*

It will help an understanding of the Malta story, as I saw it
unfold in that desperate April of 1942, if an imaginary
scenario is introduced.

Keep in the mind's eye the Isle of Wight, arguably
Britain's best-known island, with only the waters of the
Solent separating it from Southampton and the Hampshire
mainland. It is a shade larger than the 'Mediterranean
jewel', but near enough in size for the purpose. Now place
four 'targets' upon it – the equivalent of the number the
enemy was concentrating on in Malta and doing his best to
eliminate.

Cowes and its environs will substitute conveniently for
'Grand Harbour' and its surrounding towns. As to the three
airfields, a site just inland from Ventnor on the south coast
and St Catherine's Point will serve usefully as 'Halfar'. A
fair-sized spot close by Newport in the centre of the Island
will double for 'Luqa', the main aerodrome. That only
leaves 'Takali', the fighter base, to place. This much-
bombed 'target' can similarly be set on a small central area
of some 900 yards by 600 midway between Newport and
Yarmouth on the west coast.

So there, on this offshore British island, is an identikit of
Malta's close spread of targets.

But now it is springtime and imagine that the Luftwaffe
is bent upon destroying the Isle of Wight. Remember that

the Island's population of some 120,000 is less than half that of its slightly smaller Mediterranean counterpart and that the Maltese people are grouped much more tightly around or near the Axis powers' primary objectives. Malta's inhabitants are therefore more vulnerable to aerial attack notwithstanding their natural underground caves and shelters.

Moreover, Malta's population is always hungry, with little more than six or eight weeks' food stocks separating it from starvation and surrender. A convoy from the east or west is at least a month, and probably two, away. The Island's artillery is now rationed to 15 rounds per gun crew per raid. Supplies of 100 octane aviation fuel are dangerously low.

Convert that picture to the island in the Solent and that is how things would have looked on the Isle of Wight in April 1942.

The comparison must be taken an important stage further. Think of 'Sicily' and imagine that, 70 miles or so across the English Channel on the Cherbourg peninsula and in the hinterland immediately to the south, Field Marshal Albert Kesselring's Axis air force, with its 800 front-line aircraft, is deployed and ready to strike. It is a forbidding force, the more disturbing because there are usually no more than six or eight serviceable Spitfires on the Island's 'airfields' to match it.

Kesselring's orders from the Führer and the German High Command are explicit. They are to neutralize the Isle of Wight by rubbing out its three 'aerodromes' and the harbour area of Cowes and preventing any convoys from entering or leaving the place. When that is done – expectedly within a couple of months – there is a well-rehearsed plan, code-named *Herkules*, to capture this British prize with an airborne assault supported by seaborne forces. General Kurt Student, the able and experienced German airborne forces commander, is in charge. He has at his disposal two parachute divisions based alongside Kesselring's Luftflotte in Normandy. These are supported by the 2nd Italian Parachute Division, now a formidable force after training under the Germans' parachute exponent, General Ramcke, whom C-in-C South regards highly.

This is the *corps d'élite* which will spearhead the invasion if and when it comes. Backing it up in the hinterland of Normandy and Brittany are two Italian assault divisions and plenty of troop, freight and tank-carrying aircraft. Elements of the Axis battle fleet will also be available to shell the Island's strong points and cover the landings from the assault craft and troop transports.

But first must come the softening-up and immobilizing of the Isle of Wight's four 'targets' by bombing. Will it be able to stand up to what Malta had to endure in those two bleak spring months of 1942 when 4900 sorties were flown against it by the enemy in March and an astonishing 9600 in April? The Mediterranean island actually withstood in those months twice the tonnage of bombs that fell on London during the worst twelve months of the Blitz.

Compared with what Malta had to take, the Isle of Wight's 120,000 inhabitants would have had to endure 154 continuous days of round-the-clock bombing. Measure this against London's longest continual run of bombing at the peak of the attacks. This lasted for no more than a third of that time – for 54 days or 100 less than Malta had to stomach.

Take, again, the Luftwaffe's famous attack on Coventry for it makes another realistic comparison. The German Air Force dropped 260 tons of bombs on the Midland city. Thirty times that weight – 6700 tons – was dropped on Malta's Grand Harbour in six weeks of March and April alone. That's what Cowes and its people would have had to endure in the same period. Would they have stood up to such an onslaught as the Maltese did?

Would the women and children of Cowes have shown the same extraordinary resilience and fortitude in the face of such an assault as their counterparts did in Valletta, Sliema and Floriana? There would have been no question, remember, of evacuation to quieter, inland parts of the mainland. There would have been nowhere to go and nothing, anyway, to go in. And how about the Isle of Wight's 'Garrison' of 30,000? Would that number have emulated the performance of Malta's similar defending force in the spring of 1942?

These are good questions. Ponder them, for they will provide a better understanding of what the Mediterranean fortress – the 'unsinkable aircraft carrier' – was really up against in those awful times fifty years ago.

The Luftwaffe was now tightening its grip gradually around our throat. Thumbs were probing about to find the jugular. It wouldn't be long at this rate before we choked. Nor was there, at this sombre moment, any prospect that we could see of relieving the enemy's hold with the arrival of more aircraft from the carriers. There was still nothing else for it but to tough it out. The Island was at stake.

I flew only five times in April on interceptions for a total flying time of five hours and twenty minutes. Few, in my Flight, logged much more. True, such flying as we did was packed with action. Every minute of every scramble, from take-off to landing, was full of incident. One experience I had on an afternoon of blue skies and sunshine to the south-west of the Island is still cut deep in the memory.

Six of us, with the total complement of serviceable aircraft available that day, had made contact, high up, with a heavily escorted force of Ju 88s making for Halfar in the south of the Island. We had penetrated the fighter screen, unseen, from a good attacking position out of the sun and reached the bombers getting in a few good bursts. The German gunners (they were a brave lot in Lörzer's 88s) had retaliated vigorously, giving as good as they got.

Swarms of Me 109s, caught off-balance in the initial attack, now gave chase. Fierce battles were fought right down to the level of the wavetops. Then, as always, it was quickly over, with the enemy streaking northwards for Sicily and home. Wet through with perspiration, my No. 2 and I rejoined and headed back for base. A glance at my radiator temperature gauge shot a current through my body. It was already 'off the clock' and the engine was beginning to run rough. My aircraft had obviously been hit in the coolant tank by return fire from an 88 without my noticing it.

As we were about to cross the south-west coast by Dingli Cliffs at some 3000 feet, and still struggling for height, my motor seized completely. Smoke began to issue ominously from under the engine cowlings. Cutting all the switches, I realized I wasn't going to have enough height to stretch a glide with a dead stick and reach any one of the Island's three airfields for an emergency landing.

My two options had been faced by many others before. Roll over at once and hope for a successful bale-out from such altitude as I still possessed. Or pick a spot and go for a wheels-up landing trusting to the outcome on the unpromising rocky surface.

I had always had a fear of baling out. Ever since I had first learnt to fly I had made up my mind that only in the ultimate resort would I take to a parachute. My problem now was that a forced landing in Malta was roundly accepted to be an exceptionally dodgy affair and to be avoided if reasonably possible. Hundreds and hundreds of stone walls, marking myriad small plots of rock-strewn land covered the Island's white and arid surface. The consensus was that eight times out of ten it was better to bale out. The view was not shared by the commander of 'A' Flight of 249 Squadron.

The temperature in the cockpit was getting hotter and the smoke from the engine thicker. A tiny, but apparently cultivated piece of land, marked out by stone walls, caught my eye below. It was on the outskirts of a village which turned out to be Siggiewi. I now had about 1000 feet to work with. A tight slipping turn into the field with wheels up and flaps down and the speed kept just above the point of stall brought the aircraft heading into such breeze as there was with, I guessed, only a few feet to spare above the 'downwind' wall. With only 80 to 100 yards to go to the stone wall ahead, the Spitfire – aerodynamically sympathetic, the easiest operational aeroplane in all the world to 'feel' on to the ground – settled unbelievably gently on to the soft earth. A shot in a thousand, I would never have made the same job of it again.

Without so much as a scratch, a bruise or a burn, I undid my straps and jumped down quickly from the cockpit, distancing myself from the hot, smoking aircraft. I then noticed three old Maltese women in long black dresses, almost touching the ground, and black scarves covering their heads, coming stumbling over the rough ground, as fast as they could, towards me. Each was carrying some scooping implement and a hessian sack in her hand. As they came near, they stopped and, breathlessly, started shovelling earth into the sacks, intent upon getting up on to the wing and emptying the contents on top of the smouldering engine.

They could not understand English, but I explained by gestures that this wasn't sensible as there was the danger of explosion. Palpably dispirited by my caution, they turned away. The oldest and obviously the senior of the three then walked slowly back to the Spitfire and touched the wing lightly with her hand. Returning to me, she rested her hand gently on my forearm. As she did so she looked up into my eyes. A smile of benign serenity spread across that heavily lined, endearing face. Making the Sign of the Cross deliberately across her chest, she touched my arm again. With that, she turned with the others and went back to tending the land.

Here was an act of spontaneous faith which I would never forget. For a moment, in a Malta field, the Roman and the Anglican churches were as one. My fortunate escape in that small field near Siggiewi, and the heart-melting concern of those old women for my welfare, brought home to me the intimacy of this exacting life we were now leading. It seemed to increase as the precariousness of our collective state grew. It went further than the knowledge that we were 'all in this together'. Or that Malta was such a tiny place that the fortunes of the civilians were inextricably entwined with those of the military. It went well beyond that. As our prospects worsened and the dangers multiplied – and they were now very great – people were automatically drawn closer together physically and in mind and spirit.

In the fighter squadrons, with our dwindling aircraft resources and the mounting odds against us, we became more and more reliant one upon the other in the air, and upon the gunners providing a safety umbrella over the airfields, and upon the groundcrews for such serviceability as they could eke out. It all produced a closeness, stimulated by Malta's isolation in the middle of a very large sea, and the lack of any means of escape, which I was not to experience elsewhere in any other theatre of war. People wanted to be together. Even the 'loners' in the squadrons, of whom there would always be a few, became less introverted and withdrawn. It acted as a shield against adversity and as an antidote to anxiety. It made for an indomitable resolve to win through – somehow – although none could quite say how.

I remember the Canadian, Gerry de Nancrede, one of a rugged bunch of transatlantic characters we had in the Squadron, putting his finger, years later, on this feature of our island life. I wrote his words down because they seemed to me to reflect precisely the mood of those days.

'I soon found I had joined a new family. Groundcrews and aircrews were drawn together in a group that was sharing the intensity of life and death. It took time for a newcomer to comprehend it – particularly one who, like me, had come from the "political" scene of a Royal Canadian Air Force squadron. The comradeship, concern, courage and fear that joined us all has never since been forgotten by anyone who experienced it. There was something in those lines of King Henry which captured it: "We few, we happy few, we band of brothers".'

Paradoxically, one of the strange effects of this intimacy was to draw some of us – I was certainly one – closer to the enemy whose combatant activities we had brought summarily and rudely to a halt. Those whom we had shot down in 249 Squadron and, in the process, had dispatched to hospital, we genuinely wanted to go and see to compare notes. There was no question of our wanting to try to extract secrets from them about squadron strengths, intentions, comparative performances and the like. It had got nothing to do with that at all.

We wanted to see them because we were, by this time, professionals doing the same job, carrying out our duty, facing the same dangers and experiences and, generally, living the same kind of day-to-day life. There was an identity of interest between us which, for me and for a few others in the Squadron (but not, I recognized, for all), made visits to hospital compelling and curiously absorbing. Some, of course, held that this was akin to fraternizing with the enemy. I felt they were unyielding in their approach and rigid in their perception. In terms of operations, those wounded prisoners, who lay in their beds, had ceased to be actively in opposition. Their war was over. For them, it was curtains. But, in war, strong opposing attitudes were always difficult to reconcile.

There was one Luftwaffe pilot named Lauinger, a 21-year-old Me 109 pilot, whom Raoul Daddo-Langlois, Norman MacQueen and I used, now and then, to visit. Norman had shot Kurt Lauinger down in a genuine case of 'he never knew what hit him'. He had baled out and broken his leg. He told us very honestly afterwards that he had been so concerned about not losing his No. 1 in the mêlée – a first principle with the Luftwaffe as it was with the Royal Air Force – that he had eyes for nothing else. The next thing he knew he was floating down in his parachute.

Kurt was obviously a well-educated, intelligent and thoughtful German. He never expressed an opinion about his Nazi rulers, but he remained utterly convinced that his country would win the war and that, in the process, Malta would be invaded. Viewed from an airfield in Sicily in April 1942 it was a reasonable assumption. 'Then,' he said with a twinkle, 'I will be able to bring you chocolates and cigarettes!'

I asked him once how the Luftwaffe got on with the Italian pilots. With his left leg strung up in a cage, he had difficulty in turning to the right and reaching for the torch which lay on the table beside his bed. When he gripped it, he turned it on and shone it under the bed. 'We never see them,' he retorted, and in the circumstances of that time, but not later in the summer, we could only mutter 'Ditto'.

A revealing event occurred on 14 April, two days after Arthur Tedder, the Royal Air Force's C-in-C in Cairo, had visited us at Takali. The German Air Force had put on a pyrotechnic display for his benefit. As we stood on the veranda of the Xara Palace having a drink before lunch (I noticed Tedder made good use of a particularly large pink gin), looking down on the freshly devastated airfield, the 109s did a thorough job of beating up the dispersals, squirting right, left and centre as they went. One intrepid pilot made a pass at the bastions near where we were standing, for good measure. It was a salutary witness for the C-in-C. We were glad he was a spectator.

Two days later, the tables were momentarily turned when, in a nice reversal of form, Zulu Buchanan, as we then thought, picked off Hermann Neuhoff, Kurt Lauinger's Staffel Kapitan in III Gruppe of Jagdgeschwader 53. Neuhoff, who had fought in Spain, Poland, France, in the Battle of Britain, Libya and on the Eastern Front, had already notched up thirty-eight aircraft destroyed, twenty-two of them in Russia. He was clearly on his way to a maxi score when Buchanan spoilt the party. Luftwaffe pilots engaged in the combat believed, however, that Neuhoff's aircraft may have been fired on mistakenly by one of his own comrades.

Whatever the truth, we told Lauinger the next day that his Staffel Kapitan had been felled. 'Never!' he exclaimed, 'no one will shoot down Neuhoff.' He genuinely thought we were pulling his leg.

'Very well, Kurt,' I said, 'if you don't believe us, write out a note to your CO and we'll see that it is delivered to him in the hospital at St Patrick's Barracks, near Fort Madalena. We'll bring back his reply.'

Still disbelieving (such was his faith in his squadron commander's invincibility), he scribbled out a message in pencil which I still have stuck into my flying log book. In due course, we returned with Neuhoff's reply. When he read it, Kurt did not try to hide his amusement. 'Neuhoff shot down!' he exclaimed, 'And the things he used to say to me about my flying! He is in good company!' The humour was never far away.

Buchanan, then a flying officer, went to see Neuhoff in hospital to make his number with his distinguished victim. The German appeared to be greatly disappointed that his conqueror was such a junior-ranking officer. We told Kurt of this reaction. 'Neuhoff displeased because he was shot

down by an Oberleutnant! And I was destroyed by a Haupt-
mann! Now I am, how do you say, two up!'

If there were occasional visits to the hospital at Imtarfa to
see either our own or the enemy's wounded, the actual
health of the squadrons, despite the poor food, remained
surprisingly good. I recall Jack Satchell, the stockily built
and robust station commander at Takali during our first
two months or so on the Island, saying to me one day when
I had raised with him the topic of better rations for aircrew:
'You may think your chaps are underfed. I am a stone and
a half (21 lbs) underweight and I have never felt fitter!'

There was, however, one malady which used to assail
most of us occasionally and a few frequently to the extent
that they were seriously incapacitated. 'Malta Dog', as it
was called, was a pernicious form of dysentery which
brought with it extremely unpleasant symptoms the worst
of which was persistent and weakening diarrhoea. We
thought it came from drinking unboiled water or eating
uncooked fruit. It would have been of small consequence
with today's antibiotics. Without them, it was a different
and serious matter. For me, an attack every three or four
weeks in the earlier days was about par for the course.

Jeff West, a popular New Zealander,* with a penchant
for forthright criticism of anything which was remotely
substandard, was 249's chief sufferer. Every ten days or a
fortnight was about his meat. His criticism of the disease
left no one in any doubt about its effects. But Jeff was
what, in the jargon of those days, was called 'a press-on
type'. When he was over the worst of an attack, and he was

---

* Jeff West, a thoroughbred pilot, was a product of the Tangmere Wing in
Fighter Command. Himself heavily engaged, he was flying No. 2 to Doug-
las Bader on 9 August 1941 when the legless wing leader was shot down by
Oberfeldwebel Max Mayer near St Omer, in the Pas de Calais.

on the brink of being well enough to fly, a well-rehearsed dialogue would take place between him and the CO.

*Grant*: And how are you today, Jeff?
*West*: Better, sir, thank you. I could do a trip of forty minutes, no more.
*Grant*: But, Jeff, can you fart yet without danger? That's always the test.
*West*: Not yet, sir, but I don't want to.
*Grant*: Right, then, you're still stood down . . .

The ailment could attack the most experienced Malta hand. As an aside, I well remember an amusing incident happening to George Burges, the Island's famous Gladiator pilot – one of the original Faith, Hope and Charity lot – when we were in the Mediterranean some years ago, making a documentary of the battle for Scottish Television.

We were staying at a well-known five-star hotel and at dinner on the first night George regaled the party with the dangers of the Dog. He offered his 'certain advice' regarding avoidance.

The second morning after our arrival we were all down to breakfast, bright and early, in time for the filming to start at 0900 punctually . . . All, that is, except George. A call was put through to his room. Must have overslept, they said. 'I'll be down shortly,' came the reply. As we were about to get up from the table, in walked George looking glum, his face the colour of the tablecloth. 'What's up, George?' we asked.

'Been up half the night,' he said. 'I think I've got a mild touch of the Dog.'

Far worse than the Dog but, mercifully, quite rare was sand-fly fever. The locals said it came from being bitten round the ankles by ticks in the grass and dust. I caught it in April, just before the next lot of Spitfires was about to arrive. Hopes had begun to soar.

I ran a temperature of 101–102 °F for eight days. The symptoms were total lethargy and a constant and excruciating pain at the back of the neck, around the base of the skull. It was like a terrible headache in the wrong place. I daren't go to the Doc as I knew he would take me off flying, little though we were then doing of it with the paucity of aircraft. When we did scramble and we got up to 15,000 or 20,000 feet I started to shiver and my teeth to chatter as if I was in an advanced stage of Asian flu. I felt sure my voice must sound strange over the R/T, but nobody said anything.

Aspirins, taken in regulation quantity, had no effect whatever, not even temporarily to ease the pain. It went on and on and I began, almost for the first time in Malta, to worry. I was on the point of giving in and going to see the Doc when, the next day, I was on dawn readiness with my Flight. At the end of it, I had somehow dragged my feet up the hill from Takali to Mdina and the Mess. I went straight to the bar, got the barman to pour me out, unseen, a treble whisky and, taking five aspirins from the bottle, swallowed the lot, neat. I then went straight to bed under my mosquito net. I covered my naked body with a sheet.

Four hours later – it was between tea and dinner – I awoke. I had never perspired like it before or since. Everything was wringing wet, the sheets, the under-blanket, the pillow and the mattress. The water was running off my body as if I had come in from a swim and hadn't dried.

For a moment, I wondered whether I had been sensible with my drastic, self-prescribed remedy. Then, suddenly, the most marvellous realization dawned on me. The gimletlike pain at the back of my neck had gone. The relief was indescribable.

I went to the bathroom and dried myself with a towel. I couldn't have a bath because water was rationed and it wasn't my turn for a couple of days. I didn't mind. Weak, deplorably weak, though I was, the elation at feeling no pain swamped every other thought. I hadn't had an illness like it since, as a schoolboy of thirteen, I had had a bad bout of diphtheria. Then, I had been injected in my tender side with a serum. The pain had been so great that I couldn't lie still. All I could do for ten hours or thereabouts was to kneel at the end of the bed, grip the iron rail so tight that the feeling almost went out of my body and pray to God that He would come and help me.

Tomorrow, I reminded myself, would be another day. It would be 1300 hours before 'A' Flight had to come to readiness. With any luck, we might not have to scramble. I was bothered about what might happen if we had to climb to 25,000 feet or so and it was cold. After all that perspiration, I didn't want the awful shivering to start up again. It might bring back the pain.

Stop it, I thought. That's enough of that sort of fear. Besides, the pain has gone . . . Absolutely gone!

For Malta, however, there was still no relief from the agony.

# 12

# ENTRENCHED!

Of all the extraneous jobs we had to do in those impover-ished days of few aeroplanes and continual assault by the foe, the worst, by far, was filling sandbags. My diary entry for Easter Day, 5 April 1942 was explicit: 'Filling sandbags at Takali . . . Gawd! Nick Harrison to lunch.'

It was a monotonous, back-breaking and intellectually deadening activity, relieved only by the humour which it seemed to generate among the pilots, notably the Austral-ians. Gritty Australian humour, accent and all, and UK jesting had much in common – irreverence for a start. It quickly found its level when stimulated by the more mun-dane and less agreeable chores.

Apart from the monotony of the exercise, and the subse-quent building of the aircraft pens – blast pens, we called them – which it was designed to preface, it had, for 249, one thoroughly unnerving by-product. It kept us down on the airfield at a time when the Luftwaffe's onslaught against Takali and the other bases was mounting to its peak. Up to now, Kesselring's attacks had followed an unrelenting and predictable Teuton timetable. Morning, midday and late afternoon were the times when the whining of the sirens would be followed by the screech of falling bombs. To this invariable pattern was now added a fourth dimension. In the last hour or so of daylight, the enemy introduced a twilight raid which was made the more tedious coming, as it often did, at the end of a long afternoon's sandbagging or pen-building when fatigue was beginning to tell and resolve to weaken.

One notably aggressive attack on Takali, delivered out of

the western sky, had particularly disturbing consequences. My Flight was at the end of its filling and building stint in the south-east corner of the airfield. We were about to pack it in for the day when a vicious assault developed, this time without warning.

As the Ju 88s began to dive on their target from the direction of the citadel of Rabat, Bob Sergeant, Raoul Daddo-Langlois, Norman MacQueen and I took a flyer into the slit trench which had been dug beside 249's ramshackle dispersal hut. Crouching low and huddling together for common protection and courage, we were just in time to be sheltered from the worst of the blast from two accurately placed sticks of bombs which 'quartered' the southern end of the airfield from west to east. The tail-end of the package exploded with shattering ferocity less than 100 yards from our hide. Eardrums stretched like elastic with the explosions leaving one momentarily quite deaf.

As the raiding party headed east out to sea, like some mammoth thunderstorm passing through, a period of blessed quiet followed. Gingerly, we dragged ourselves out of the trench, covered with dust and debris. As we shook ourselves down and looked westwards across the pockmarked airfield and into the fading light, I suddenly saw two Me 109s in loose line abreast, no more than 50 feet up, diving at speed straight in our direction firing their cannon and machine-guns as they pressed a resolute attack. Shells from the flashing gun ports were cutting a swath across the dusty field, kicking up earth and stones as they tore towards us. With two or three bounds we were back in the slit trench, heads down, cringing and waiting for the worst.

The danger passed as the roar of the Daimler-Benz 601 engines drowned the staccato crackling of the Bofors guns now retaliating in anger around the landing strip. As we clambered above ground again, dusted ourselves down once more and stood erect, each of the four of us was shaking –

not so much from fright as with the shock of what had so suddenly, and unexpectedly, descended upon us.

The experience was instructive. All four of us had been on the Island as long as any of the other Spitfire pilots, and maybe longer. We had all had our share of aerial combat against odds with the full gamut of emotions which this had often brought. Yet, as we talked it over in the Mess later that evening, with soothing refreshment in our hands, each of us agreed that those very few minutes we had spent together in the slit trench an hour or two earlier were infinitely more deranging than anything we had experienced in the air.

The explanation was, of course, simple. When we were in the cockpit of a Spitfire we had something pretty lethal to fight with. Moreover, we had a blind confidence in the aircraft. The odds may have been outrageous, but the equipment was superb, and we knew it. At this stage, there wasn't a pilot on the Island who would have picked a Me 109F in preference to a Spitfire VB or C. Man for man, we were certain that we had the edge.

But crouching in a slit trench with first bombs and then bullets flying about, the circumstances were different. Here we were helpless, impotent and virtually at the mercy of the Hun, with no means to retaliation. We were cornered, yet we had nothing to fight our corner with. Well might Kesselring and his cohorts recite that piece of catching, Easter doggerel:

> 'Tis Holy Thursday let us snooker
> All these bloody Spits at Luqa,
> Fill the sky with every Stuka
>     Hallelujah!
>
> Hail Good Friday – Halfar's turn.
> Watch those bloody Swordfish burn,
> Won't the buggers ever learn.
>     Hallelujah!

Easter Saturday – that's fine.
Make Takali toe the line,
Here a rocket, there a mine.
> Hallelujah!

Christ! The Lord is risen today!
Let's bomb the harbour, bomb the bay,
Bomb the bloody place all day.
> Hallelujah, Hallelujah!

Easter Monday – let 'em rip,
God we'll give those boys the pip,
TEAR 'EM OFF A SAFI STRIP.
> Hallelujah!

> *Colin Davis, Squadron Leader*
> *Command HQ Dentist, Malta, 1942*

That momentary brush with Death certainly did one thing for us. It confirmed in us the knowledge that for the ground-crews, and the long days they had to spend down at the dispersals, working on the aircraft, open to most forms of attack, the routine demanded not only a combination of technical skill and nerve, but an excess measure of guts as well.

When, a little later on, Jumbo Gracie gave up the leader-ship of 126 Squadron and became an outstanding station commander at Takali, he struck a blow for the ground-crews which had an instant psychological effect. He did three things. First, he declared that any airman working on the airfield who wished to be issued with a rifle and ammunition would be provided with both forthwith. At the same time, he established a ring of machine-gun posts round the aerodrome which the airmen could man and operate during a raid. Third, he had printed at the head of Daily Routine Orders a sentence containing eleven short English words: 'It is the duty of *every* airman to kill the Hun.'

The effect was electric. The sight of an airman – or 'erk' as he was called – grabbing a rifle or racing to a machine-gun and blowing off at the 109s, 87s and 88s, a few thousand feet up, like some inexperienced game shot trying to fell a high pheasant turning on a brisk December wind, gave an immediate fillip to the spirits.

It was an act of genius on Jumbo's part. There would be several others to follow.

One early morning, when Takali had been put out of action, I flew over to Luqa with three others from the Squadron to come to readiness. I hadn't visited this principal airfield since we had operated from there while the ill-fated March convoy had been fighting its way through heavy seas to Grand Harbour. I was impressed at once by the paucity of multi-engined aircraft in the widely dispersed pens. Many were empty. Two months before, when we had first arrived on the Island, there were Wellingtons and Marylands, a few Blenheims and Beauforts, all of which had been maintaining an offensive role either against Axis supply ports or against the convoys plying a dangerous passage southwards across the Mediterranean to Rommel and his Afrika Korps in Libya.

This was the card which Hugh Pughe Lloyd had been briefed to play when he first took up his command a year before. The attacks from Malta against Axis shipping, although disturbingly costly, were very effective. These earlier operations, pressed to the limit by the gallant Blenheim crews, were justification enough for holding the Island at all costs. They were a symbol of the AOC's aggressive style of leadership.

The experience of Ivor Broom, one of the most intrepid of all the Blenheim captains, who was to finish the war with a telling operational record, makes the point.* Then a

* Later to become Air Marshal and be knighted, Broom had collected a DSO and three DFCs by the war's end.

21-year-old sergeant pilot, Broom had been detailed in the United Kingdom to take an aircraft and crew out to the Far East, stopping in Malta and Egypt, when Lloyd intervened on the crew's arrival at Luqa. Instead of staying the night, refuelling and flying on to Egypt the next day, the pilot was informed by the AOC that he was to tarry on the Island 'for a few days' before moving on.

Within hours, Broom and his crew found themselves on the battle order of 105 (Blenheim) Squadron, briefed for a murderous low-level attack on a southbound Axis convoy – one of those daylight attacks which produced just about the highest sustained casualties of the war. Having survived that, and three similar operations in the next four days, Broom was quietly relieved to hear that 105, seriously depleted by losses, was to return at once to the United Kingdom. Once again, Egypt and Malaya beckoned.

Lloyd ordered things otherwise. The sergeant pilot and his crew were now transferred to another Blenheim squadron – 107, detached from 2 Group of Bomber Command in England. Instantly, they were in the thick of it.

Four months and goodness knows how many more 'low-level daylights' later, only two of the Squadron's original crews had survived. Broom was still with them. In this time, 107 had sunk twenty-four ships for the loss of twenty-four crews. In the middle of the carnage, when no officers were left and a new CO had been sent for, the sergeant pilot was summoned to the AOC. It was a brief exchange. 'You are now,' said Lloyd, 'a commissioned officer. Put your stripe up at once. The paperwork will be sorted out later!'

It was Hugh Pughe Lloyd at his typical and individual best. The stay of 'a few days' had turned into a months-long saga of horrendous missions – a time of which Lloyd, the original hijacker, was himself later to write: 'Everyone

realized that the chances of surviving a tour in Malta were very remote indeed – which was the stark truth . . .'*
Such was the AOC's way and such was the effectiveness of his offensive that, at its climax, between 70 and 80 per cent of Rommel's supplies failed to reach their destination.†

But now I could see that the picture at Luqa was materially changed. Gone, as far as I could discern, were most of the Wellingtons. Of the torpedo-carrying Beauforts, and their supporting Beaufighters, no more than six or eight were visible. Such Marylands as I could spot appeared mainly to be wrecks.

The position had not, moreover, been improved by a singularly unfortunate shipping strike which had taken place far to the east of Malta on 16 April. A force of eight torpedo Beauforts – all that could be mustered that day – with an escort of Beaufighters, had suffered a pulverizing reverse. Two aircraft were lost over the target, three more near the Island on the way home, and a sixth on landing at Luqa – a loss of 75 per cent for the Beauforts. The escorting Beaufighters claimed two of the attacking Me 110s destroyed. Two gains for six losses do not win wars.

So the message was clear enough. The thorn which had been piercing Rommel's side for months had ceased to fester and had now been removed. The patient was recovering quickly and regaining his strength. This was bad news for Auchinleck and the 8th Army in North Africa. Such pricks as the enemy was now feeling were barely breaking the skin. The great panzer general's 70–80 per cent losses in supplies had now been cut dramatically to between 20 per

* Air Marshal Sir Hugh Lloyd, *Briefed to Attack: Malta's Part in African Victory*, Hodder & Stoughton, 1949.
† *The Memoirs of Field Marshal Kesselring*, William Kimber, 1953.

cent and 30 per cent – still significant, but small by comparison with what had gone before.*

With 70–80 per cent of the Afrika Korps commander's convoys getting through, the stage was being prepared for the Germans' planned advance through Cyrenaica and into Egypt – code-named *Theseus*. It was just what Malta was there to prevent. But if things looked bleak now, in a few days' time the picture would be even worse.

*ibid.

# 13

# TREADING ON TOES

He who has nothing to assert has no style and can have
none: he who has something to assert will go as far in
power of style as its momentousness and his conviction
will carry him.

*George Bernard Shaw*

Having reached this pass, signals to the summit from
Governor-General, C-in-C or AOC, in the field, were of
small avail in underscoring the gravity of the crisis which
was now upon us. A clued-up emissary, fresh from the day-
to-day fighting, was needed to bring home to the highest
authority the circumstances with which the Island was
having to grapple. Lloyd, with his searching mind, could
cut through the dross. If, as he knew, Malta's salvation now
rested upon obtaining 'fighters and still more fighters', a
personal representative must immediately be dispatched to
dump the responsibility squarely on a few desks in Whitehall. His man for the job was the Englishman Jumbo Gracie
– Squadron Leader Edward John Gracie, CO of 126 Squadron, a blunt and thick-skinned officer, whose methods
bordered on the ruthless, but whose resource and ability
were never in question. I was personally in no doubt that
Jumbo, with his tenacity and pungent views, was the man
to bear the harsh tidings 'from Aix to Ghent'. He had the
courage to do it.

If things were bad this determined character could be
relied upon to make them sound a damned sight worse. If
there were sensitive toes to tread on, Gracie's heavy foot
would find the sorest spot. He would have no compunction whatever about employing any subterfuge designed

to increase the impact of his message. His great characteristic, as we were to see now, and again a little later on, was that he was a tough-headed go-getter who knew exactly what he was after. If a senior officer's door was shut, he would put his stocky, medium-size frame against it and give it a shove. For one who had been a serving officer in peacetime he was surprisingly insensitive to protocol. 'Yes' was the answer he expected, not 'no'. In a phrase, Gracie was now The Man for the Hour.

I had taken at once to this restless pirate as soon as he had arrived at Mdina. In ten minutes, he had given the impression that he had been there for a year and owned the place. It had nothing to do with bragging or boasting; he wasn't like that at all. It was much more that his natural stance was to be 'in charge'. He felt more comfortable that way. That mischievous little chuckle which accompanied any dig at 'authority' brought his personality nicely into focus. I knew very well that I wouldn't have wanted to be a flight commander in his squadron – I was much too happy serving Stan Grant's urbane and contrasting correctness: but, kept at arm's length, Gracie, who smoked V for Victory and Belle of the Orient cigarettes through an extra-long holder, was a compelling comrade to have on one's side.

What this London visit actually achieved, other than to underscore more dramatically the gravity of the Island's plight, is questionable. So much had, in any case, been ordered by Churchill, the War Cabinet and the Chiefs of Staff in an attempt to redress Malta's imbalance with the enemy that some imaginative hand would probably have been played anyway. One thing Jumbo did do, however, was to have word sent back to Lloyd in Malta, for onward transmission to the squadrons, that 'something important' was soon going to happen. Coming fresh from our man's mouth, it acted as an instant stimulant.

Woodhall came over to the Xara Palace the same evening that Gracie's message had come through. Over his customary pink gin he confided the news. 'Jumbo says it won't be long now before the reinforcements are here.' Buck McNair – Flight Lieutenant Robert Wendell McNair – my splendidly assertive opposite number in 249, gave the Group Captain the collective reaction. 'And about effing time too . . . *sir!*' Buck had a ready knack of picking up the mood and giving it graphic expression.

Churchill had already been at work using his considerable persuasive power, and his special relationship with the US President, to obtain the loan of one of the US Navy's vast carriers for the next reinforcing operation. It was one thing to be able to fly sixteen Spitfires off *Eagle* into the Island at one go. It was something else altogether to be capable of dispatching fifty aeroplanes, or thereabouts, at one stroke.

We knew, and Lloyd was fully aware, that a good-sized fly-in of aircraft in one reinforcing mission would give us the chance of meeting the Hun in genuine strength. Such was now the confidence we felt in the cohesion and quality of 249's and 126's flying that, given enough resources at one time, we were certain we could cut the Luftwaffe down to size. And to hell with the odds.

This period of restlessness and waiting to which we were being subjected had, paradoxically, its advantages. The unrelenting pounding of the Island by the enemy, the interceptions of heavily escorted raids of anything up to 150 or so strong by the customary handful of Spitfires, the lack of decent food and the persistent feeling of hunger, the irregularity of mail from home – all this, and more, tested character to the limit and exposed man's actual worth. Little could be hidden for long. Personality, attributes and defects were worn on the sleeve.

A little over a year before, on 27 February 1941, Winston Churchill, intervening during the Second Reading debate on the Macdonald Bill* in Parliament, had said this about membership of the House of Commons:

I must admit I may be biased in favour of the House of Commons ... I have lived all my life here, and I owe any part I have been able to take in public affairs entirely to the consideration with which I have been treated by the House ... I do not hesitate to say that five or ten years' experience as a Member of this House is as fine an all-round education in public affairs as any man can obtain ... We get to know something about each other when we work together in this House. We see men with their qualities and defects.

For House of Commons read a fighter squadron in Malta in April 1942.

I thought at the time and, fifty years on, with ten years' membership of the House of Commons intervening, I still think that Churchill's assessment had a precise application for the relationships which existed between us at Takali as Malta fought for its life.

In 249 Squadron, we came from widely disparate backgrounds, lands and education. We spoke with different accents. Our peacetime occupations (for those who were old enough to have had one) had been extensively spread from the great professions and commerce and industry to the manual trades. We were a broad mixture of officers, NCOs and other ranks. In 249, we probably had the most diverse mix of all, and yet through all the ups and downs of the fighting the blend was complete.

Differences there may have been in outlook, temperament and attitudes, but we lived together in robust harmony and

---

*A wartime measure, designed to enable Malcolm Macdonald, Minister of Health, to become High Commissioner in Canada while still retaining his seat in the House of Commons.

fought as one. We were a classless society, dependent one upon the other for our future. The unity of our existence in those days makes a mockery of much that I have since seen written, and portrayed, of the class divisions which were alleged to have existed in the operational squadrons. In my experience and belief – and I saw it all as a wing leader, a staff officer, a CO of three quite separate squadrons embracing a variety of nationalities, and as a station commander – the contention is nonsense, served up for cash and controversy.

Apart from one isolated and quite exceptional instance which will be recounted later, I do not recall either as a flight or squadron commander in Malta ever having to deal with problems arising from difficulties in human relations or, for that matter, with deliberate acts of ill discipline. The ground rules were laid down and understood just as they were in the air and, once comprehended, all played to the whistle and followed a direct and commonsense lead.

When I look today at the differences in our society, and the excesses which are deliberately inflamed between the various 'sides' in our national life, I marvel at the unity we obtained in those rough times when just about the only 'extreme' we thought about was the simple difference between Life and Death.

This universally held attitude had nothing to do with courage or fear, exceptional ability or a lack of it. It had, I believe, everything to do with honour, personal common sense and decency and the ready acceptance of reasonable discipline and respect.

If a man was genuine and doing his best for the Squadron, pulling for the same common end on the ground and in the air, it mattered not one whit whether he possessed skills above the average or qualities beyond the general run. If he was genuine and average and dedicated, he was a 'good bloke', a 'nice guy' or a 'regular cobber' and accepted. He formed the indispensable backbone of the unit.

Of course, we had in 249 in those tenuously balanced days, when Kesselring and Lörzer were bent upon knocking Malta out of the game, an exceptional collection of 'characters'. I doubt whether there was a squadron in the Royal Air Force at that or any other time which could have bettered, on the ground or in the air, the quality and the talent which were there.

A roll-call told its story. Standing four-square behind Stan Grant, we had, among the UK representatives, Norman MacQueen from Rhyl in Wales, Ron West from Lossiemouth on the shores of the Moray Firth, Pete Nash, the printer from *The Times* in Fleet Street, Philip Heppell, a surveyor, the joker in the pack, with his ages-long Northumbrian family background, and Norman Lee the architect, whose rather diffident approach cloaked more than his fair share of purpose and resolve. To these we could add Raoul Daddo-Langlois and Bob Sergeant, originals on this mission, material that would pass my test.

The United States gave us the redoubtable Harry Kelly, a worthy son of the 'Lone Star' state. From the Dominions and the Colonies, apart from the already 'starred' Jeff West from New Zealand, came the two dominant Canadians, Buck McNair and Bud Connell, the exceptionally able Rhodesian pair, Plagis and Buchanan, and from Australia and New Zealand, the 'twins', Paul Brennan and Ray Hesslyn, who would soon be surrendering their sergeants' stripes in favour of the thin blue line of the pilot officer – and cause the 109s, 87s and 88s more misery than most. Laurie Verrall, too, kept the New Zealand standard flying and confirmed the mark a few of us had seen him make in 66 Squadron in England.

The undeniable fact was that we were now relatively so strong all round that we were being obliged to surrender a few of our promising newcomers. Thus, Jack (Slim) Yarra, the clearly able Australian, had to leave us for 185 at Halfar, there to contribute hugely to his squadron's success. Others were to follow. Our trouble was that the HQ staff in Valletta knew we could afford these transfers even when, eventually, an improvement in the aircraft supply position increased substantially the pilots' work rate.

What surprised me at this time was the extent and the depth of the talent which the Squadron was able to attract when the need arose. When the original stalwarts either fell by the wayside or came to take their rests, we were at once able to attract to our side ability which proved to be well above the Island's average. Everyone will always want to join a good and successful team. We now enjoyed that happy reputation so when vacancies arose we never had to look far for replacements. The remarkable thing was the speed with which the newcomers lifted their sights when they began to operate with us and when the improved flow of aeroplanes gave them their fair chance. As 'characters' they became as unforgettable as their predecessors.

The names come tumbling down. Canada provided renewed support with Gerry de Nancrede, Mickey Butler, the two Chucks – Chuck Ramsay and Chuck MacLean – Ozzie Linton, Bob Middlemiss and the two Johns – John McElroy and John Williams, alias Willie the Kid. Then came George Beurling to add fresh lustre to his country's name. It was a formidable contingent which moulded readily with our mix.

Jack Rae, one of our undoubted 'finds', brought with him not only a natural flair for air fighting but also the constancy which seemed to me so often to bear the New Zealand stamp. I looked upon Jack as one of our 'bankers'. Then Dallas, Texas, provided Tex Spradley with a zest for combat and with a southern, homespun humour which brought life to readiness during the more anxious hours.

Australia made up for the 'stealing' of Slim Yarra by coming up with Alan Yates to march easily in step with his proven compatriot Paul Brennan, who, by now, had risen to a spot near the top of 249's high-scoring league. Nor did the United Kingdom fail us with its new intake. Berkeley-Hill mixed youth and special charm with an extrovert craving to engage the enemy, while Les Watts, with 'made in Birmingham' stamped all over him, lightened our time with a recipe for provoking laughter when there was precious little to smile about. His was an invaluable contribution.

Losses there would be – occasionally they were heavy – for the 249 stable, but seldom did they occur before the victim had enhanced the Squadron's record.

There was another contributor to the daily round at Mdina whose appeal and intellect set him apart. Tim Johnston – Flight Lieutenant Hugh Anthony Stephen Johnston, Johnny, perforce, to the squadrons – had the best mind that I personally came across in Malta. A shade older than the rest of us, with a sparkle which often lit a smile, his ability had earlier won him an Exhibition at Brasenose, his college at Oxford and, subsequently, at the end of his undergraduate years, a narrowly missed First in Modern Greats. Thereafter, he had pursued a career in the Colonial Service to which he would return, with signal distinction, when peace came round again.*

Johnston was at work in the African bush when war

---

* Johnston, who had learnt the art of air fighting with Bob Stanford-Tuck in 257 Squadron, rose to lead a wing of P-51 Mustangs before the war's end. To his two Distinguished Flying Crosses in war, he added a CMG and a CBE for his work in the public service in peace. Sadly, he died prematurely in 1967, aged fifty-four.

broke out. It was an occupation he could have followed throughout hostilities had he chosen to do so. But that wasn't his way, for Tim was a patriot and the Colours had an irresistible appeal. He made his way back to the mother country, there to volunteer for aircrew. Within eighteen months he had realized his obvious promise by being appointed to command a Flight in 133, the third of the three American Eagle Squadrons in the Royal Air Force. His translation to the same office in 126 Squadron, now operating mainly from Luqa, was probably predictable given the strength and exceptional calibre of the Eagles' volunteers who came to Malta to make our cause theirs.

Like most able games players, Tim could fly aeroplanes, but in the context of his sojourn in Malta, he had two horrific escapes. The first of his two bale-outs would have finished me for good. The second, forced upon him after a volley of cannon shells from a 109 had found their mark, did indeed bring his time on the Island to a summary and hideously painful halt.

On the first occasion, he had been mixed up with a heavy Ju 88 raid on Luqa. He was about to land when a pair of 109s made a determined pass at the airfield. Off he had gone in pursuit. Unable to catch them, he had returned to base, there to make a run at 50 feet over the smoking aircraft and runway to check for craters. As he did so a delayed-action bomb exploded with a blinding flash right underneath his aircraft. The blast was fierce enough to propel his Spitfire straight up another 1,500 feet, destroying some of the important controls in the process.

Miraculously, Tim was able to extricate himself from the aeroplane, take to his parachute and open it only seconds before he hit the ground. Suffering nothing worse than a bruised heel, he was flying with the Squadron the next day.

There was a sequel to this bizarre tale. Johnston was mildly superstitious. He always flew with a little white elephant hanging from his neck. This day, he had mistakenly left it in the pocket of some trousers when he changed his clothes. He didn't realize it until too late. As he came to readiness, he was concerned that, without it to preserve his luck, 'something untoward might happen'.

Many operational pilots used to carry a talisman of some sort with them. Dizzy Allen, my second CO in 66 Squadron in England, always used to fly with what he alleged was the seventh veil of a seven-veil dancer. He used to chew one end of it, I remember, when he became agitated. George Beurling, when he was with the Squadron in Malta, invariably had a small Bible in a pocket. Once, when he was shot down into the sea, his rescuers found it floating on the water nearby. Beurling's relief at its recovery was greater than his concern for the badly damaged foot which he had just sustained.

My own wartime companion was a small pigskin purse. In it I carried five treasured objects, wrapped in muslin. There was a gold French 20-franc piece and a little ivory elephant like Tim Johnston's. They had been given to me as I went away to war by an old friend, Jack Izod, who ran a well-patronized and fashionable shop at 49 Conduit Street, just off Bond Street, in London's West End. He had carried them safely with him through years in the trenches in the First World War.

There was also a silver US dollar, given me by a special girl in 1936, on my first visit to the United States. My mother had contributed her own choice of a tiny St Christopher medal, made of silver and tied to a piece of Cambridge blue ribbon. When I arrived in Malta, I added a Maltese Cross, fashioned as a brooch, which I acquired from a silversmith in Valletta.

I never flew without my pigskin purse in Malta, or,

for that matter, on any other day or night operation during three tours of flying against the enemy in World War II.

I survived without a scratch.

# 14

# SPITCHERED!

Say not the struggle nought availeth
  The labour and the wounds are vain
The enemy faints not, nor faileth
And as things have been, things remain
                                    *Arthur Hugh Clough*

A new transitive verb was now gaining currency in the Anglo–Maltese vocabulary – 'spitcher'. Mainly it was used in the past tense – 'spitchered'. Fowler might, at the time, have considered including it in any new edition of the *Concise Oxford Dictionary*. Had he been circumspect enough to do so (the word would have had an important relevance today), the entry, with abbreviations, might have run along these lines: '*Spitcher*: v.t. blot out, efface, erase, destroy, leave few traces of: attrib. bombing: sl. (Aeron: ref. Spitfire).'

As Kesselring and Lörzer increased the weight and frequency of the raids against Takali, we looked down daily from the bastions in Mdina upon the familiar, yet pitiful, sight of yet another aircraft going up in smoke in its pen. 'Spitchered!' became the normal and repetitive epithet. It was explicit, graphic and apposite. Moreover, it was final. Soon, its application became all-embracing, from bombed aircraft and buildings down to the destruction of even the smallest personal item. Everything became 'spitchered'. Broadly based, it suited the scene and the mood.

It wasn't long, however, before it was being freely used in an altogether more serious context.

At Greenock, hard by Glasgow, on Scotland's river Clyde, 47 Spitfire Vs were being loaded on to the US

Navy's jumbo-sized carrier *Wasp*, the outcome of a deal between Prime Minister and President. The transportation of these aircraft from the supply bases to Scotland, first to Prestwick and thence to Renfrew, by the pilots of the Air Transport Auxiliary, had been accompanied by a catalogue of trouble, compounded, at one point, by a spell of atrocious weather.

The last stage of the journey by road in Royal Air Force 'Queen Mary' transporters, in police-escorted convoys of six, to the carrier now lying alongside, had fully lived up to its earlier pattern. It was an inauspicious start to a critical enterprise. Fortunately, the pilots destined to fly the aircraft to Malta weren't aware of the problems until, eventually, they went aboard the carrier.

Two famous Auxiliary Air Force units were engaged: 601, the County of London's Squadron, and 603, its counterpart representing the City of Edinburgh. Squadron Leader John Bisdee, former scholar of Marlborough, exhibitioner of Corpus Christi, Cambridge and a peacetime product of the Unilever Group of companies, who had already made his mark fighting throughout the Battle of Britain with 609, Yorkshire's West Riding Squadron, led 601. After Malta, Bisdee was to lead the Squadron in the Western Desert.

Squadron Leader Lord David Douglas-Hamilton, from the centuries-old Scottish family, the youngest of four remarkable brothers, all of whom became squadron commanders in the Air Force, was well placed at the helm of 603. David, a boxing 'blue' at Oxford, and I, a golfing counterpart at Cambridge, were already friends. Sport had brought us together during our respective undergraduate years. Little did we think then what might be lying in store for us now!

Jumbo Gracie, fresh from his exchanges in Whitehall, and steeped in Malta's jungle lore, was to head the reinforcing operation, code-named 'Operation Calendar'. He would lead the mission from the carrier to the Island.

None could say that this promised to be an uneventful sortie. Having passed through the Irish Sea with its escort, *Wasp* would then head out into the Atlantic before changing course again and sailing through the Gibraltar Straits to the customary fly-off point 50 miles or so south of Algiers. Gracie and the two squadron commanders would then be left to lead their formations over the last 650 to 700 miles to Malta. As before, with the German Air Force now very much in control of the central Mediterranean area, the passage of the reinforcements would be shadowed throughout. It didn't then require a genius to estimate the projected time of arrival of the Spitfires at Takali and Luqa. Lörzer's *staffeln* and *gruppen* would thus be standing by to strike, with no more than the usual handful of Spitfires serviceable for island defence.

More worrying in some ways than the prospects for Operation Calendar was the leak which, for much of a week, had been going the rounds of the bars and clubs in Valletta. The Island-based squadrons had been warned no more than twelve hours beforehand, and in the greatest secrecy, of the impending touchdown time for this all-or-nothing venture. Yet what amazed us, when we heard about it, was that the outline of the story about a massive fly-in being prepared – even naming the nationality of the reinforcing carrier – had been common knowledge among those 'in the know' of the Island. In certain respects – mail censorship for one – security in Malta was exceptionally tight, yet here was an irregular and thoroughly disturbing example of laxity somewhere. It certainly fuelled my contention that there could be very few secrets in this tiny Mediterranean outpost. The place was just too small, with civilians and the military too closely intertwined.

When the fly-off did get under way, it was Jumbo Gracie, of all people, who put his foot in it first. Four decades afterwards, Philip Heppell, 249 Squadron's joker, could still barely conceal his mirth when he told the story on a television programme we did together. 'You'd never believe it,' he said, 'of someone who was so widely experienced as Gracie. First off from *Wasp* at around 0600, he started heading west, with other aircraft formating on him, straight back for Gibraltar. In Royal Air Force jargon, he had put what we called "red on black", meaning that he was flying a reciprocal course to the one he was supposed to be following!

'Despite the strictest radio silence being maintained, a sergeant pilot in the formation, a forthright character, not much given to subservience, called him up on the R/T. "Say, Red Leader," he inquired, "when do you propose setting course for the Island?"'

Jumbo never lived it down.

In a different bracket altogether came the inexplicable defection of the American, Sergeant Walcott, from David Douglas-Hamilton's squadron. Walcott was one of three Americans in 603. Like many others among his countrymen, he had volunteered to fight with the Air Force long before the United States had entered the war. He was in many ways a perplexing character. He had once apparently landed in the Irish Republic for no particular reason – another case, perhaps, of a coming event casting its shadow before it.

None read Walcott in 603 better than Tony Holland, an officer of quality and humanity. Holland was to fight all through the spring and summer battles and emerge, at the end of his time, as one of the Squadron's unqualified successes. His first-hand witness of this curious episode still sticks in my memory.

'Walcott,' said Tony, 'was instantly distinguishable by his close-cropped dark hair and eyebrows which met over his nose. He was a strange person who delighted in practising his skills as a hypnotist on anyone who was willing to volunteer. His success at this curious practice was achieved by applying pressure to a nerve or blood vessel at the back of his "victim's" neck – very probably highly dangerous for aircrew waiting on readiness.

'On board *Wasp*, he shared a cabin with a Canadian, Flight Sergeant Buckley. But after take-off, he was never seen again and certainly never turned up in Malta. When David Douglas-Hamilton started making inquiries, Buckley disclosed to him that, during the voyage from Greenock, Walcott had confided that he had no intention of ever going to Malta and that he had, in fact, applied for, and obtained, an interview with the ship's padre. The padre had apparently told him there was nothing he could do to intervene to alter either the circumstances of his posting or his intended destination. What else the padre may have said isn't known.'

There was a sequel to this extraordinary happening. Some while later, after Holland had returned from Malta to the United Kingdom, he was recovering in Halton Hospital, near Wendover in Buckinghamshire, from a broken femur. In the bed next to him in the orthopaedic ward was a young Cornishman, one Flying Officer Michael Giddings, who was later to become an air marshal and a knight with an impressive cluster of decorations. Giddings had served in Malta after Holland's and my time there. Let Tony complete the story.

'According to Mike Giddings, it was apparently confirmed that an American pilot had, indeed, crash-landed a Spitfire on the south side of the Atlas Mountains. Thereafter, he had made his way to a US consulate in Algeria, claiming to be a lost civilian pilot. His story stuck and eventually he obtained repatriation back to the United States.'

Other versions of the tale have since come to light, notably one told by a survivor of the cruiser *Manchester*, which was sunk during the August convoy – code-named

'Operation Pedestal'– to Malta. He and others in the ship's company had fetched up in a detention-cum-prison camp sited in an oasis in French territory in the Sahara Desert, a truly dreadful place. One of the detainees was alleged to be Walcott who later escaped in a provision lorry as it was leaving the camp. Having made good his escape, he was eventually repatriated to the United States.

Whatever the truth, the fact remains that, when forty-six Spitfires landed on the Island's two bases in mid-morning on 20 April 1942, Sergeant Walcott, in the forty-seventh, was not among them. Running quite contrary to all our experience of these dedicated US volunteers, it was certainly a very rum story.

The arrival of the new aircraft at Takali was a memorable affair. 249 Squadron's dispersal in the south-east of the airfield had been heavily attacked the previous evening – 'spitchered' – so this day we were using its counterpart on the west side of the pock-marked surface under the shadow of Mdina and the bastions. Most of us were down on the airfield waiting for the arrival of these treasures. Word had just come through from Ops that they were now west of the Island and would be landing in a few minutes.

Soon there came the distant and unmistakable roar of a formation of Spitfires flying tightly together. Gradually it got louder and louder until, suddenly, there they were, a dozen or so aeroplanes flying tightly in three sections in line astern, wing-tip to wing-tip, nose to tail, streaking in over the top of the citadel of Rabat, sitting up on the hill above us. We were astonished to see them flying like that. No one in his senses had flown that sort of super-tight formation in weeks and months – or even at all – in Malta. For one thing, we hadn't got that number of aircraft to formate with and, for another, there were usually too many Me 109s floating about to make such a drill sensible.

'They'll soon learn,' we said, as they fanned out to land . . .

The new arrivals hadn't been on the ground an hour before the plots from Sicily had started building up on the Ops Room table in Valletta. Ju 87s and 88s, with a greatly increased escort of 109s, started coming and kept coming.

Around 1300 hours, six of us old hands – Raoul Daddo-Langlois, Buck McNair, Junior Tayleur, an Englishman in the Squadron, Ray Hesslyn, Zulu Buchanan and I – really got stuck into what turned into one of the heaviest raids to date. There were pickings all round, although Junior Tayleur had the cockpit canopy of his aircraft shattered by cannon fire from a Me 109 which had attacked him from head-on. Despite being badly cut about the face and bleeding freely, Junior had carried doggedly on, probably destroying an 87 before landing his Spitfire, with wheels and flaps down, at Takali and immediately being carted off to hospital at M'tarfa.

Raoul had had a similarly unnerving experience. It was the only one of its kind that I had heard reported in my time on the Island. Like the rest of us, he had been mixed up with the 109s. Then, just as he was extricating himself from them, he saw one coming straight at him, head-on, with guns blazing away. Returning the fire, he held his bead on the German attacker. Each refused to give way, with a closing speed of some 500 or 600 m.p.h.; neither broke in time. They collided, the tip of Raoul's starboard wing catching the root of the 109's wing, severing it completely and sending the aircraft spiralling earthwards.

Only the outer section of the Spitfire's wing had been severed. Bringing the aircraft in with excess speed, wheels and flaps down, Raoul had let it run down the strip until he saw he was going to overshoot. Then, as the undercarriage was whipped smartly up, the run was brought to a halt with the pilot leaping from the cockpit just as a *schwärme* of four 109s was beginning an aggressive run across the airfield, all guns firing.

Raoul tore for the nearest slit trench and threw himself into it as the German fighters, spitting venom, passed overhead, leaving layers of surface dust, and a badly damaged Spitfire, in their train.

I knew Raoul so well that when we went out to him, covered with dust, but otherwise quite unharmed, I could see he was greatly deranged, not from the beat-up of the 109s, but from the earlier collision in the air. Typically, he played it off. 'Nice to know,' he murmured, 'that a Spit is tougher than a 109!'

The AOC called all the pilots of 601 and 603, and the rest of us, to the Xara Palace the same evening. Woodhall came with him. The setting and the circumstances, and the expectancy of the new arrivals, all contributed to a good sense of theatre . . . The new coming to the aid of the old . . . Forty-six new aeroplanes (less those which had been 'spitchered' that day) to boost the existing serviceability . . . Malta right up against it . . . Everyone in it together . . . All eyes now on this beleaguered Mediterranean outpost . . . The call for a supreme effort . . . The ingredients were tailor-made for one of Hugh Pughe Lloyd's stirring, ten-minute (never any more) addresses, spoken without notes. He was good at this sort of talk . . . pauses, nuances, asides, and all. He played well to an audience of pilots.

He was nearing the end of the essence of his message and approaching his peroration when the air raid sirens began to wail for the umpteenth time that day. Whisky-and-soda in one hand and a cigarette in the other, he went on undeterred:

I will leave you, then, in not the slightest doubt. The arrival of

133

these new aircraft today means that the climax of this battle is upon us. On its outcome will depend Malta's future as an attacking base against the Axis. On your ability to retain it against the odds will rest not only our own and the Maltese people's fortunes, but those of the 8th Army slogging it out with Rommel in the Western Desert as well. We must hold Malta at all costs and despite all dangers. That, gentlemen, is your task.

It was exhilarating, almost Churchillian stuff. Amid the din gathering all round, Lloyd ploughed on, his twitchy audience still gripped:

To discharge that task, your job is to destroy the enemy wherever you find him. Get in close, press home your attacks, see the whites of his eyes before you shoot. Then just pop him in the bag ... Mark my words, if you don't get him, he'll get you –

The rest of the sentence was drowned by the mounting crescendo of the Harbour barrage and the crackling of the Bofors batteries, manned by the marvellously brave Army gunners, barking out their defiance around Takali only a thousand yards or so away.

As the bombs began to fall, a 2000-pounder, screeching and screaming vengeance, seemed to have our names on it. It was too much for the old campaigners. Led by the Australians and the New Zealanders, there was a headlong dive for the cover of the billiard table ... The bomb missed by a few hundred yards ...

Sheepish figures emerged from under the table. Lloyd, with Woodhall still beside him, was standing erect, whisky-and-soda remaining in one hand, cigarette in the other. The faintest smile spread across that Indiarubber face as he looked, slightly patronizingly, around the room. 'You will now see, gentlemen, what I mean!' The rest was predictable rhetoric until he came quite abruptly to his closing sentence, spoken dead seriously and still without a note: 'Win this island battle and all the rest of your life you will be entitled to say with pride, "I was there."'

Forty-eight hours later, after an unremitting bombardment, only seven of the forty-six reinforcing Spitfires remained fit to fly. It was our Darkest Hour, no doubt about that. Hopes, momentarily, were buried. The old hands, looking tellingly at one another, said little, for there was little to say. We understood.

Daybreak seemed as far away as ever.

# 15

# BACK AGAINST THE ROPES

*Prosperity doth best discover vice, but adversity doth best discover virtue*

*Francis Bacon*

I had become convinced of one thing about our AOC: he was at his best when he was right back against the ropes. And, make no mistake, that's where he was – where we all were – now, as Kesselring looked for the knockout.

But, with the contest moving fast to its climax, Lloyd's ring-craft, and the unruffled control he exercised over his reflexes, never left him. From a defensive but defiant John Bull stance, he went on boxing his man, determined, somehow, to stay in the fight until the bell, and the next round of Spitfires, brought respite and renewed strength.

In the face of all the punching and pummelling, there remained about the man a serenity and confidence which, I felt, must have been deliberately contrived. There was no other explanation for it.

The façade – if, indeed, that's what it was – was immensely impressive; infectiously so. Whether he was talking to aircrew at dispersal, issuing orders from his office at Air HQ, or, again, exchanging thoughts socially and informally over a drink in the Mess at Mdina, there was always about him this same governing impression of poise. If there was turmoil in his mind at this lowest point – and he would surely have been inhuman if there weren't – he never let it show. The image was one of composure even when the bombs were whistling down. In these unsettling times, he epitomized to a T the age-old advice given by the great

British ambassador to his son as he started out on a career in the diplomatic service. 'Try,' said the father, 'to be like a duck, calm and serene on the surface, but paddle like hell underneath.'

That was Hugh Pughe Lloyd in Malta in the fateful spring of 1942.

The AOC selected this moment to make one of his no-holds-barred signals to Tedder in Cairo. Parts of it merit extraction. It was dated 23 April, and sent after three days' blasting following the arrival of the last lot of aircraft from *Wasp*.

Both places (Takali 377 tons of bombs ... Luqa 122 tons) a complete shambles in spite of soldiers working day and night ... Have made every effort to get Spitfires off the ground ... All Spits in pens widely dispersed, some with complete cover from blast ... In spite of this, 9 [out of 46 delivered] destroyed on the ground – direct hits, 29 damaged [by] splintered rocks. Owing to heavy fighter escort, our battle casualties eight Spitfires destroyed and 75% of remainder damaged in combat ... Army filling bomb holes day and night. Airmen work all day and, in shifts, throughout the night. Cannot do more to protect Wellingtons or Spitfires. Here everything liable to attack. German intention appears to be air blockade into submission ... Aim now is to destroy harbour facilities so that when convoy arrives it will be difficult to unload ... Also to destroy aerodromes and all equipment for handling aircraft. To hold this Island must have abundance of Spitfires and hope to get them into air before next raid which was 90 minutes on this [last] occasion.

It is worth adding a postscript to the AOC's graphic signal. It is taken from the Air Historical Branch's unpublished Narrative on the Malta battle:

The delay in getting aircraft of 601 and 603 into the air (it actually took three hours) was due partly to excessive security in Malta which prevented administrative staff from making adequate preparations for the receipt of aircraft. Also, in spite of the most explicit instructions from Air Ministry, the aircraft cannons had not been air-tested before leaving the UK, and there was trouble with faulty ammunition.

There seemed now to be no end to the bad news. Punch-drunk from it, all we could do was stand our ground and take it on the chin. A day or two after the last reinforcements' disaster, MacQueen, Daddo-Langlois and I had bicycled over to Luqa to see Harry Coldbeck. Harry, with his highly regarded partner, Les Colquhoun, and the redoubtable Flight Sergeant 'JO' Dalley, was now working overtime, covering the Axis airfields and ports in Sicily and southern Italy in the unarmed, blue Spitfire, bringing back vital photographic evidence of the enemy's dispositions. No one's contribution counted for more – or was more up to date – at this period in the Island's affairs.

We found Harry near to what purported to be PRU's* dispersal, clearing up after a mission earlier in the day. He was by himself and, for a moment, seemed uncharacteristically distracted and preoccupied, his thoughts miles away. 'What's new Harry?' we asked, trying to bring him back to reality. The answer brought no comfort. We all knew that an Axis invasion was on the cards anytime and PRU's leader seemed to bring it a step nearer.

'They look to be getting ready to take gliders on quite a large scale around Gerbini on the eastern Catanian plain,' he retorted. 'It doesn't seem too healthy.'

Earlier in the year, Admiral Raeder, German's invasion C-in-C, Field Marshal Kesselring and (at that time) General Rommel, supported by the Italian High Command and Mussolini, had made it clear to Hitler that if the Afrika Korps was to achieve its objective of dominating North Africa, Malta would first have to be captured. Raeder, Kes-

*Photographic Reconnaissance Unit.

selring and the German Naval C-in-C in the Mediterranean, Vice-Admiral Weichold, were all of the same mind that the neutralization of the Island by bombing was no substitute for the real thing – invasion.

Hitler had reservations. 'Operation *Herkules*' would place extra-heavy demands upon German resources at a time when they could ill be borne. There would have to be withdrawals from the Eastern Front, from North Africa, Crete and Greece. Besides, the serious losses incurred in the invasion of Crete in the previous year had signalled doubts about the wisdom of attempting a similar operation against Malta with its unfavourable terrain and a Garrison and people who could be relied upon to fight to the last ounce of blood. Moreover, the Führer doubted the outcome of the inevitable clash between the Italian Navy and the Royal Navy's Mediterranean Fleet.

Kesselring, in particular, had pressed his hand to the limit – and beyond – convinced that the case for invasion had been made.

Over and over again I urged Hitler and Goering to stabilize our position in the Mediterranean by taking Malta. I even persuaded Rommel to back me up. It was not until February 1942 that I succeeded in getting my plan approved ... at the *Führer's* GHQ in Berlin. Tempers ran high. Hitler ended [the conference] by grasping my arm. 'Keep your shirt on, Field Marshal Kesselring. I am going to do it . . .'*

Mid-July was set as the provisional date for the operation.

Coldbeck's disclosure about the Gerbini pictures, taken on 21 April, was, to say the least, disturbing. The last thing that Harry, with his stable temperament, wanted to do was to raise the alarm or otherwise create apprehension. But for

* *The Memoirs of Field Marshal Kesselring*, William Kimber, London, 1953.

someone of his transparent honesty, it was plainly unaccept-
able to withhold, or even temper down, what he knew to be
the truth. That wasn't his form with trusted friends.

The fact was that the interpretation of the pictures had
left not the slightest doubt about the Axis intention behind
the preparations. The details confirmed it. Close by Gerbini
airfield, some 25 miles south of Mount Etna, a rectangular
area 1500 yards along by 400 yards wide, and marked out
by a plough, was seen to have been prepared. By 24 April,
three days after the original pictures had been taken, a strip
had been cut and identified. By the end of the month, two
further strips had been added. Ten days later, all strips had
been completed with supporting huts erected and underground cables laid.

Further evidence that these installations were intended for
glider operations – that principal plank upon which the airborne invasion would rest – came when it was noted that the
strips had been sited close to a railway station. This was on the
direct line from Messina where a ferry connected Sicily with
the Italian mainland. The location was thus ready-made for
the passage of glider components and airborne troops . . . *

As we cycled the few miles back to Mdina in the dusty
heat of the late afternoon, Harry's news weighed heavily.
Two questions dominated our thoughts. When would the
next tranche of Spitfires arrive from the carriers and would
this be before Kesselring chanced his arm with an invasion?
And how, when the Spitfires did arrive, could we avoid a
repetition of the abysmal outcome of the previous operation?
To the three of us, nothing else seemed to matter on that
torrid afternoon. As we dismounted and trudged wearily
with our bikes the last quarter of a mile up the hill into
Rabat, I cannot say our hearts were exactly full of joy.

*

* Air Historical Branch Draft Narrative: Malta (unpublished).

The PRU Flight at Luqa provided a fascinating study in opposite personalities. On the one hand, we now had the dogged New Zealander Harry Coldbeck, with a capacity for taking infinite pains. On the other, there had been the contrasting flamboyance of Adrian Warburton, whose previous performance and way-out lifestyle had prospered signally under the gaze of an AOC whose own individualism and resource had complemented that of his legendary subordinate.

Warburton (everyone called him Warby, including the groundcrews in 69 (GR) Squadron)* lived his own life and wrote his own ticket. He was an original entrepreneur, good-looking in a fair, flaxen-haired way, pencil-thin and independent. He was brave to the point of being virtually nerveless.

In an island of exceptional individuals, Adrian cut an engaging figure not least because his character was by far the most difficult to read. He lived well apart from the fighter squadrons; that was his choice. But, despite this, I did not feel that, anyway, he would have wanted to become 'one of us'. He was too remote, too insular, too separate for that. In any case, I did not think that he would have felt particularly comfortable with, say, 249 or 126, or all those clubbable characters who made up our number.

He had small regard for convention. He was a crusader and his crusade was to fight the Axis in his own imaginative way – individually, and dressed mostly as he pleased – casually. He usually wore a curiously shabby mixture of Army and Air Force garments with a cravat covering the V of his open-neck shirt. The attire was a pose, a prop, maybe, for the play-actor and a means of appearing to be 'different'.

Like most publicists – Montgomery and Patton among

*No. 69 (General Reconnaissance) Squadron.

them – Adrian thrived on adulation and glory. Legend, true or apocryphal, fed on legend. He liked to be identified and be readily identifiable. He was a paradox with flair. One moment, he would be painting extrovertly on a broad canvas and splashing about with plenty of colour. The next, he was a withdrawn and secretive loner, introverted and, let's face it, pretty selfish with it.

He could be insensitive and unthinking, never with his own people – his crew, his fitters and riggers, NCOs and subordinates – but with any contemporary officer who might challenge his ego. I guessed this sprung from a desire to be the one in the spotlight, occupying centre stage. In racing parlance, he liked to be 'in the frame'.

Warby made his name in Malta and Malta made Warby. There was no other theatre in which he could have performed with the same latitude, the same disregard for convention, the same sterling results, the same imagination and panache, and with the same instant access to an AOC. Malta – and the Middle East – formed his parish. He held a long lease of the area and was regarded as a rare and prized tenant.

But, as with our Canadian 'ace' in 249, George Beurling, the Mediterranean island was built for Warburton's methods and style. That was where he felt at home. Had he and Beurling been obliged to spend their war operating from the United Kingdom and over the Western Front, where conventional rules and disciplines applied, it is at least arguable whether either would have shone and made a name. It wouldn't have been their scene.

What I saw of Adrian (as I told him, I much preferred his attractive Christian name to the commonplace soubriquet to which he answered) during my early days on the Island, I found appealing. I was sorry when, with the advance of spring, he was posted away to Egypt on what was euphemistically called 'a rest'. When he returned at the end of the summer, I was gone. All my life I have always had a regard for the unpredictable individualists who have played things their way and have said what they thought. Life has been the richer for their presence. Malta lapped up Warburton's idiosyncratic style and habit, and the fables which surrounded his feats.

The problem about getting to know this character as he was instead of the personality which he wore on his sleeve was that he spent so little time on the station – less, probably, than any other operational pilot on the Island. He had a compelling reason for absence. With an earlier marriage that was clearly no impediment to free expression, he was in love with an attractive girl named Christina Ratcliffe who lived in a flat in Vilhena Terrace, Floriana, nicely placed for Luqa.

Christina, an English cabaret dancer, who, with the rest of her troupe, had been caught on the Island when war broke out, worked as a civilian in the underground Ops Room in Valletta. At a time when Malta was largely devoid of entertainment, she and the other girls became the mainstay of the Raffians' Concert Party, alias the Whizz Bangs. They did their stuff with manifest courage and verve, even when the bombs were falling; yet when, in 1943, British Empire Medals were awarded to Christina Ratcliffe, and others among the girls, eyebrows were raised, particularly among members of the Royal Air Force's HQ staff who had given years of devoted service on the Island, starting in some cases in their very early twenties and enduring through the roughest part of the fighting. Understandably, they found the awards difficult to stomach . . . But life has always been unequal.

What is, however, undeniable is that Adrian Warburton, at the time of his achievements, was sustained by Christina, and Adrian, in his turn, and in so far as he was content to provide it, gave Christina his love. When, later in the war –

on 12 April 1944, this enigmatic character was lost on a one-off mission to southern Germany from Mount Farm, near Benson, PRU's base in Oxfordshire, a burning light went out of Christina's life. Four decades later, she was dead, a heartbroken alcoholic.

Coldbeck played things quite differently from Warburton. For one thing, by the time he picked up the reconnaissance mantle from his predecessor, the circumstances had changed fundamentally. With the build-up of the Axis air strength in Sicily, southern Italy and Sardinia (including elements of the Regia Aeronautica, Kesselring now had a front-line strength of 900 aircraft under his control), and with the imminent threat of invasion, the tasks were altogether more formidable. Left substantially to his own initiative and devices by a squadron commander who, on his own admission, knew little of this esoteric photographic work, the New Zealander was quite clear about his own, critically essential role. It was a scholarship examination paper. The questions were there to be studied with meticulous care and the answers (with every question answered) had to be provided accordingly. It demanded taxing application and long periods of concentration quite apart from all the hazards of the air.

Harry avoided histrionics. He approached his missions rather as an accountant would prepare a consolidated balance sheet for the company's year-end accounts. His aim with his pictures, and with the interpretation which followed, was to present a true and fair view of the state of the enemy's affairs. He didn't want to have any qualifications when it came to the audit. He was, in a phrase, a painstaking professional, the ultimate perfectionist.

That Coldbeck flew an aircraft alone, without a crew, without guns and without any other means of defence save that of altitude and speed, mattered not. It did not trouble him that he did not possess the means of retaliation or of shooting down any stray enemy aircraft he might see. That wasn't part of the reconnaissance remit. In any case, he had been a fighter pilot once: all that was behind. His task now could be summed up simply: to find the target unobtrusively, to get the best pictures and to bring them home safely.

In that tortuous late spring and summer, while his predecessor was 'resting' at No. 2 PRU at Heliopolis, Harry and his mates, Colquhoun and Dalley, had a potentially lethal danger to face. With Lörzer's fighter strength in Sicily at its zenith, the Me 109Fs with the Daimler-Benz 601 engine and, later, the Me 109Gs with the DB 605 unit, were an ever-present threat to a lone Spitfire assigned to cover targets far up in the north of Italy. The perils escalated as the chances of being headed off on the return flight increased. Tracked up and down the mainland by radar, and with the Sicily-based 109s having all the time they wanted to gain both altitude and position for an interception of the returning intruder as he ran the gauntlet for Malta, it became an oft-repeated nightmare.

By comparison, the so-called 'milk runs' to the heavily defended airfields and ports of Sicily and southern Italy, and their counterparts along the Libyan and Tunisian seaboard, became 'routine' – although some of us would hardly have described them as such!

Equally testing on a single, Rolls-Royce Merlin engine was the surveillance of enemy naval vessels and convoys, and the long all-sea flights, sometimes approaching 500 miles' radius, which this entailed. It was all hazardous operational service which earned, for some, minimal rewards. Coldbeck, with more than 150 missions and 500 operational hours in his log book, knew the form. His concern for his subordinates ensured that his frequent representations to the AOC about Colquhoun and Dalley brought recognition and eventually commissioned rank.

Arrangements at Luqa were primitive in the extreme. Pre-dawn take-offs in the blackout, in an aircraft unequipped for night flying, increased risks. Taxiing after an airman trotting along with a torch and trusting him to thread a passage past old craters and obstructions was one thing. Lining up on a runway devoid of lighting, with the odd delayed action bomb lying about was another. It was scarcely an uplifting start for a long and arduous flight ahead. It called on the reserves of discipline and courage.

Coldbeck's, Colquhoun's and Dalley's work, unlike Warburton's, was never highly publicized. It went unsung. They did not seek the limelight. That wasn't their way. Yet we thought in 249 Squadron at the time, and half a century on I still think it today, that here at Luqa, in the face of adversity, photographic reconnaissance was touching the limits of human endeavour. It placed the highest premium upon personal character and integrity.

Like X-ray pictures of the human frame, PRU's cameras exposed it all. The pictorial evidence confirmed our 'feel' that we had now reached the crunch. The next material move, from whichever side it came, would surely be decisive . . .

# 16

# CUTTING A PIECE OF CAKE

Often do the spirits
Of great events stride on before the events
And in today already walks tomorrow
*Samuel Taylor Coleridge*

We were warned at lunch-time that Group Captain Wood-hall would want to see the five of us at the Xara Palace later the same day. We guessed at once that something was afoot.

Stan Grant, our CO, the two flight commanders, Buck McNair and myself, and, additionally, two of our stalwarts, Ronnie West and Raoul Daddo-Langlois, were to be ready by 1900 hours to meet the Group Captain when he arrived from Valletta. It was often his habit to look in at the Mess at Mdina around this hour for a sundowner, but this obviously was different. There had been fresh rumours for several days that another delivery of Spitfires from the carriers was imminent and this meeting, we felt, probably had got something to do with it.

Woody didn't waste time when he met us. Having got us drinks, he took us along to the intelligence room at the far end of the terrace overlooking Takali where we could be alone. He came straight to the point. The AOC had asked him to come over and see the five of us because there was important news. After the disaster of the first lot of Spitfires from USS *Wasp*, arrangements had apparently been made at a high level to allow the US Navy's huge carrier to make a second run down the Med with a further batch of forty-eight Spitfires on board. The ship had gone back to the Clyde and was now alongside at Greenock waiting for the new aircraft to be loaded. As soon as everything was ready she would be sailing again for Gib and the Med. The operation would be code-named 'Operation Bowery'.

As she passed through the Straits, the plan was for her to join up with *Eagle* with a present complement of sixteen Spitfires (seventeen at a squeeze). The two carriers and their escort of a battleship, a cruiser and numerous destroyers – Royal Navy and US Navy – would then sail through the night to the usual fly-off point just north of Algiers. The sixty-four aircraft would take off early in the morning and, as they approached the Island some three-and-a-half hours later, would fan out into three groups to land, this time at Takali, Luqa and Halfar.

After the fly-off, *Eagle* would then return to Gib, load up again with a further consignment and make a second run a few days later. This way, something like eighty aircraft could be expected to reach the Island in the next two to three weeks. It would give us the clout we so badly needed.

New and elaborate arrangements were to be made on the three airfields for the reception of the reinforcements. Each aircraft would be plainly numbered and, after landing, would be directed to a similarly numbered blast pen. There, five members of the groundcrews and Army would be waiting to refuel the aircraft from five-gallon cans, rearm it as necessary and make any technical adjustments needed to maintain serviceability. The aim would be to have each aircraft fully operational again within thirty minutes and probably less. Experienced Malta pilots would be standing by to take each new aircraft over as soon as it arrived in its pen. They would be at advanced readiness for the rest of the day. All would be prepared to meet the enemy's attacks which must be expected to develop as soon as the delivery had been made. We should thereby stand the best chance of avoiding a repetition of the previous fiasco, when far too long had been taken to turn the new arrivals around with the result that many had been caught on the ground when the enemy struck.

Woody then came to the reason why the five of us had been singled out to see him. 'The AOC,' he said, 'has decided that it is essential for the next reinforcements to be led in by experienced Malta pilots, not by people who don't know the Island form. He wants 249, as probably the most experienced squadron here, to head this up. The five of you will therefore be leaving Luqa for Gib in a Hudson* tomorrow night. Wing Commander J. S. McLean will be in charge of the operation in Gib and he will see that you are all fully briefed. You should go prepared to be away for between about ten and twenty days.'

He added a rider of which we hardly needed reminding. 'I don't have to tell you fellows what is at stake with this operation. Everything will hang on it. It's make or break and it has just got to succeed . . . You'll be told what time to be at Luqa tomorrow evening. Meanwhile, no flying till then, and the best of luck to you all.'

This new responsibility made an instant impact. While none of us was exactly comforted by what he knew would lie in store, all of us felt proud that we – and 249 – had been picked out for the job. Now and then in a lifetime one feels instinctively that one is walking in step with destiny and playing a part – albeit a comparatively humble one – in some great, even historic, event. How historic this mission was to prove would not be seen until the European war had pretty well run its course and things could be looked at rationally in retrospect.

The truth was, of course, that the previous operation, after the fly-off from *Wasp*, had fallen far below the level of events. When 601 and 603 had flown in, apart from John Bisdee, 601's CO, and a very few others, there was found to be an appalling paucity of genuine operational strength among the pilots. It was totally wrong that this should have

---

* Lockheed Hudson, transport aircraft.

been allowed. Tedder, on hearing about it in Cairo, had referred to the quality of the pilots as 'also rans'. The facts justified the epithet.

Of the twenty-three pilots who had flown in with 601, seven had no operational experience at all, while a further twelve had under twenty-five hours on Spitfires, and 603's experience was no better. Nine of their number had never fired their guns in action, while a further thirteen had had less than twenty-five hours on Spitfires. What was, perhaps, worse, seventeen of the Squadron's most experienced pilots had been posted away during the two months immediately preceding the unit's departure for Malta.*

Malta was just about the most unsuitable theatre to which to send inexperienced pilots, no matter how courageous and keen. In the face of some of the fiercest aerial fighting of the whole war, against the most unfavourable odds, the Island was a place for hardened aircrew not the 'also rans'. Moreover, it was grossly unfair to the tried Malta hands, who had been slogging it out with the enemy for weeks, suddenly to find that survival in the air could be dependent upon a bunch of greenhorns.

Woody assured us that the C-in-C, with his sharp perception, had got the issue gripped and had seen to it that this nonsense was stopped. The next batch of pilots coming from the United Kingdom would have been properly bloodied and accustomed to mixing it with the Focke-Wulf 190s and the Me 109s high up over northern France.

The Lockheed Hudson, piloted by Flying Officer Matthews, a confident aircraft captain, was airborne from Luqa shortly before midnight on 30 April. A raid had just passed, but the all-clear hadn't yet sounded. All five of us were a-twitch and it felt uncomfortable not to have control of the aircraft

---

* Air Historical Branch Draft Narrative: Malta (unpublished).

oneself. But the take-off was uneventful and in no time the pilot's mastery over the aeroplane was apparent. Eight hours and forty minutes later, after flying through a moonlit Mediterranean night, we were running thankfully down the wide runway in the shadow of the Rock.

The peace and plenty of the place, after weeks of privations and hammering, enveloped us. It made us want to slump back and do absolutely nothing. We hadn't, of course, realized what the last weeks and months had taken out of us or how taut our nerves had become. In your twenties you don't think about that sort of thing.

We soon made our number with the admirable Wing Commander McLean, the well-decorated officer of whom Woody had spoken the night before we left Luqa. Based at the Rock, he was in charge of all preparations for the reinforcing operations. And 'in charge' was the phrase. Here was an officer of energy with a mind which cut through difficulties like a laser. Full of operational experience himself, efficiency oozed out of him. No detail escaped his notice. McLean had been responsible for previous fly-offs into Malta and now had the procedures buttoned up. He had seen at first hand some of the previous cock-ups which, for someone of his precision and temperament, must have been exasperating.

As to the mission which lay ahead, he regarded it – as he did most of his responsibilities – as a 'piece of cake'. It was a phrase with which, by the finish of the operation, we were to become very familiar, accompanied, as it was, with a disarming smile and a chuckle. Everything, no matter how bad, frustrating or hopeless, was met with the same uncompromising rejoinder. There wasn't a problem or a task in Gibraltar which fell outside this category. Psychologically, it had an unusual effect. It instilled confidence. McLean very nearly got the old Malta sweats to believe that the whole operation would be, genuinely, 'a piece of cake'. He was a master of the con.

But in so far as it was possible to have an uncomplicated understanding of the plan before us, Mac had it. The timing of the first fly-off of sixty-four aircraft from *Wasp* and *Eagle* together was dependent upon actions now taking place in Scotland. He couldn't influence these, but what he could do was to control the work which still had to be done in Gibraltar to assemble the Spitfires from parts which had been sent down by sea and have them ready for loading on to *Eagle* so that the eventual rendezvous with *Wasp* would be comfortably achieved.

He was confident this could be done because he had won the cooperation of the groundcrews on the Rock who, even without the spirit of a squadron to stimulate their efforts, were still 250 per cent dedicated to the task on the successful completion of which Malta's continued existence in Allied hands would depend. Working under McLean, his engineer officers and senior NCOs, they matched in every way the tradition of their counterparts in the operational squadrons.

On Mac's best estimate, the first fly-off from *Eagle* and *Wasp*, in unison, would take place within about a week, perhaps a day or two longer. Stan Grant would be at the head of the leading formation with Ronnie West in the van of the next. This would leave Buck McNair, Raoul Daddo-Langlois and myself to sweat it out for a further week in Gib to give time for *Eagle* to return to the Rock and be loaded up with another consignment of aircraft before setting sail, with her escort, for the customary fly-off point.

It became plain, therefore, that if McLean's estimated timetable turned out to be within gunshot of the actual timing, the three of us assigned to the second reinforcing party would be in this haven at the western entrance to the Mediterranean for a fortnight, perhaps a little more. At the outset, the prospect greatly appealed. A couple of weeks' rest and good living in the bright lights of the Rock, would serve as a tonic before returning to the rigours of the battle.

I had no doubt that Buck and Raoul were of the same mind. Each had drawn heavily upon his reserves to contribute not only to the Squadron's success in Malta, but also to the Air Force's collective effort. Yet, within three or four days of arriving at this station of rest, we were bored and anxious to get back to the fight.

Robert Wendell McNair, who was quick to complain about what, operationally, we might be missing 800 or 900 miles away, was a Canadian of easily recognizable calibre. He was, by nature, a critic of anything or anyone he thought to be substandard. He spoke his mind and never hedged his bets. He did not suffer fools gladly, as was borne out by an incident which occurred in the circuit at Takali during the worst of the spring fighting. The 109s were hanging about after a raid, waiting to pick off the Spitfires as they attempted to land, short of fuel and out of ammunition.

Buck sent his relatively inexperienced No. 2 in to land first while he maintained a watching brief above. The unfortunate wingman, with half an eye on the 109s circling like vultures overhead, made a poor fist of the first attempt at a landing. Off he went round again. It was too much for Buck. 'For Christ's sake, Blue 2,' he said over the R/T, 'Pull your effing hook out and land next time. If the 109s don't get you, I will!'

He was, of course, a first-rate fighter leader, aggressive to the extent of being ruthless, yet inside him was a private worry which he confided in me – that his eyesight was deteriorating and might not last the war. He lived with the fear that at some point the medics might discover his defect and take him off ops. For Robert McNair, in the middle of World War II, that would have been worse than the end.

In fact, his eyes did last the course with something to spare, and Buck ended the war with a record of leadership which had few parallels in the Royal Canadian Air Force.

For the moment, however, here in Gibraltar, he was soon at his restless worst, putting excessive pressure on McLean and Stan Grant to let him take part in the first fly-off instead of having to kick his heels with us and wait for the second. Inactivity was anathema to McNair.

One morning, down on the airfield by the Rock, he exploded in front of McLean. 'Let's get on, *sir*,' he gibed, 'and get ourselves a slice of this effing piece of goddam cake that we hear so much about . . .'

Mac played it deadpan. 'All in good time, Buck,' he said, 'all in good time.' The additional chuckle diffused the tension.

McNair didn't know it, but the words of the preacher would turn out to be wise.

# 17

# 'SO YOU FINALLY MADE
# PAGE ONE!'

In one respect, I was able to put the time we spent on
the Rock to what my journalistic mind suggested was good
use.

I was fed up – we all were – with the level of Allied
propaganda which was coming out of Malta and finding its
way into the national Press at home. The popular newspapers, with their four wartime pages, usually arrived weeks
late. What we read there, for instance, about the state of
play between the two opposing Air Forces, bordered on the
grotesque in its inaccuracy. It wasn't the newspapers' fault;
the misjudgements could be laid at the door of those who
were propagating the information. Isolation, security and
censorship all combined to ensure that only the well-
doctored stories were filed from the Island.

Most of the great war correspondents like the Alan Moore-
heads, the Alex Cliffords, the O. D. Gallaghers, the Alan
Woods, the Colin Bednalls, the Quentin Reynoldses, the
Drew Middletons, the Chris Buckleys – stayed away. For
one thing they weren't welcome. An extra mouth to feed
wasn't wanted.

So, walking one day into the orderly room of Station HQ
on the Rock, I noticed an uncovered typewriter on a desk.
If I came back later that evening, I thought, when few were
about, I could probably knock off 1500 or 2000 words on
what was actually happening in Malta and then get someone
who was going back to England to post the envelope in the
United Kingdom. Express Newspapers were still paying me
a proportion of my peacetime salary, so I wanted to do

something in return. Using the well-known 'lobby rules', I reckoned I could let John Gordon, the editor of the *Sunday Express*, or Arthur Christiansen, the editor of the *Daily* – or both – know something of the real background to what was going on with the Island battle.

To stretch a point, if I provided this background from Gibraltar, none could say I was deliberately flouting the Island's rules. In any case, this would be 'background briefing', not a story written for publication. I had to be careful because it was common knowledge in Malta that I had worked for the *Express* pre-war and suspicions would be easily aroused.

I had made friends with one Flight Lieutenant Bradley, a Catalina flying boat captain, stationed at Gib. He had already given me nearly three hours' dual instruction doing circuits and landings on the water, well away from the harbour – a captivating experience, incidentally, for a mere fighter pilot. Bradley was, I knew, returning soon to the United Kingdom. He was just the sort of dependable chap who could be relied upon to post a letter if asked.

There were only one or two orderlies about when I returned to Station HQ and they took no interest; so I wound a few sheets into the typewriter and let my mind run. Within an hour or so, I had recorded a rough impression of the Malta picture. I was careful to avoid exposing sensitive facts. I didn't need to as there was quite enough copy as it was. At the same time, I was determined to do an honest reporter's job and tell the story shortly just as I had seen it at first hand.

I sealed the envelope and addressed it to a friend in England whom I knew to be close to E. J. Robertson, the Express Group's all-embracing general manager, Gordon and Christiansen. His address was far removed from Fleet Street. In my covering note I asked him to pass on the enclosed piece, 'Robbie, John or Chris' (omitting the surnames) 'might be interested.' Bradley did the rest. I then put the matter out of my mind, satisfied that I had discharged my purpose. There had been a strong sense of loyalty to the newspapers pre-war and I hadn't forgotten it.

Three weeks or so later and a week after we had returned to Malta, I was sitting out on the balcony of the Mess when the Station Commander – now Jumbo Gracie – came up. 'The AOC wants to see you this evening.' Seeing my surprise, he elaborated. 'Don't say I said so, but I think it is something to do with some article he thinks you've written for the *Express*. We'll organize transport for you to Valletta.'

The news stopped me in my tracks.

Lloyd motioned me to a chair after I had saluted. He then passed a copy of the *Daily Express*, dated Saturday 23 May 1942, across his desk. 'I take it,' he said perfunctorily, 'that you wrote this?'

I looked at the front page. There, all the way down column one was my piece, just as I had written it. I doubted whether a word had been changed. There was a three-sided rule round the head.

## AIR KNIGHT OF MALTA WRITES HOME
### Battle of Britain Had Nothing on This

There was no by-line, but I felt my blood run cold as I read the intro: 'The *Daily Express* publishes below the first story from one of the gallant band of Spitfire pilots who are defending Malta.' Seeing my evident embarrassment, the AOC pressed his question. 'Did you write that?', pointing to the front page.

Obviously, I had to come clean. 'Yes sir,' I replied, 'I did, but not from here, not from the Island. I wrote it when we were in Gib waiting to fly the aircraft off the carrier.' I felt I had to make the best of it. The AOC wasn't responsible for Gibraltar.

Lloyd went on. 'You obviously know, as a journalist, that you are not allowed to communicate with the Press without authority, so why did you do it?'

Better to come out with it, I thought. 'Yes sir,' I said, 'I am aware of the rule, but, to be honest, I never intended it for publication. I didn't write it with that in mind at all. I sent the piece as a 'lobby briefing' so that the editor might have it as background to counter some of the ridiculous propaganda which is being written about the fighting here and which, to be frank, sir, makes us sick.'

The AOC seemed to be a bit appeased by my explanation, but he wasn't going to leave it there. I had to put up a black and he was resolved to see to it that I knew it.

'I quite understand your feeling,' he said, 'but you must have known that, if this sort of stuff got out, true though it is, it would cause trouble. It has certainly caused trouble in London as you can see by the speed with which this copy of the paper has got here.'

There comes a point in this sort of interview when an apology is the only way out, and the fuller it is made the better. 'I quite see it has caused trouble, sir,' I said 'and I am bothered that you have been troubled with it when you have so much on your plate. All I can plead is that I never intended that it should come out like this. I just wanted the truth to be known as background.'

Lloyd was never one for keeping alive differences. 'All right,' he said, 'you've said you're sorry and I accept the apology. But you must promise me that you won't do it again.'

The undertaking was readily given. It was small beer in the AOC's life. 'I want to hear now how you found the organization in Gib,' he went on. 'The two operations have come out splendidly. Full marks to 249 for the part the Squadron played in them.' In a moment, he had the recalcitrant flight commander eating out of his hand. He was a past master in the art of humouring aircrew after he had turned on the heat.

Unbeknown to Lloyd, the ripples from this incident spread wider. A week or so after my interview with the AOC, an envelope with OHMS stamped on it arrived for me at Mdina. Inside was a copy of the offending issue of the *Daily Express*. Clipped to the front page was a note containing a single sentence written with one of those thick, black 'subbing' pencils we used to use in the office. The handwriting was familiar. 'So you finally made Page One!' It was signed with the single initial 'C'.

Chris always had a word of encouragement for a young reporter who had produced a good story. But where he got the OHMS envelope from, God only knew.

Nor was this the end of the saga. Quite a short while after I had received the copy of the paper from Christiansen, a letter arrived for me from E. J. Robertson. It was very short. 'Lord Beaverbrook has asked me to say that he is thrilled by the exploits of your Squadron. We have paid £50 into your bank account in England. It could be handy just now.' A few days later, another letter came from Robbie. It was equally concise. 'Lord Beaverbrook tells me we haven't paid you enough. Another £50 had been passed to your bank in England.'

With all the aircraft plying between Malta and Gibraltar, news travelled fast between the two places. One morning McLean brought us terrible tidings. Norman MacQueen had, he said, been shot down over the Island on 4 May and been killed. The news stunned us. Indeed, at first, we couldn't credit it. Norman, who was standing in for Grant as CO of the Squadron at the time, had been such a success right from the start of our days together that we had come to regard him as almost invincible. With a total of eight aircraft destroyed already and several more probables – and with an exceptional ability to go with it – he had never suffered so much as a single bullet in his aircraft in all these weeks. He was one of our stars – like Nash, Plagis, West and McNair.

Apparently, he had been shot down late in the day from about 5000 feet near Naxxar. A lone Me 109, returning home after a raid, had pulled up under him, unseen, from dead astern, and given him a strong burst of cannon and machine-gun fire. The Spitfire had seemed to falter, but then correct itself, before diving straight in, pouring white glycol smoke.

It was thought that Norman's R/T must have been dead. Fred Almos, the American, formerly of 121, the US Eagle Squadron in the United Kingdom, flying No. 2, had called him over the radio to warn of the approach of the 109 and to break. There had been no reaction, whereas, in the normal way, MacQueen's reflexes had been like quicksilver. Poor Mac, he was dead when they got to him, the probability being that he had been killed when the German pilot attacked.

We felt his loss deeply for he was universally liked with his sunny and modest personality which bore ill to no man. Life was a game to be played to the full until the final whistle. For Norman, 'no side' had come cruelly early.

There was a revealing sequel to this depressing end. A few weeks before, I had had a fine Kodak camera stolen from my room in the Xara Palace which I shared with Daddo-Langlois and others. I had bought it in America a year before the war and prized it greatly. Photography was a hobby and the loss cast me down. Norman, with his generous, feeling heart, knew how I felt. He, too, was a keen photographer and possessed an equally treasured, German-made Kodak-Retina camera with a Schneider Kreuzmach f 3.5 Xenar lens and Compur-Rapid shutter. He always flew with it tucked inside his battledress pocket.

'Look here,' he said to me one evening, 'I can't forget the loss of your camera. If I should ever get bumped here and not survive, I would want you to have my camera. We'll find the adjutant and tell him so he can be a witness to my wish.'

I never felt that Norman ever had a premonition that he might not see out the battle. He was much too happy and jolly to harbour any such maudlin thoughts. The gesture was simply a manifestation of the natural goodness and generosity which adorned his mind.

The camera was found on his dead body, apparently undamaged. The adjutant passed it to me. 'I am quite satisfied that it was Norman's wish that you should have it if he did not survive.'

It took splendid pictures, as some of the illustrations in the work will testify. When I returned to the United Kingdom, I told Lieut.-Colonel J. T. C. Moore-Brabazon (later, the first Lord Brabazon of Tara), an old family friend who had been, first, Minister of Aircraft Production and then Minister of Transport in Churchill's National Coalition. Brab had been forced to resign over some intemperate remarks about the Russians which had been deliberately leaked from what he thought was a private gathering. Now a director of the Kodak company in the United Kingdom, and himself an able photographer, he insisted that I let him ask the firm's technicians to examine the camera minutely for any damage. The examiners gave it their blessing. 'We have dismantled and examined the camera piece by piece. It is in perfect condition.'

I still have it in use today, one of life's treasures, but ever a poignant reminder of a much-loved friend's sacrifice.

I suppose Raoul Daddo-Langlois and I took Norman's loss the hardest, for, with Bob Sergeant, we had formed a quartet of friendship which had been smelted in the furnace of battle. We had spent hours together, on and off duty, in one another's company, grateful for the chance which had brought the four of us into a close-knit partnership.

But now, as Raoul and I absorbed the awful news, another reverse struck. On 11 May, only a week after MacQueen had been killed, Bob Sergeant came through Gib on his way home, posted back to the United Kingdom, 'non-effective sick', as it was called. We were astonished to see him. He had been, we knew, the victim of a rare misfortune which had banished him summarily to hospital. But we expected him soon to recover.

Tony Holland, who, by now, had established himself as one of David Douglas-Hamilton's linchpins in 603, was up on the roof terrace of the Xara Palace one morning with several others, watching a full-scale Luftwaffe blitz on Takali. He was a first-hand witness of the incident.

'As the attack went in,' he said afterwards, 'and the bombs were falling, the Bofors batteries blazing away and the Spitfires mixing it up above with the 109s and 88s, Bob Sergeant came running up the stairs on the terrace from the floor below. He had barely called out "What's happening?" when he was hit by a stray bullet which fell from the sky. It clipped his lower lip and jaw before lodging dangerously in his chest. It was a chance in a million, but an object lesson in the sense of tin-hat wearing.'

(It's fair here to say that Holland and his friends in 603 knew all about tin-hat wearing. On their first night on the Island after flying the Spitfires in from *Wasp*, they had slept under canvas in an olive grove on high ground quite near Mdina. Tony was sharing a tent with John Buckstone, a very good type and 603's 'B' Flight Commander, and Paul Forster. They had awoken soon after first light to the sound of cannon and machine-gun fire from 109s strafing Takali and our precious Spitfires. Canvas was hardly bullet-proof so Buckstone, who had been married just before leaving the United Kingdom, stretched out a languid hand for the tin hat which was lying on the table beside the camp bed. Still on his back, John placed the hat slowly and gently over the vital area of his lower torso, thus displaying, they said, 'all the right priorities'!)

Bob Sergeant's wounds, it turned out, had been quite sufficient to terminate abruptly, and for good, his doggedly successful run with 249. After weeks of unequal combat since the Sunderland bringing out the original Spitfire party had touched down in Kalafrana Bay, Bob was entitled to expect better from Fate's hand.

Now, in Gib, the three of us recalled the prophetic question he had posed that February day, three months before, as the train in which we were travelling was steaming its way through the West Country to Plymouth at the start of what all three sensed would be for each an historic mission: 'I wonder how many of the first ten will come back?'

In fact the figure of ten should have read sixteen for that was the total complement of the first group. Of that number, six, or 35.5 per cent, had already perished, and a further four, victims of wounds, illness or exhaustion, were no longer on the Island's operational strength of pilots. Of the original sixteen, therefore, 62.5 per cent had either sacrificed their lives for a noble cause or had otherwise fallen by the wayside. It was a salutary token of Malta's pressures and hazards. It did not compare with the appalling carnage of the Island's Blenheim crews of 1941 and early 1942, but the wastage was still heavy enough.

As for our own tight-knit quartet, which had meant much to us while it survived, my factual diary entry for 11 May lays bare the truth. 'Gibraltar: shopping with Raoul. Bob Sergeant arrives from Malta *en route* for England. So with Mac's [Norman MacQueen's] death, our original four is split in half.'

Malta was going to be a different place when we returned.

# PART THREE

# 'THE BATTLE IS TURNED'

# 18

# AN ISLAND'S SALVATION

Now's the day, and now's the hour;
See the front o' battle lour!
*Robert Burns*

Gibraltar had much of the magic and expectancy of a West End or Broadway 'first night' as Operation Bowery was about to begin. It was 8 May 1942, the rehearsals were over and the last touches had been made. The props were in place and the cast, with Stan Grant and Ronnie West playing the leads, was ready. McLean, the producer, now aboard *Eagle*, and still fidgeting with details, was confident of success ... With plenty of 'pieces of cake' being handed out. There was nothing else for it now save wait for the curtain – and for the show to sell itself.

The timing looked good. As *Eagle*, with seventeen Spit-fires aboard, moved off to join *Wasp*, with her complement of forty-seven, the Royal Navy and the US Navy escort slipped naturally into place. A few hours' sailing in darkness and the fly-off of sixty-four priceless aeroplanes would begin, as planned, soon after first light. Britain and the United States, locked together in an historic enterprise, were setting forth to rescue the Island.

For 249 Squadron of the Royal Air Force, and its five representatives, the cards were down on the table, face up. We understood the plan. We knew the risks. None of us had ever flown off a carrier before. We had been warned to 'watch it', one problem being that, for take-off, *Eagle*'s flight deck of 667 feet overall was perceptibly shorter than

*Wasp*'s with 720! In practice, however, when the aircraft were stacked aft on the deck, the leaders had markedly less length to work with. And after that hazard had been surmounted, there would then be the business of leading and navigating a bunch of aircraft over 700 miles or so of water to a small piece of rock sticking out of a very large sea. And, if at the end, the enemy should challenge, then so be it. The force would be ready to fight.

None of us gave failure a chance. All we thought about was getting on with the job and having done with it. McNair, Daddo-Langlois and I envied our comrades their places in the van of the mission with its now promising meteorological forecast. We would have given much to have changed places, gone first and got it over. There was no comfort in having to stay behind, sit around Gib for another week and wait for *Eagle* to return, be reloaded and sail a second time. Besides, said Buck, we'd be missing 'some goddam good opportunities' on the Island. But such was to be our lot.

Meanwhile, as all this was going on, Churchill and the War Cabinet had their collective eye not only on events in the western and central Mediterranean. Their gaze was also fastened on the Libyan Desert. On the same day as *Eagle*, with her US Navy counterpart, was steaming towards the launch point north of Algiers, the Prime Minister sent an unequivocal message to General Auchinleck, C-in-C, Middle East. The signal deliberately underscored the importance of Malta's future in relation to the projected operations in North Africa.

The Chiefs of Staff, the Defence Committee and the War Cabinet have all earnestly considered your telegram in relation to the whole war situation, having particular regard to Malta, the loss of which would be a disaster of first magnitude to the British Empire, and probably fatal in the long run to the defence of the Nile Valley.

2. We are agreed that in spite of the risks ... you would be right to attack the enemy and fight a major battle*

As if to dispel any possible doubt about the concern felt in London for the future of the Island and its Garrison, Churchill, two days later, on 10 May, again signalled Auchinleck, this time in even more direct terms.

The Chiefs of Staff, the Defence Committee and the War Cabinet have again considered the whole position. We are determined that Malta shall not be allowed to fall without a battle being fought by your whole army for its retention. The starving out of the fortress would involve the surrender of over 30,000 men, Army and Air Force ... Its possession would give the enemy a clear and sure bridge to Africa, with all the consequences flowing from that. Its loss would sever the air route upon which both you and India must depend ... Besides this, it would compromise any offensive against Italy and [other] future plans ... Compared with the certainty of these disasters, we consider the risks you have set out to the safety of Egypt are infinitely less, and we accept them.†

It was no coincidence that there occurred at this finely balanced moment a change at the top in Malta. Months of agonizing stress and responsibility had worn Sir William Dobbie down and left him not only exhausted but unwell. With his faith to support him, he had run his course as Governor heroically. However, soon after announcing to the Maltese people that the George Cross had been awarded to the Island by King George VI – a tellingly calculated stroke, Dobbie stepped down. His place was taken by Lord Gort, John Standish Prendergrast Vereker, then fifty-five years old, sixth Viscount, 'a warrior of the truest mettle',‡

---

*Winston Churchill, *The Second World War*: vol. II, *Their Finest Hour*, Cassell, 1949.
†ibid.   ‡ibid.

holder of the Victoria Cross, the Distinguished Service Order and two bars and the Military Cross, commander of the British forces at Dunkirk and as hard a piece of granite as might be found. He was transferred from Gibraltar, where he had been acting in the same capacity. His was a significant selection. He epitomized to his fingertips the ethos of the Island, the resolution of its people and the bulldog resolve of the armed forces to fight for its protection to the last bullet – and then, if necessary, with bare fists.

Gort had the Guards officer's touch. Came one June dawn, soon after I had taken over command of 249 from Stan Grant, I was sitting in my Spitfire at Takali at advance readiness. It was barely light, but already our radars were picking up the enemy moving south from Sicily. I heard a heavy thump on the fuselage of my aircraft. Looking down to my left, I was astonished to see the Governor and C-in-C, by himself, red tabs and all. Whipping my flying helmet off, I made as if to get down from the cockpit only to be met with a brusque, 'Stay there, squadron leader, stay there, please.'

Gort nipped up on to the port wing of the Spitfire and held out his hand. 'Good morning, squadron leader, my name's Gort. I'm the Governor. I just called in to see the Squadron. I know how well 249 has been doing and I wanted to say so to you personally. Keep it up and good luck to the Squadron.'

With that, he jumped down off the wing and started to talk to my groundcrew clustered round the blast pen. He knew their worth and, I gathered afterwards, saw to it that they understood it. Gort knew there was only one place from which to lead – from the front . . .

The fly-off of the Spitfires from *Wasp* and *Eagle* on 9 May, upon which so much rested, was a huge success and vindication of Grant's immaculate leadership – no flap and everything buttoned up tight. Of the sixty-four aeroplanes launched from the two carriers, sixty, or 93.7 per cent, reached the Island. Of the arrivals, sadly one, the twenty-year-old, but experienced, Flight Lieutenant R. H. C. 'Ray' Sly, who had been a member of the Royal Australian Air Force's 452 and 457 Squadrons in the United Kingdom, was killed after touching down at Halfar.

The Me 109s were treating the newcomers to a customarily lively reception as they joined the circuit on Malta's southernmost airfield. One of the arrivals from *Wasp* with Sly was the Canadian John Sherlock, who was later to make his contribution to 185 Squadron during the ebb and flow of the summer's fighting. John was a first-hand witness to Sly's demise, recording a note in his diary at the time of the unfortunate incident. He and another compatriot, Pilot Officer C. A. ('Cy') King, each critically short of fuel, were following Sly in to land.

There were several 109s in the circuit as we came in; some had actually got their wheels and flaps down to fox us! Cy, now completely out of fuel, was gliding in for a landing in front of me, wheels and flaps down. As I still had some petrol left, I moved off to one side of him, intending to go round again. I was surprised to see Cy's plane swerve a little as he fired at a 109 which passed in front of him! He was about 500 feet at the time, and continued to land.

I was a couple of hundred feet above Cy when I saw another Spit – Sly's, it was, in fact – which had landed OK but which then attempted to take off again. Aircraft which were taxiing in were being strafed. It was, I think, to try to avoid this that Sly had another go at getting airborne (not downwind, as some have suggested). Obviously, he didn't have enough flying speed to make it; he bounced off a pen and that was that.

Sherlock ended his diary entry on a happier note. Writing of 'Old Tex Vineyard', a flight sergeant in the RCAF, who was eventually to transfer and become a US Marine Corps flyer and shoot down Japs in the Pacific, he painted a memorable picture.

Tex was strafed after he had landed at Halfar. He actually jumped out of his plane while it was still doing about 40 m.p.h., going ass-over-teakettle in the process as his Spit came to a pilotless stop!

While all this was going on, we were also hit by some Ju 88s and Eyetyes ... It was a day when the ages-old question: "Are you happy in the Service?" would have received a very negative answer!'

As for the four non-arrivals from *Wasp*, they made up a remarkable mixed bag. One, Sergeant E. F. Sherrington, another Canadian in the RCAF, took off with his airscrew in the coarse pitch,* a heinous pilot error, difficult to comprehend in the exceptional circumstances. His resultant lack of flying speed meant that his aircraft barely got airborne, dropped off the bows of the ship and was chopped in half as the carrier knifed through it.

Yet another Canadian, Pilot Officer Jerrold Smith, was more fortunate. On these reinforcing operations down the Mediterranean to Malta, there were only two worthwhile options open to a pilot if, after getting airborne, it became clear that, for one reason or another, he wasn't going to be able to make it to the Island. He could climb up, bale out and trust to luck that one of the many naval vessels below would pick him out of the water. Otherwise, he could fly south into French North Africa, force land, destroy his aeroplane and then do his best to make it back home.

Jerry Smith, whose younger brother, Roderick, was to become one of the RCAF's well-decorated wing commanders and, later, a distinguished Vancouver lawyer, had lost his 90-gallon belly tank on take-off. Eschewing the two

---

* Like starting a car in the wrong gear.

options, he went for broke, trying for a landing back on *Wasp* without a tail-hook to check him. This was an alternative which was greatly discouraged and, in the case of *Eagle*, actually forbidden. To everyone's amazement, Smith made it at his second try, the first time a Spitfire had been landed on the flight deck of a carrier without arrester gear. But he had one exceptional piece of luck.

The Landing Signals Officer in *Wasp* for Operation Bowery was one David McCampbell (later Captain David McCampbell), who was to become one of the US Navy's most gifted and successful pilots in the Pacific theatre. Long afterwards, McCampbell recalled this hair-raising incident.

Fortunately, I had given all the Spitfire pilots a briefing to acquaint them with operations aboard ship. I told them that if anyone saw me jump into the net alongside my platform, he would know the plane coming in was in trouble and must make a new approach.

On his first approach, Pilot Officer Smith was much too high and too fast . . . so I simply jumped into the net. He got the news real fast. Next time, I got him to slow down and make his approach a little lower. I then decided to give him the 'cut' signal [to land] . . .

He landed with his wheels a few feet short of the forward part of the flight deck . . . That night in the wardroom, we presented him with a pair of Navy wings!*

Jerry Smith joined us in Gib the next day – with a secret. When they took him down to the wardroom of this supposedly always 'dry' US man of war, Douglas Fairbanks Jr, *Wasp*'s liaison officer, 'surreptitiously pressed the largest Scotch-and-soda you ever did see into my hand. "Here," he said, "drink this quick!"'

Jerry's luck didn't hold. Within three months, this bright

---

*Captain David McCampbell, *Wings of War*, ed. Laddie Lucas, Hutchinson, 1983.

and attractive character, who, at school, had always been in the first two or three in his class, had been lost in circumstances which all regretted.

Having flown into the Island with us from *Eagle* on the carrier's next run eight days later, he had joined 601 Squadron at Luqa and quickly settled into the cut and thrust of battle. When, early in July, the Squadron was moved from Malta to the Western Desert, a sharp bout of sand-fly fever kept him behind. Remaining in Malta, he was transferred to 126 Squadron, there to join his younger brother who, at Jerry's request, was soon flying as his wingman. With only a year between them in age, they made a pair of special quality, on the ground and in the air.

On 10 August, the Squadron was on readiness at Luqa, with Rod Smith paired, as usual, as No. 2 to his brother. With a lull in activity, 126 was eased to '30 minutes available'. Rod at once took advantage of the easement and the proximity of an Army dispatch rider to get a lift over to station stores there to replace, both for himself and for his brother, the worn silk inner liners for their flying gloves.

Things changed in the moments he was away from dispersal and Jerrold Smith's section was scrambled in answer to a sweep of Me 109s east of Grand Harbour, a sergeant pilot standing in for Jerry's brother.

It was the last the Squadron ever saw of the 21-year-old pilot officer who always flew with an electric torch in his battledress. Flying north, away from some minesweepers which were plying their trade to the east of the Island, Jerry and his unfamiliar wingman became separated. Nothing more was heard or seen of the section leader although there was some vague report of a parachute having been seen by a section of aircraft from Takali.

It was a terrible reverse for the surviving brother for the two were very close, but he gave no visible sign of his inner feelings. 'I just followed the practice I always adopted on memorial occasions. I immediately put into neutral that part of my brain which ponders such matters, and carried on quietly.'

But Rod Smith did more. Remembering that his brother had always carried a flashlight with him in his aircraft, he asked his flight commander whether he might make a dusk take-off and have one last search of the Island's eastern approaches. Permission was at once granted, but the darkness kept its secret . . .

About the other two non-arrivals, with Jerry Smith, from *Wasp* there was also something of a mystery. The loss of the two flight sergeants, Charles Napoleon Valiquet and John Vaughan Rounsefell, both of the RCAF, was said to have resulted from a mid-air collision during some brush with the Regia Aeronautica near the island of Lampedusa 100 miles or so south-west of Malta. The information came from the enemy, but it was a strange way to lose a couple of Spitfires in a reinforcing operation of this kind.

For the rest, however, the overwhelming success of Operation Bowery transformed the Island's picture almost overnight. The effectiveness of the new reception arrangements meant that, on arrival at a specially designated blast pen, a Spitfire was turned round not in thirty minutes, as was originally being anticipated, but in ten and sometimes less, as the procedure developed. With a Malta-trained pilot then ready to take over, it was a triumph of planning and organization in which Army and Air Force each played its full part.

At a stroke, the serviceable strength of the defending fighter force was increased fivefold. Astute operational management of these new-found resources, coupled with Woodhall's imaginative and agile controlling of the squadrons in the air, meant that the Luftwaffe was now confronted by an opposition infinitely more formidable than anything it had encountered over the Island before.

For Lloyd and Woodhall, it was now a matter of being offered a choice. They could wholly disregard, if they wished, Kesselring's fighter sweeps, palpably designed to tempt the defending fighters into battle. Or, again, they could select, for interception, only those enemy raids which would yield the highest dividends, and cause the maximum hurt to the opposition. The heavily escorted raids by the Ju 88s (the vulnerable Ju 87s were no longer so much in evidence) now became the currency in which Lloyd and Woodhall could afford readily to deal.

For the first time, they could risk being choosy – to shun the fighters, but tear into the bombers. Furious battles were fought out on 10 May and subsequent days under these new rules with results which brought the hard-pressed islanders, with their unquenchable spirit, cheering on to the ramparts. Terrible hardships and privations would still be with them and their families for weeks to come. But, with their marvellous faith to sustain them, they now began to feel sure that Someone had been listening to their prayers.

Meanwhile, back in Gibraltar, our period of waiting, with its good food, rest and all the comings and goings of friends, was almost over. There was still our reinforcing operation to come under McLean's increasingly buoyant direction. No matter how many 'pieces of cake' the first part of the mission might have drawn from him there was still our hurdle to clear. And we didn't forget it. Nevertheless, God willing, we would soon be back on the old treadmill of bully beef, bitter bread, gharry grease and the perennial Macon-achie's stew.

Even in times of waiting and boredom, humour was never very far away – certainly not when the Australians were about. There was always something rich and tasty and open about their joking. It was simple, direct and didn't have too much regard for human feelings. We laughed (and moaned) more spontaneously with the Aussies than with anyone else. They were the salt and the pepper of the earth.

One morning, Raoul Daddo-Langlois and I were watching, with a couple of others, the well-established Ceremony of the Keys which, in the early summer of 1942, was performed occasionally for the onlookers' benefit on the square in front of what was then called Government House. It had attracted a sizeable gathering with all the spit, pomp and polish of the parade ground. The two neighbours on our right were both Royal Australian Air Force sergeant pilots. A likely looking pair, they were dutifully attentive throughout the ceremony. They seemed to know the procedure off pat.

At one point in the parade, the Sergeant of the Guard called out in stentorian tones 'Whose keys?' At which there was a shout from the back 'Sire! The Governor's keys' or some such phrase.

This day, we reached the *moment critique*, with the Sergeant of the Guard bawling out the question 'Whose keys?' Whereupon, right on cue, and a split second before the anticipated rejoinder, the Aussies were ready with their retort. 'MaconaCHEES!' they bellowed, exactly in unison, to a roar from the astonished spectators.

You could have cut the accent midway between Melbourne and Brisbane.

# 19

# FLIGHT TO FORGET

The Royal Navy of England has ever been its greatest
defence and ornament.

*Sir William Blackstone*

For the two cricketers among the three of us, it was rather
like going in to bat after a long opening stand. Our two
openers, Stand Grant and Ronnie West, had taken the score
confidently past 100 and had paved the way for a big total
from the rest. Now it was up to Nos 3, 4 and 5 in the
batting order – McNair, Daddo-Langlois and myself – to
consolidate the gains and profit from a good start. It was
just the kind of situation to give McLean, now on his fifth
successful reinforcing operation from *Eagle*, good grounds
for asserting that the second and last stage of the mission
could undoubtedly be regarded as another 'piece of cake'.

It didn't look like that to the rest of us. Too much was
still to play for. Too many hazards lurked along the way.
Too many things could still go wrong. Besides, after a long
wait in the pavilion on a bright day, it always took time to
adjust to the light. Still, we were experienced and ready.
The balancing seventeen aircraft to be flown into the Island
– they were Spitfire VCs with four cannons each – had all
been air-tested. We had done it ourselves. Indeed, in the
time we had been waiting at Gib, we had done little else
but air tests and spells of precautionary readiness in antici-
pation of an unlikely Axis attack. Now that the aircraft had
been loaded aboard the carrier, it would be up to us, and
those whom we would be leading, to finish off the job.

We were certainly well up on our toes. The enemy, after

all the activity of the last fortnight, would be on the alert and waiting for the new arrivals. None of us could be accused of being a purveyor of alarm, but each knew that McLean's remarkable run of success with the fly-offs from *Eagle* (he had now seen forty-eight Spitfires delivered from this carrier to Malta without loss) could not last forever. There was bound to be a reverse before long. However, we were reassured of one thing. Tedder's earlier representation to the Air Ministry from Cairo about the lack of operational experience among pilots being sent out to Malta had borne fruit. There wasn't an 'also ran' among the ones who were now to fly off with us.

Life aboard *Eagle* was instructive. The ship was again under the command of Captain L. D. Mackintosh RN, himself an experienced Naval Officer, who had been through the gamut of these reinforcing operations. He had had to endure the bad times and clearly didn't expect any more. He was a tolerant and understanding man, but he worked on a short fuse when it came to inefficiency.

The relationship between the Royal Navy and the Royal Air Force, after the initial hiccups, was good. McLean had had a lot to do with it and he and Mackintosh were much of the same feather. Things were now on a professional basis with everyone knowing the drill and exactly what was expected of him.

There were big differences between our two Services, but I had become drawn to the Royal Navy, its characters and disciplines. Crossing the Atlantic early in 1941 in the armed merchant cruiser, *California*, after learning to fly in Canada, had given me the chance to study the senior Service at close quarters under strictly operational conditions. Moreover, on that run from west to east, we had had on board with us the crew of a submarine under its commander, Richard Raikes. They were returning to England from Halifax, in Nova Scotia, and had quickly become friends.

A short extract from my diary, written a year before, while we were heading for Reykjavik, in Iceland, recaptured the present ethos of *Eagle* as we steamed eastwards down the Med for the fly-off next morning.

I fancy the Navy has the tightest discipline of all. Take this ship; to all intents we are permanently on the alert, for U-boats are operating ... In the Navy everything is done at the double. There's no questioning an order. There is the clipped summons from an officer, the coming to attention, the brief and direct order, an 'Aye, aye, sir', a salute and away you go.

There's a noticeable division in this Service between officers and other ranks, much more so than in the Royal Air Force. Yet, paradoxically, the relationship is close. It seems to have much to do with trust. Everyone knows his job and the crew appear to be perpetually busy. Things are done precisely. Divisions (prayers), said first thing each morning, are taken sincerely and said in earnest.

When there's scrubbing to be done it is done thoroughly. The Navy's ships don't smell of rubber like the liners I've sailed in in peacetime. They're like the Service itself, clean and tidy – a Service which sports starched white collars, black ties and tunics with every button done up. I'm in the Royal Air Force and very proud of it, so this is a tribute to another Service, a first-hand and, I believe, well-deserved accolade.

After a night of fitful sleep, we were up well before first light, waiting for our designated aircraft to be brought up on to the flight deck. Everyone in the ship's company was on edge. You could feel it. There had been three quick – but unsuccessful – attacks by U-boats as night turned into day, one torpedo passing much too close for comfort. Destroyers, looking wonderfully agile, were chasing about all over the place in a protective screen, dropping depth charges galore. Unbeknown to us, it was the shape of things to come, for in a later convoy operation *Eagle* was caught fair and square by a torpedo and sent to the bottom.

McLean was moving about among the pilots like an attentive schoolmaster among his class, offering a comforting word here, a piece of cautionary advice there. I got the feeling that these fly-offs must have been nervy affairs for him – as nervy for him as they certainly were for us. So much was at stake. But he didn't show his emotions. He couldn't afford to. If he had, no one would have believed all those 'pieces of cake'.

The wing commander handed each one of us personally a flight card with every conceivable detail we might need on it . . . heights, speeds, courses and times to fly and much other information. These cards were typical of McLean's precise, sharp and invariably tidy mind. He forgot nothing. Operations which were thoughtfully conceived and meticulously planned in wartime seldom went wrong. The success of these reinforcing missions from *Eagle* owed much to the care McLean devoted to them. The track of the flight, which he made the leaders superimpose on a small-scale map of the Med and the Algerian and Tunisian coastline supports, too, the thoroughness of his approach (see map illustration in the second photograph section).

I had memorized his written instructions – a fail-safe against dropping the card in the cockpit. Its possible loss became a pre-flight nightmare despite its being strapped to the knee. I had also made up my mind exactly how I would lead my eight aircraft over the 700 miles or so of water – steadily, at a constant airspeed and height, with the minimum of variations. Uniformity and constancy, that was the key. Life was comparatively easy for the man who was leading. It was for Red 2 and 4 and Blue 2 and 4 flying out on the flanks, that erratic leading meant increased fuel consumption, and therefore worry about petrol reserves near the end of the flight.

With an estimated 40 m.p.h. wind from due south at 10,000 feet, there should be sufficient endurance to make Malta provided the leading was properly and sensibly done.

There had been sufficient earlier examples of erratic and inexperienced leading, resulting in excess fuel consumption – and loss, to teach their lessons. Too many of Tedder's so-called 'also rans' had been given the job and made a cock of it. No. 249 Squadron knew better. All being well, I thought, Buck, Raoul and I would see to that.

Buck's formation was off first in the early morning of 18 May, all his aircraft disappearing ominously, one after the other, beneath the bows of the carrier as they left the flight deck before appearing as the undercarriage of each Spitfire came up and its airscrew bit into the air. We, who were to follow, would have preferred not to have witnessed this disturbing scene!

I had known more relaxing moments in my Service career as I sat, strapped into my aircraft, waiting for McLean to give me the all-clear for the second eight to take off. The sequence was predictable ... Airscrew in fine pitch, trim correctly set, throttle gradually eased forward against the brakes until the aircraft wouldn't be held any longer, and the tail unit was beginning to lift ... Then let her go ... Maximum boost ... Nose held straight at all costs along the flight deck, no swinging ... And trust Rolls-Royce to do the rest ...

There was a nasty, unsettling 'sag', with some sloppiness, as the aircraft cleared the bows ... Then wheels up in-stantly, stick held well forward to keep the nose down and build up flying speed ... And the relief of it as lateral and fore-and-aft controls firmed up and the aircraft was coaxed into a climbing turn to port with *Eagle* now visible down below, still cutting through the waves at maximum knots as the last of our eight aircraft gathered pace along the flight deck and the pilot went through the same traumas which, a few minutes earlier, had been for me a personal and, if the truth be told, a most deranging thing ...

Formed up now into two sections of four aircraft in wide

open line abreast, and setting course on a heading of 095° at 10,000 feet and at an indicated airspeed of 165 m.p.h., with Raoul leading the second, we felt that, barring accidents and some untimely intervention by the enemy, we were over the worst. All the same, there would still be another three hours and more of listening for the slightest sound of roughness in the faithful Merlin engine with nothing but sea and sky in sight.

In peacetime, the sparkling blue of the Mediterranean on this early summer's day would have been an inviting tourist attraction. But now, as we passed the enemy-held island of Pantelleria, housing, we knew, a squadron of Me 109Fs, manned by the Axis, the blue ocean was a menace we hoped to avoid.

A hundred miles out from Malta, with all eight Spitfires looking rock-solid in the stable air, an unfamiliar English voice, with just the trace of a foreign accent, came over the R/T. After nearly three hours of absolute radio silence, it gave me a jolt. 'Hello, Spitfire leader, steer zero-two-zero for base . . . Vector zero-two-zero for forty-five minutes for base. Do you hear me?'

The Germans had tried this sort of homing subterfuge before either by W/T* on some unsuspecting navigator or, as now, in plain language over the R/T, to entice an unwitting pilot to Sicily. With 249 Squadron, it cut no ice and only a few minutes later there came the deep, and immensely reassuring, voice of Group Captain Woodhall speaking to Buck McNair, whose formation, nearly thirty minutes ahead of mine, was now approaching Malta and about to touch down at Takali. It was another ten minutes – perhaps a little longer – before I heard the same distinctive voice called 'Balsam Red One', my call sign. It was comforting to respond. 'Hello, Gondar, Balsam Red One here, loud and clear. Everything OK. Over.'

* Wireless Telegraphy.

Back came Woody, speaking, as he always did over the R/T, conversationally and naturally, even when things got very rough. He preferred Christian names to call signs.

'Good show, Laddie. Keep a good lookout as you approach base. There are some little jobs* about. Your friends will be covering you. You'll see them soon.'

'OK, Woody. Thanks. Out.'

It was like old times. But did I detect just a slight lessening of the tension?

I sent Raoul, with his four, in to land first at Luqa, followed by the three newcomers who had been flying with me. Exhausted and damp with sweat, I followed the other seven in to a thankful touchdown. When I taxied to my allotted dispersal pen, I found Norman Lee waiting to take over my aircraft and the groundcrew ready to refuel it. It was a relief to feel that this operation, which we had been worrying about for a fortnight, was over.

The entry in my log book was factual and explicit: '18 May 1942: Spitfire VC BR 115: Self: HMS *Eagle* to Malta: 3 hours and 30 minutes: O Lord, deliver us from such a task again!'

Yet this had been a fortnight which would turn a battle – and, maybe, the war.

* Enemy fighters.

# 20

# ULTRA SECRET

A clandestine operation of capital importance to the Malta battle was presently being conducted deep underground in Valletta. Nothing whatever was known of it in the squadrons or at station HQ on any of the three airfields. It was probably the most preciously guarded secret of the whole struggle. Its benefits were known only to four, perhaps five, of the most senior officers perched at the Island's summit and who, locally, held Malta's destiny in their hands.

The breaking of the enemy's code by the intelligence organization known as Ultra at Bletchley Park in the United Kingdom achieved results of inestimable consequence for the Allied cause. Nowhere was this more true than in Valletta and Cairo.

Thanks originally to the perception, vigilance and pluck of a Polish mechanic, the busting of the seemingly unbustable German cipher machine called Enigma, and the securing of the top-secret intercepts which this produced, gave us an advantage in the central Mediterranean which went some way to offsetting the odds with which we were daily contending.

Ultra's brilliant deciphering of the enemy's inter-HQ and inter-unit coded signals gave us invaluable advance insight into the opposition's tactical and strategic intentions. Often the means were not there to allow advantage to be taken of this priceless information. Nevertheless, when they were there, the profit accruing to the Island's Governor and C-in-C, and to the Service heads, became a significant factor in enabling them to take the right measures in support of Malta's defence. Ultra's special liaison unit (SLU) on the Island was one of the organization's key posts. To this was added what was called the 'Y' Service, a supplementary listening process which gathered its information from a round-the-clock coverage of W/T and R/T transmissions between Axis aircraft, ships at sea and their related bases and units. Some of us in the squadrons knew about the 'Y' Service and tasted its fruits.

The men and women who staffed the SLU and 'Y' posts worked long and concentrated hours below ground in conditions which, in normal circumstances, would not have been tolerated; and yet their contribution to the Island's defence, and survival, necessarily had to go unsung. Indeed, except for a few, their activities were unknown.

There was an interesting example of the lengths to which our High Command went to camouflage even the faintest suggestion that the Allies might be reading the Germans' Enigma ciphers. It was to be found in the work of the Royal Air Force's Photographic Reconnaissance Unit at Luqa. Harry Coldbeck, now commanding the PR Flight, was performing, at this new stage, a service of signal quality to the Allied cause. In strictly intelligence and surveillance terms, the results which the New Zealand flight lieutenant, backed by Les Colquhoun and 'JO' Dalley, was freshly achieving was certainly now matching, and may even have been surpassing, the earlier performances of his illustrious predecessor, Adrian Warburton.

We in the fighter squadrons were the better able to recognize Coldbeck's achievement for he had once been 'one of us'. We knew, at first hand, his character and his worth, and we knew, too, what was involved in these increasingly long, solo round-trips of 800 and 1000 miles, deep into enemy territory or over great expanses of the cruel sea. The curious thing was that for the CO of 69 Squadron, the PR Flight might have been a separate entity lodging outside his operational ken. Photographic reconnaissance in a single-engine aeroplane, unarmed and without escort, and flown at excessive altitudes far beyond the radius of any air-sea rescue capability or air-to-ground radio contact, was an acquired taste without wide appeal. The work was alien to that normally undertaken by the crews of a general reconnaissance squadron equipped with multi-engined Marylands or Baltimores.

The work rate which Coldbeck was now undertaking with his two supporters was higher than that averaged over weeks at a time by any other of the Island's continuously operational aerial units. Coldbeck's log book showed him to be notching up sixty and sometimes seventy operational hours a month – on a single motor. Because he was left to his own devices and initiative, the New Zealander operated from the station's intelligence office, aided by Luqa's Intelligence Officer (IO), Flight Lieutenant Kerridge, and two seconded Army officers, Ian Gammidge of the Buffs and John Tucker of the Dorsets. It was a tight-knit and effective surveillance team.

There was a direct line from the intelligence office to Air HQ in Valletta. When, unbeknown to Coldbeck, Ultra's 'advice' was having to be deliberately camouflaged, his contact at the top was always the Senior Air Staff Officer, first, Air Commodore Bowen-Buscarlet, and then his successor, Air Commodore Riley. It puzzled him why he was required on these occasions to deal at this level. He expressed his puzzlement to us one afternoon when Daddo-Langlois and I had gone over to Luqa to see him soon after our return from Gibraltar.

Not only did he find this difficult to understand, he also thought it strange that Air HQ seemed often to have advance information regarding the sailing, movement and location convoys moving across the Mediterranean.

'There's something odd,' he said, 'about the calls I've had of late from the SASO.' He cited one which had taken place on the previous day when Bowen-Buscarlet had asked him to cover a particular area of sea far out to the north-east of the Island. The grid references had been given. Pictures were to be taken of any shipping sighted in the locality provided cloud and light allowed. Also strange was the request that any sighting should be reported at once in obviously coded language over the VHF R/T. Normally, such reports awaited the pilot's return.

In this event, a convoy was sighted, photographed and a report at once given 'out loud' over the R/T. Plainly foxed by it all, Harry dismissed the affair with a perfunctory comment. 'Anyway,' he said, 'with this and the other times it has happened, I've done what has been asked. The SASO seems quite pleased . . .'

What neither Coldbeck nor anyone else, save those at the very top, had any inkling of was that Ultra's SLU had already provided the AOC with information about this particular convoy's sailing from a Sicilian or southern Italian port, its direction and other details. By asking for this special surveillance and VHF report, Air HQ's intention was to leave the impression with the enemy, whose own listening posts would have been at work, that this was nothing more than a chance discovery – certainly nothing of which the Allies had obtained prior information by their deciphering of a coded signal.

Any subsequent attack by a strike force of Beaufort torpedo aircraft would thus be regarded as an expected consequence of PRU's 'lucky break' . . . Truly a case, if ever there was one, of Churchill's 'riddle wrapped in a mystery inside an enigma.'

These convoy sightings, in fact, brought no joy to Cold-beck. 'By the time I get back here to base,' he explained, 'the Beaufort crews are usually getting ready to go off on the strike. With all the awful casualties which these ops bring, it is really a grim prospect for them. The anxiety shows on their grey faces. I try to avoid their eyes . . .'

*

There was another interesting instance of the part Ultra was playing in the Malta battle. Looking back now, with all the constraints of secrecy removed, it is possible to comprehend why the Chiefs of Staff in London, acting on Ultra's 'advice', reacted as they did to PRU's disclosure of the Germans' preparations to take gliders and airborne forces near Gerbini on Sicily's Catanian plain. The revelation of General Kurt Student's activities and those of his Fliegerkorps XI had elicited some disturbed signals from Valletta to Whitehall. It would have been a comfort to us at the time had we known what Ultra, and those at the top, knew. The Royal Air Force's historians have since been able to fill the gaps. The picture now becomes quite clear.

On the 26 April, the German Air Force Enigma disclosed that . . . units of [Lörzer's] Fliegerkorps II were preparing to leave Sicily [for Russia and the spring offensive, and North Africa]. On 2 May, the same source showed that two *gruppen* were already withdrawing and that more were to follow. On the same day, the Chiefs of Staff [in London] used this evidence to reassure the Governor of Malta [then General Dobbie] that he could discount the danger of invasion*

By then, of course, the German High Command, against Kesselring's and the Italians' best advice, had decided to defer *Herkules* until mid-July in preference to allowing Rommel and his Afrika Korps to launch Operation *Theseus* – the capture of Cyrenaica and, with it, the garrison of Tobruk, and the advance through Libya to the threshold of Egypt. Thereafter, the Axis would come back and polish off Malta before reverting again to North Africa, the capture of Egypt, the advance to the Nile Delta, and ultimately to the rich oilfields of the Middle East.

Such was the opposition's buoyant scenario.

*

* Air Historical Branch Draft Narrative: Malta (unpublished).

There was, for me, one textbook experience of the effectiveness of Malta's 'Y' Service as its operators listened to the transmissions passing between the aircraft of Lörzer's Fliegerkorps II and their Sicilian bases. It transcends in my memory all the other similar instances in which 249 played a squadron's part. Indeed, I doubt whether a better example exists of the value of the service which these dedicated men and women were providing from their stuffy and ill-ventilated underground fastness in Valletta.

It occurred one early summer's morning of heaven-sent beauty when my Flight was on readiness at Takali. Wing Commander W. R. Farnes, who, in peace, would rise to the top echelon of the Bristol Aeroplane Company, was the duty controller down in the Ditch in the bowels of the capital. Bill Farnes had become, by now, highly proficient at this advanced art. To his experience of 11 Group of Fighter Command in the United Kingdom, he had added weeks on the Island working with Woodhall than whom there could have been no better mentor. Woody was presently in a class of his own and much of his expertise had rubbed off on Farnes.

The tea cart had just come round to 249's dispersal accompanied by the usual supply of hard, 'World War I' unsweetened biscuits. Pilots and groundcrews were talking together when the operations telephone rang in our bombed-out premises. Picking up the receiver, I heard Farnes's voice at the other end.

'We think there may be some activity south-east of the Island,' he said, 'about 60 miles out. There seems to be a bit of traffic in that area, possibly a shipping reconnaissance or something of that sort. There are no plots on the table so whatever it is is probably operating low down on the water. It might be worth sending a section of four aircraft out for twenty or twenty-five minutes on a heading of one-two-five degrees. If nothing is seen after twenty-five minutes, the section shouldn't hang about, but come straight back. There must be absolute R/T silence until the aircraft are at the end of the outward leg. We feel it's worth a shot.'

I recognized at once the source of the information.

Bill knew the form from A to Z; he was himself no mean pilot and understood the work from the squadrons' standpoint. I told him I would go myself with three other aircraft.

'Don't be cross if you don't see anything, will you?' His rejoinder was predictable.

My Red Section was steeped in Malta experience. Flying with me was my usual No. 2, Frank Jones, from Montreal, an able and quick-witted section leader in his own right; but, selflessly, he was always prepared to string along with me when I was leading. We felt comfortable together. Frank had come to us from the Biggin Hill Wing and a season of sweeps, tangling with the 190s and 109s over northern France. He had a pair of eyes which could see from Nova Scotia to British Columbia. On my right were two other competent performers from our strong Canadian contingent – Ozzie Linton at No. 3 and Basil (Mickey) Butler at No. 4. The four had a nice, efficient 'feel' about it.

We crossed out at Marsaxlokk Bay in the south-east of the Island and settled down at once on to the given compass heading. The clean morning air was beautifully stable, no bumps and virtually no wind. Below, the Med, shining and quite still save for a slight swell, looked like oil. In front, the sun was just beginning to push up above the horizon to see who was about. Overhead, night had given way to a cloudless sky of misty powder blue. Before we took off, the temperature was beginning to rise; by midday it would be in the nineties. It was an attractive time to be flying an aeroplane.

Nothing, except the seagulls, seemed to be moving on the outward leg. I was just looking at my watch for the end of the 25-minute stretch, when Jonesie's high-pitched, nasal twang made me nearly jump out of the cockpit.

'Tiger leader (my call sign), two Ju 88s at eleven o'clock right down on the water, flying east.' Frank's acute eyes had picked up the 88s' grey-green camouflage against the water. The enemy had already spotted us, 1000 feet above, silhouetted against the brightening sky. A reconnaissance of this sort carried no 109 escort. The pilots of the two aircraft, with throttles now wide open and hugging the still water, had moved into quite close line-abreast formation to give each other maximum protection, with the rear gunners providing mutual crossfire.

'OK, Jonesie,' I said, 'I see them. You and I will take the aircraft to port and Lint, you and Mickey take the aircraft to starboard. Lint, we'll get ahead of them on either side and then turn in to the attack together. Jonesie and Mickey will follow us in.' Red 2 and 3 acknowledged the instruction. I added a caveat. 'You fellows must watch the sea level. The water is dead calm and it's easy to misjudge the height in the breakaway.'

We got our attacks spot on. With all the advantage of height, each pair made a nicely judged, beam-into-quarter attack from opposite sides, pressed right home to near-point-blank range. The four 20 mm cannons from our Spitfire VCs struck hard at the prey.

The shooting was good, so one attack from each side was enough to do it. As, first, Jonesie and then Mickey pulled away, I saw the port Ju 88 start terraplaning over the water before rearing up and sinking amid a cloud of spray. Moments later, the second 88 did much the same.

We circled the spot for a full five minutes, climbing up to give fixes for the ground station (and, no doubt, the enemy) to pinpoint the area. There was no sign of survivors, only two patches of spreading oil and debris. I was sorry, for each crew and, in particular, each rear gunner had fought the attack in the best tradition of the Luftwaffe. But such is war.

We re-formed, climbed to 5000 feet and set course for home. I called Gondar, the ground station on the R/T, for I guessed Farnes and the staff in the Ops Room would be athirst for news. Bill answered. 'Bill,' I said, 'you win, game, set and match.'

'Good show, Tiger leader. Thanks. Roger. Out.' It was in his nature to play it deadpan. Yet the victory was down to the operators of the 'Y' Service in Valletta and to Farnes at ground control.

It wasn't quite all over. Ten minutes from the Island, I was horrified to see my radiator temperature gauge going 'off the clock'. Obviously, one of the 88s' rear gunners had hit my aircraft in the coolant tank before he succumbed. Until then, he had given as good as he got with his return fire. Frank Jones confirmed my suspicions. 'Tiger leader,' he said, 'white glycol smoke is pouring from your aircraft. I'll stay around.'

I had gained enough height, I guessed, as we approached the coast, to be able to make Halfar, the Island's south-easternmost airfield. My engine was now seizing so I told Farnes what I was intending to do. 'OK,' he said, 'I'll warn them.'

With switches cut and a dead stick, but with wheels and flaps down, I went straight in to a good landing as red Very lights, fired from Halfar's flying control, shot into the sky to warn off all comers.

Six weeks later, when I did the same thing on the same airfield, there wasn't such a good story to tell.

# 21

# MISJUDGED TIMING

*In life, as in footer, it's the last 20 minutes that count.*
*Dr Cyril Alington, former Headmaster of Eton*

Malta now felt quite different. An old hand, returning afresh to the Island, could recognize it at once. Yet it was difficult to credit the change. The Spitfire reinforcements of 9 and 18 May, flown in so quickly one after the other, had given the defence a new impetus. The advent, within nine days, of almost eighty new aeroplanes, piloted for the most part by well-fed, battle-hardened officers and NCOs, who were fresh and looking for trouble, had transformed the ethos of the place.

Thanks to the superhuman efforts of the Army – the Manchesters, the Royal Irish Fusiliers, the Buffs, the West Kents, the Dorsets, the Devons and others, 27 miles of dispersal track had been completed (often under fire) and 260 dispersal points built, immeasurably improving the protection of the newly-arrived aircraft. The atmosphere of those awful days of March and April – of the

> tired waves, vainly breaking,
> and seeming
> here no painful inch to gain

had given way to buoyancy and hope.

Things would, however, remain critically poised for weeks. Taxing air battles would still have to be fought, literally, to the death and no real improvement in food or living conditions, or life on the Island, could properly be expected until it was possible to run convoys through with some reasonable chance of success. The Luftwaffe would return in strength to aid the Regia Aeronautica. Bombings and losses would continue. Movies and haircuts in Valletta would still be interrupted by the wailing of the sirens. The Malta Dog would flatten the newer arrivals and the gastronomically unwary . . .

All this – and much more – would be with us for weeks, but nothing could disguise from those who had lived through and survived the roughest fighting the overriding feeling that a great air victory had been gained and that, come what might, nothing for the Luftwaffe would ever be quite the same again.

For Field Marshal Albert Kesselring who, six months earlier, had been given a 'final briefing by Hitler in the presence of Goering and Jeschonnek'* to neutralize Malta by bombing, the Island's new-found strength must have been a shaker, particularly in the context of the withdrawals now known, via Ultra, to be taking place from Sicily. 'When Kesselring announced to the General Staff [in Berlin] on 10 May "our task completed", his statement could not have been worse timed.'†

If the timing was ill-chosen and his information flawed, the process by which the C-in-C South had arrived at his erroneous conclusion was scarcely credible. Indeed, it flew straight in the face of the commonly held belief that the German military mind was methodical, stereotyped and adhered strictly to the set-piece principles of the textbook. Individualism and unorthodoxy were qualities to be played right down.

For a Luftflotte commander and a general staff officer of Kesselring's calibre, who had had all the experience of command during the Battle of Britain to draw on, his tactical direction of the neutralization policy bordered on the irrational.

* *The Memoirs of Field Marshal Kesselring*, William Kimber, 1953.
† Air Historical Branch Draft Narrative: Malta (unpublished).

In spite of the policy laid down, Luftflotte 2, in its offensive against Malta, *failed to keep any scientific system of target priorities.* [Author's italics]. Due to the consequent dispersal of effort, the power of the enemy offensive always fell just short of the Island's recuperative ability. Airfields were put out of action and then a respite followed, with a diversion of effort to other targets, giving time for the airfields to be put back into commission again. In this way the Luftwaffe never, except for very short periods, prevented the Royal Air Force from being able to hit back*

The paucity of the German intelligence network may well have had much to do with it. In the Battle of Britain, the High Command's fatal decision to switch, on 7 September 1940, the Luftwaffe's attack away from all the paraphernalia of Fighter Command – the sector stations, the airfields, the aircraft, the radars – and on to London, when it had the contest just about made, cost the German Air Force the battle. Hitler's desire to go for London in retaliation for Bomber Command's attacks on Berlin was, politically, quite understandable. But if the High Command's intelligence sources had been sufficiently effective to have revealed to the Führer the real state of the game – and how close Fighter Command, with its grave shortage of pilots, was to defeat – it is inconceivable that this diversion would have prevailed for more than a few retaliatory raids 'to get even'.

The fact that Kesselring had made a comparable miscalculation in his judgement of Malta's capacity to survive, and then strike back, suggests that the German intelligence machine was as ineffectual in southern Europe as it had been two years before in the west. As it was, with elements of Luftflotte 2 now being transferred to the Eastern Front, North Africa, Greece and Crete, 'Kesselring believed mistakenly that these transfers could be made without the Royal

---

* Air Historical Branch, op. cit.

Air Force regaining air superiority in the Mediterranean. Thus Malta got its midsummer respite.'*

There was another factor, much smaller by comparison, but nonetheless vital in a detailed sense, which had now come into play in Malta's defence. *Welshman*, the Royal Navy's fast minelaying cruiser, which, with her sister ship *Manxman*, had been performing wonders during the Island's heroic resistance with her life-saving runs from Gibraltar, through the Narrows to Grand Harbour, had made another unescorted dash down the Med to coincide with the arrival of the sixty Spitfires from *Eagle* and *Wasp*.

With Captain Dennis Friedberger RN in command, and carrying a cargo of essentials – of powdered milk, canned meat, dehydrated foodstuffs, ammunition, aero engines and other Spitfire spares, she had berthed soon after 0600 on 10 May and had at once become the Luftwaffe's Target for Today. The Army had fallen upon her as she came alongside and, despite the air raids, had unloaded her precious wares within some six hours.

Fourteen hours later, minimally refuelled and empty, and still camouflaged as a French destroyer, flying French colours, *Welshman* was heading back for Gib at her customary 40 knots only slightly damaged by the Luftwaffe's relentless pounding.

What we should have done in the fighter squadrons in those impoverished days without this ship, her captain and crew, and the additional replenishing support of the Royal Navy's submarines of which *Upholder*, and her gallant captain David Wanklyn VC, were a paragon, really doesn't bear thinking about.

The change which had overtaken Malta in little more than a fortnight was beginning to be shown in diverse ways. As

* ibid.

the arid summer heat mounted to a crescendo, and the intensity of the Luftwaffe's attacks began temporarily to lessen, so 249 Squadron's chances of taking an occasional day's break at the Rest Camp, down by St Paul's Bay in the north-east of the Island, increased.

The villa at St Paul's, with its idyllic setting, was a haven from the dust, heat and glaring whiteness of Malta's central expanse – if you could find a way of getting there. It was a stiff 5-mile bicycle ride from Takali: 10 miles or so there and back with one leg of the journey normally being pedalled in the hot sun.

The lawn at the back of the house, sloping down towards the water, overlooked the Bay and the little island of St Paul beyond. Here, Paul of Tarsus had found sanctuary from tempest and shipwreck 1900 years before and here, on this tiny island, a statue of the missionary, with preacher's arm raised, stands on higher ground, a symbol of Malta's spiritual strength.

And when it was day, they knew not the land: but they discovered a certain creek with a shore into which they were minded . . . to thrust in the ship . . .

And falling into a place where two seas met, they ran the ship aground; and the forepart stuck fast, and remained unmoveable, but the hinder part was broken with the violence of the waves . . .

And when they were escaped, then they knew that the island was called Melita.*

The house across the street, opposite the Rest Camp, was numbered, somewhat inappropriately, 109. 'Get that changed at once,' remarked Paul Brennan, 249's forthright Australian, the first time he saw it, 'otherwise we'll get no rest!'

To the rear of the villa, the bathing platform and mooring was reached by a circuitous path which wound its way past

*Acts 27:39–44, 28:1.

a profusion of honeysuckle and through a blissfully cool, covered avenue of trees, down many steps to the quietly lapping waters below. All was private and none of it was overlooked. 'Nice place this, for a honeymoon,' said Paul, allowing his mind to run a little.

From the platform, 249 Squadron, in a state of partial or total undress, would, now and then, pile into the Rest Camp's rowing boat and row the mile across the Bay to the little island for a naked bathe and a picnic. Sandwiches made of bitter, 'half-cast' bread, spread with 'gharry grease' and filled with bully beef, tasted surprisingly good after a turn at the oars.

One day we were halfway across to the island when the air raid sirens started wailing out their misery. Soon the unmistakable 'blue note' of the Daimler-Benz engines was to be heard up above as a couple of *staffeln* of Me 109s, at around 8000 feet, swept in ahead of the incoming raid. Suddenly, and apparently for no good reason, two of their number peeled away from the rest and started down a fast, curving dive towards the Bay. Could they really be going to draw a bead on our boat?

Mostly naked, except for our hats to keep the sun off, we prepared to leap bravely into the water while Philip Heppell, 249's Northumbrian jester, sitting right up in the bows, kept a jocular commentary on the 109s' progress and intentions. Quickly, he changed his tune. 'Take your hats off, fellers,' he shouted, 'they'll see we're officers!'

The 109s passed right overhead, straightening out at about 50 feet at the bottom of their hell-bent dive. Why they did that if they weren't going to fire we weren't quite sure.

That evening we celebrated what we thought must have been St Paul's blessing at the little fish restaurant in the village. This the intrepid local fishermen kept freshly supplied, netting their catches in the Bay apparently quite oblivious to the marauding ways of the Messerschmitts.

Grilled over a charcoal burner and accompanied by several glasses of the recommended 'plonk', the fish reminded me of the delicious Dover soles we used sometimes to get in the Mess at Hawkinge, in East Kent, after the local fishing fleet had ventured out. Wilton's in Jermyn Street, SW1, could never have bettered it. It made the bicycle ride back to Mdina seem half the distance.

Things were looking up, too, at Takali. Since Jumbo Gracie had given up command of 126 Squadron and taken over command of the station, he had really set about trying to improve the squadrons', and particularly the ground-crews', lot. With virtually nothing to do it with, he had contrived to inject new vitality into the airfield and made the airmen feel he was running the establishment for them. Heads were held higher, backs were straighter and the meagre food ration seemed to take on more variety as he tapped local sources for supplementary produce. A new broom was certainly sweeping clean.

Quite short-tempered and impatient, Jumbo was intolerant of inefficiency and of those who did not toe the line. Excuses didn't wash with this dynamo.

Tony Holland told us one day of an incident which exposed the wing commander's quick, but short-lived, temper. The Luftwaffe, much to Gracie's annoyance, were in the process of giving Takali a thoroughly good going over. Bomb holes were scattered about the airfield and the Bofors gunners were loosing off at the attackers. For some reason, the signal for the aircraft to scramble had come late.

At this moment, Tony, now a star of 603, and Pete Nash, one of 249's outstanding successes, were last into their Spitfires, taxiing out behind the others which were throwing up clouds of dust. Pete, uncharacteristically, hit an unseen steamroller with a wing. Tony, right beside him, sank the port wheel and oleo leg of his aircraft into a recently filled, but not yet compacted crater, with consequential damage to all three blades of the airscrew. Annoyed and dejected, the two officers returned to dispersal, pursued by an irate station commander who had witnessed the damage. Holland described the sequence.

'Without waiting or asking for an explanation, Jumbo launched into a tirade of admonition. Fortunately, he was stopped in his tracks by an airman shouting at him. "Look out, sir, bomb coming."

'With that, airman and wing commander flung themselves flat on the ground, swiftly followed by Pete and myself. Just then, a single bomb from a lone 109, passing fast overhead, disturbed the peace, shattering what remained of the dispersal hut.

'Getting slowly to our feet, Pete and I braced ourselves for the remainder of the tirade, only to see Jumbo stumping off to inspect some other damage, flinging an 'I'll see you both later,' over his shoulder as he went. He never mentioned it again!'

Poor Pete Nash! he was lost only a few days later, with $13\frac{1}{2}$ enemy aircraft and several probables already standing to his credit on the Island. He and Laurie Verrall, the New Zealand flight sergeant in 249, who had served with Harry Coldbeck, Raoul Daddo-Langlois and myself in 66 Squadron in the United Kingdom, and was well practised in the day-fighting art, had encountered five Me 109s high up over Grand Harbour. A vigorous dog-fight had developed in which Pete and Laurie had each scored. What happened after that is unclear. While Verrall disengaged from the mêlée and landed safely back at base, Nash did not return. There were reports that a Spitfire and a 109 had been seen falling almost simultaneously, suggesting that there may have been a collision, but this could not be confirmed. Whatever the true outcome, the loss left an unfilled void in the Squadron, for Pete was, day in and day out, probably the best of some exceptional performers and, maybe, the most accomplished fighter pilot on the Island during the worst of the battle.

I had found that I was, by now, hardened – inured – against loss. Life would have been intolerable, with so many casualties, had this not been so; but to lose two such close and respected comrades as Pete Nash and Norman Mac-Queen – two 'invincibles' – in as many weeks, tested my armour to the limit. We were learning that in this kind of struggle, between two First Division sides, even the 'inde-structibles' could be felled.

Gracie stamped his style on the station and played things very much his way. For a peacetime-trained officer, I thought he worried surprisingly little about the niceties of King's Regulations. For Jumbo, results were what counted, not so much the means by which they were obtained.

Who, for instance, among the run of Royal Air Force station commanders, would have contemplated erecting four gibbets at Takali as a deterrent to any Maltese workman, engaged on the airfield, who might be considering 'acquir-ing' a can or three of petrol or fuel oil – valuable commodi-ties on Malta's black market?

It never ceased to amaze me how the Maltese people who, through no fault of theirs, had seen war come to their island home in 1940, and had then been subjected to a gathering hell for the next three years, could have remained so loyal, brave and patriotic. It would never have surprised me if, given their affinity with the Italians and their common religion, they had run an underground Fifth Column within the fortress.

Deportations there certainly were from Malta to Uganda in 1942 – rather less than fifty of them – and in the same year there was the celebrated capture of the so-called spy, Borghi Pisani, alias Caio Borghi. A Maltese of pro-Italian sympathies and a member of Mussolini's Fascist Party, he had gone to Rome pre-war to study art at the Regia Academia dei Belle Arti. When, on 18 May, he was landed by motor torpedo boat and dinghy at the foot of the cliffs between Dingli and Imtahleb, a most unsuitable stretch of coast on the west side of the Island, he was to be a plant working for the Axis.

After easy capture, criminal trial and conviction, Pisani was sentenced to death and, on the warrant of the Governor, hanged. But this was exceptional, for there was precious little of this kind of thing in wartime Malta. Petty pilfering, however, there was among an isolated few of the Maltese working at Takali. I had, for instance, little doubt that it was a civilian batman who had lifted my camera from my room in the Xara Palace. But this was small stuff.

Nevertheless, Gracie was determined to put a stop to what there was of it on the airfield. He did this by resorting to his gibbets at the same time publishing in Orders that anyone caught stealing petrol or other stores from the Royal Air Force would be hanged. His action, regarded as a great joke by the squadrons, caused a frightful row. Someone took a photograph of the gallows and got the picture smuggled out to the United Kingdom where, not surprisingly, it found its way into the London office of the *Daily Mirror*.

It started quite a fluttering in the dovecotes at the Air Ministry which at once demanded of Air HQ in Valletta a full explanation. The Royal Air Force's military police on the Island visited a photographer in Sliema, bought up all his pictures of the gibbets and made him give an undertaking, on pain of the confessional, that he would neither print nor sell any more.

Gracie had cut his mark deeply upon the Malta scene. Unpredictable and always unconventional, he was never dull.

# 22

# EVENING FLIGHT

The light had already begun to fade as the operations'
telephone rang in 249's dispersal at Takali. The sun had
long since dropped behind the higher ground to the west.
The citadel of Rabat, the bastions of Mdina and the hills
running north-westwards round to M'tarfa, were silhouetted against the western sky. To the east, over Grand Harbour and out to sea, night was drawing in. Another
three-quarters of an hour and it would be dark.

When the telephone rang I felt pretty sure it would be
Ops telling us to stand down. It had been a long, hot
day of maximum effort. 'Operation Harpoon', code name
for the vital June convoy sailing from Gibraltar, was in
the final throes of its run to Malta having fought the opposition, day and night, for the last two days.

Six merchantmen had left Gib, with their escort of one
battleship, two carriers, four cruisers, one minelayer, seventeen destroyers and four minesweepers, four days before.
Now, only two of the cargo ships remained. This was all
that stood between Malta and starvation. The second
convoy from Alexandria – 'Operation Vigorous' – with its
eleven merchantmen and escort, which was to have been
run through concurrently from the east, had had to turn
back. Once again, the Italian Fleet and the dangerous narrows between Crete and the Benghazi blister had proved
its undoing.

I picked up the receiver. It was Woodhall. He had been
down in the Ditch controlling all day long. I knew he must
be all in. He sounded like it.

'There are twelve-plus big jobs* at angels twelve†
flying south from Sicily obviously heading for the ships.
It looks as if the attack is timed to go in at last light.
There are no little jobs‡ about. I know it's late and will
almost certainly mean night landings, but we'd like you
to send out a section of four aircraft, with four experienced chaps, to see if the attack can be intercepted and
broken up. The convoy has been taking a pounding all
day and we'd like to try to give this support. The leader
should start out on a heading of two–seven–zero degrees –
due west – climbing fast to 14,000 feet. I'll contact him
when he's airborne. He should be able to see the big jobs
against the western sky.'

'OK, sir,' I said. 'I'll be going with my Tiger Red section.
Jones, Linton and Watts will be with me. They're all clued
up, sir, and quite able to handle this sort of thing. We'll get
off at once.'

'Good show, Laddie,' said Woody, 'I'll call you when
you're airborne and give you other vectors.'

Jones, my trusted No. 2, and Linton, at No. 3, were old
hands by now. Les Watts was newer, flying at No. 4, but as
sound a bit of brass as ever came out of Birmingham. He
had come to us quite recently from the fire of 11 Group and
the sweeps over northern France. I had been much impressed with his competence and dry and uncontrived
humour. Wattie was a reliable trooper.

It was one of Woody's virtuoso performances. Variations
in vectors were given in that deep, measured and always
confident voice. 'You should see them quite soon now
against the western light. They're a little below you.'

Search as we might, we could not see them. If we were
above them, I thought, we're trying to pick them out
against the darkening sea down below. I dropped a couple

*Bombers.    † 12,000 feet    ‡ Fighters.

of thousand feet which, anyway, gave us a bit of extra speed. Amost at once, I saw them, standing out plainly against the western sky.

'OK, fellers, I see them. Eighty-eights at two o'clock, flying south. Same level. About a dozen of them.'

The Ju 88s were flying straight and level in quite tight boxes of some four aircraft each. They hadn't seen us coming out of the darkening eastern sky. I gave the instructions. We would dive another 1000 feet and, with all the speed we wanted, pull up from underneath and attack from the quarter into astern position. Lint and Wattie would take the starboard box, and Jonesie and I the one to port. Then both pairs would have a go at the centre formation if we could. This would give the best chance of breaking up the attack. After that, it would be each man for himself.

Our assault came off to a T. The rear gunners never saw us as we attacked upwards from underneath, against the dark waters below. It wasn't until we had closed to 150–200 yards' range and the flashes from the four cannons in our Spitfire VCs and the strikes from them began to drive home that the German crews realized what was happening. Then there was mayhem, with the 88s breaking all over the place, not knowing how many Spitfires were attacking them. There might have been a couple of squadrons of us for all they knew.

It was a splendid steal from which we extracted about as much as we could reasonably expect in the fading light. It was difficult to see the results, but Wattie and I reckoned we had shared an 88 between us, Jonesie got another – a flamer – while Lint and I felt we had severely damaged an additional 88 apiece. But more important than the score was the fact that the attack had been thrown into disarray. The Luftwaffe really had little idea what had hit them.

Woody came on the blower. 'Tiger aircraft, put your backs to the light and fly zero-nine-zero degrees for base.

Put the light behind you and steer due east for fifteen minutes. We'll see you home.'

'OK, Woody,' I said, 'message understood.'

I called Red 2, 3 and 4, individually, in that order. We were all separated and it was too dark now to think of trying to re-form. An elated acknowledgement from each brought relief. All were intact and humming.

With, apparently, no other plots on the table, Woody got flying control at Luqa, in the centre of the Island, to light the lead-in path and the flarepath for us. Takali wasn't on for night landings. I sent Wattie in first, followed by Jonesie and then Lint. Drenched with sweat, and limp after the tension, I touched down immediately after them, stopping to allow two airmen with torches to lead me safely off the runway. Running ahead of the Spitfire, they guided me to a dispersal pen which seemed all of half a mile away.

I had flown many interceptions under Group Captain Woodhall's ground control by now, but never had his genius shone through as with this one. On this single sortie – my fourth that day, as it happened – he had brought the whole art to life. Sitting down there in the Ditch below Valletta, reading the plots on the ops table, he had made it seem as if he was talking his own way through the attack.

Unforgettable experiences often provoke strange reactions. When I saw that gaggle of Ju 88s silhouetted against the western sky, it had momentarily reminded me of my boyhood at Sandwich Bay, in East Kent, flighting duck of an evening with my father, on the marshes beside the River Stour. Then, in those tense fifteen or twenty minutes, as twilight turned into night, first the teal, then the widgeon and last the mallard, would come 'whooshing' in from the sea, heading for their feeding grounds, visible only as dark specks against the fading sky.

This evening's flight had been made of sterner stuff. In place of the duck there had been the 88s. Yet, between wildfowler and fighter pilot, I felt there was an unmistakable affinity.

*Above:* Nonpareil in victory: Group Captain A.B. Woodhall, fighter controller extraordinary (*Laddie Lucas*)

*Above right:* A sparkling Anglo-Canadian pair: Buck McNair (*left*), soon to lead a Cannuck wing in the UK, and Lossiemouth's able Ronnie West (*Laddie Lucas*)

*Right:* Stamped with class: Cranwell-educated Stanley Grant (*right*), CO of 249 after Turner, and the personable Raoul Daddo-Langlois (*Laddie Lucas*)

*Below:* Something to laugh about? When Stan Grant gave up 249 in June 1942, the author, aged 26, took over command (*Daddo-Langlois Collection*)

Lull before the storm. Spitfires at Gibraltar waiting for loading on HMS *Eagle* for fly-off to Malta
(*Laddie Lucas*)

Under the whip: pressure-wait for the take-off from *Eagle*
(*Laddie Lucas*)

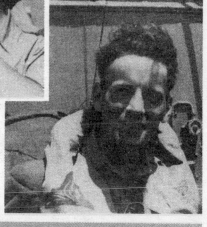

*Above:* 'Piece of cake': the astute Wing Commander J.S. McLean, mastermind of Spitfire reinforcements, aboard *Eagle* (*Laddie Lucas*)

*Right:* Jerrold Smith, brother of Roderick, from Canada, aboard *Eagle* after landing his Spitfire on USS *Wasp* without tailhook (*Laddie Lucas*)

*Below:* Historic fly-off from USS *Wasp*, 9 May 1942. Within 10 days, this new contingent had helped to turn the battle

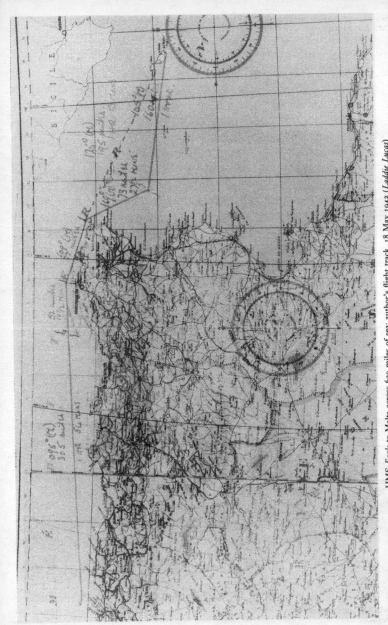

HMS *Eagle* to Malta across 629 miles of sea: author's flight track, 18 May 1942 (*Laddie Lucas*)

esting moment: Spitfire, with just enough flying speed, getting airborne from short flight-deck
f HMS *Furious*

aftwaffe welcomes new arrivals at Takali! Picture taken from terrace of Xara Palace, our Mess in Mdina
*addie Lucas*)

Relentless bombing devastated Valletta,
but natural air-raid shelters and casualty
stations, fashioned out of rock and cave,
saved countless lives

Indomitable under attack: while Maltese men cleared the ravages of bombing, their womenfolk tended the island's myriad, lattice-work fields

In a stroke of genius, King George VI bestowed the George Cross upon Malta on 15 April 1942 at the nadir of the Island's desperate fortunes. (*Above*) Chief Justice Sir George Borg receives the award from the Governor, Lord Gort VC, at the presentation ceremony on 13 September in Palace Square, Valletta (*below*) amid all the spit, polish, pomp and glory which could be mustered

# 23

# ARM OF COURAGE

You could not be successful in such an action without a
large loss. We must make up our mind to affairs of this
kind sometimes, or give up the game.

*Duke of Wellington*

The fighting over the convoy on 15 June, as attack after
attack went in, was a tormenting business. There was so
much and yet so little that we could do as the last two
surviving merchantmen, *Troilus* (7500 tons) and *Orari*
(10,500 tons), with their Naval escort, struggled to reach
Grand Harbour.

Furious combats took place around the periphery, and
even over the top of, the ships as relays of Spitfires from
Takali, Luqa and Halfar flew out to offer support. Working
at extreme range, the fighters only gave up their vigil when
fuel reserves became critical.

There were triumphs and losses against an enemy who
knew as well as we did what was at stake. The Luftwaffe
and the Regia Aeronautica were both giving it all they had,
going for the maximum penetration of the Royal Navy's
defensive screen. Their success, and that of the Italian
Navy's surface ships, could be measured by the fact that, of
the six merchantmen which had set out from the United
Kingdom, and three days ago had sailed through the Straits
of Gibraltar, only three were still afloat as they entered the
penultimate day of the convoy. *Kentucky* (5500 tons), the
vital US oiler, had already been lost and, of the three
remaining merchant vessels, one was belching quantities of
thick black smoke and destined to die. Thereafter, the Axis
were going flat out to deny the Island the gains which even

two well-laden ships would bring. And all of this had to be seen in the context of the failure of the larger convoy from Egypt to force a passage through to Malta. It was a sombre picture. So much had been promised; so little had been gained.

Even with the docking of the two merchant ships – and yet another intrepid dash from Gibraltar by *Welshman*, carrying her invaluable necessities – we would still be fighting for survival. Belts, already too tight, would have to be pulled in another couple of notches.

As we looked down upon this battle at sea, we were like the parents of a dangerously sick child lying in hospital. The best had been done – and was being done – to bring succour. No effort had been too great, no opinion disregarded. But the virus would not yield. The child's future, it seemed, must rest on faith and a prayer.

This is how we saw things in Malta at the time. There were, however, other considerations, other views and another side of the coin. None of them could we know in the squadrons. While Rommel, with his successful attack at Gazala (Operation *Theseus*), was driving the British 8th Army helter-skelter out of Cyrenaica and capturing Tobruk *en route*, the picture in the desert and central Mediterranean appeared just about as bleak as it could be. Nevertheless, the Royal Air Force's historians, seeing things years afterwards in retrospect, could put a very different construction on these midsummer events arising from what we saw as the appalling reverse with the convoys.

The arrival of these [two] ships from *Harpoon*, at a time of great crisis in the Mediterranean, was one of the turning points in the war in that theatre ... The blockade of Malta, for which the Axis air force had been fighting for so long, and at such heavy cost, had been broken ... [while] a high proportion of the enemy air strength, which should have been concentrated against the 8th Army, as it retreated from Gazala towards El Alamein, presenting a series of unparalleled air targets, was diverted against the convoy ... [Moreover], it permitted Malta to resume her role of an offensive air and naval base. This led to a remarkable diminution in the enemy's supplies at a time when, with his offensive in full swing, Rommel was in greatest need of a steady stream of supplies and reinforcements in order to allow the *Panzer* army to exploit the success of his offensive in the Western Desert and the fulfilment of his long-term plans (Operation *Aida*) for the occupation of Egypt and a drive to the Suez Canal ... Admiral Weichold [German Vice-Admiral in Rome in charge of Hitler's Naval forces in the Mediterranean from June 1940 to March 1943], who, as a Naval man, had a very shrewd idea of the bearing that the war of supplies was having on the fortunes of the *Panzer* army in North Africa, wrote: 'The cargoes brought by the two supply ships *Troilus* and *Orari* enabled Malta to keep going a few more months. In this respect, the western part of the British operation *Harpoon* had been a success despite the losses incurred.'

The Island was now able to last out until late September.*

Had we known the German High Command's reaction to the fall of Tobruk on 21 June, at this depressing juncture in the Island's story, we might have slept easier in our beds: 'With the capture of Tobruk, the situation is completely changed. The conquest of Malta is no longer necessary ...'

Operation *Herkules* would later be resuscitated in a half-hearted form, but in reality this was the end of the invasion threat which, for three-and-a-half months, had haunted our lives.

What the operations surrounding the June convoy had done for us in the fighter squadrons was to consolidate the good rapport which we had already established with the crews of the Fleet Air Arm's Swordfish and Albacore squadrons at Halfar. They were a rugged, well-disciplined and buoyant body with some dreadful jobs to do.

* Air Historical Branch Draft Narrative: Malta (unpublished).

Flying their antiquated biplanes at speeds which would have shown up poorly in the fast lane of a modern motorway, they performed prodigious feats both by day and by night. None of us would have changed places with them. They were indomitable in adversity.

One operation, flown by the crews of four Albacores, which I witnessed at first hand when the convoy was still rather more than 100 miles west of Malta and some 70 south-east of Pantelleria, has been riveted upon my memory ever since. Two Italian warships with their formidable fire power, were known to be lurking in the Bay of Hammemet, north-east of Sousse, off the Tunisian coast. They were plainly manœuvring for position for an assault upon the remaining merchantmen.

The orders for the four torpedo-carrying Albacores were clear enough. Attack the warships before they can strike. My instructions from Woodhall at Takali were equally plain. They were to take a section of four Spitfires out on a heading of 290° at 8000 feet for a given time and at economical cruising to a point roughly 20 miles east of the target. From there, after rendezvousing with the Albacores, we were to cover them in to the ships and for the initial part of the withdrawal, then, another section from 249 would take over, leaving us to return directly to base. The fuel factor would be critical as we would be operating at the effective limit of our fighting range. The Albacores would be flying tight down on the water. If there was to be an attack upon the Fleet Air Arm aircraft, it would come from the fighter version of the Ju 88 or from the Me 110s based in Sicily. A sprinkling of Macchi 202s or Me 109s, based on Pantelleria, might also come into play. After picking up the biplanes, I would have freedom of action with only the safety of our 90-knots charges to consider.

I had known easier tasks.

It was a cloudless Mediterranean morning of high

summer with unlimited visibility. A moderate southerly wind was blowing from the Sahara and off the North African land mass – the wind that, in summer, always seemed to bring with it days of uninterrupted sunshine, blue skies and great heat. Down below us, the Mediterranean was twinkling and sparkling like sequins.

To my intense relief, we picked up the biplanes, which hardly seemed to be moving, at the same moment as we spotted their target. The two Italian warships, shining elegantly in the bright sunlight, were running north-east in line ahead towards the convoy which was now no more than 20 or 30 miles away. As we made rendezvous, I spotted three Ju 88s at two o'clock 5000 feet below us, making for the attackers. As we dived and turned towards them, they spotted us and made off. We could not afford to give chase; petrol had to be conserved.

When the Albacores were some 3 miles or so short of their target, the ships, which were now going full bore, opened up a barrage of fire which cut the water up around the aircraft throwing showers of spray over the top of them. Undeterred, the crews pressed on into this inferno until the port aircraft of the four, when only a few hundred yards short of the ships, was obviously hit hard and pulled help-lessly away in a climbing turn to the left, but not before it had unleashed its torpedo.

Still the remaining three aircraft flew on with a courage which defies description, letting their torpedoes go at a minimum range. One fish hit the leading warship with a flash which outshone all the other pyrotechnics that were then erupting as the aircraft broke away to starboard, their task marvellously discharged.

Down now to 3000 or 4000 feet, we spotted the Ju 88s again, this time at nine o'clock as we headed east away from the ships. A bit late in the day, they were obviously bent upon making a pass at the Albacores, but when we turned to face them head-on they thought better of it and made off. As they did so I was thankful to see, well above us, the relieving section from 249 appearing from the east, dead on cue. A greeting over the R/T established contact and we were left to head straight back to base, with Merlin engines throttled well back and anxious eyes scanning our petrol gauges.

I had seen many acts of unusual bravery at close quarters by then, starting, in the summer of 1941, with those hideous low-level, daylight attacks by the Blenheims of 2 Group against heavily armed convoys plying their way round the Frisian Islands and the north Dutch coast across anything up to 150 miles of North Sea. They were lethal affairs and the casualties among the attackers crippling. We observed the carnage from our so-called long-range Spitfire IIs, as we provided the escort, and marvelled at the guts of the crews.

But nothing, absolutely nothing, that I personally saw in wartime matched the courage of those four Albacore crews on that Mediterranean morning in June, 1942. The entry in my log book was no more than factual: 'June 15. Spitfire VC-TK: Cover for Albacores. Sighted two Eyetye warships. Saw Albacore score direct hit.'

Two or three hours later on the same day and in the same Spitfire, I witnessed a similar, but less fruitful, Fleet Air Arm search: 'Cover for Swordfish. Saw little save a vast column of smoke from bombed British tanker.'

I have often thought, since those days, of the quality of those Naval flyers who played so telling and aggressive a part in the Malta battle, some surviving and some not – the Hopkinses, the Osbornes, the Watsons, the Heads, the Roes, the Fosters and others. In a varied war, I saw much of their number close to and, now and then, under the whip – in *Eagle*, in Malta itself, in 616 Squadron in Fighter Command in 1943, when I was commanding, and when Nigel Hallett, one of their stand-outs, and others of his comrades, were seconded to us. I came across them, too, at the Fighter Leaders' School at Charmy Down, near Bath, when, for three months, I was instructing, and several of their numbers were 'pupils' on the courses. They were with us again during our rest periods from flying on the Command HQ staffs, to which they brought their rare seaborne experience.

Some were professionals from peacetime, who had started their Naval life at Dartmouth, others were wartime amateurs in the Volunteer Reserve. Irrespective of their background and circumstances, they seemed to me to possess one noticeable common characteristic beyond their other more obvious and notable qualities. Whatever their inner thoughts may have been, they contrived to give the outward impression of utter confidence in their ability to do the job set for them – and then deliberately to play its importance right down. This had nothing whatsoever to do with false modesty, which was an altogether different thing.

David Foster, a lifelong friend, and one of the Fleet Air Arm's well decorated 'stars', who was later to lead the attacks on the oil refineries at Palembang, in Sumatra, during the last months of the Pacific War, seemed to me to epitomize, as well as any of his contemporaries, this attitude of confident understatement.

I asked him once, for the purpose of a work I was then undertaking, to write a few hundred words on his impressions of the Malta conflict to which we had each made a contribution. His relatively short time on the Island had followed an exacting, but successful, spell in the Western Desert in 1941 and 1942 when, after recovering from a bout of malaria and paratyphoid, which would have put paid to operations for most, he returned to fly, for fifteen pressing months, under Royal Air Force command, forty-six night bombing missions with the Fleet Air Arm's 821 (Albacore)

Squadron, attacking Rommel's armour and his supporting port facilities.

Scheduled for overdue home leave, and then reappointment, he was thwarted by the timing of the 8th Army's plans for attack on the Afrika Korps. With Rommel's subsequent retreat, there arose for the Fleet Air Arm an urgent need for more torpedo bombers to fly to Malta to harass and sink Axis shipping crossing the Mediterranean.

Of these hazardous but successful missions he mentioned nothing. Instead, he allowed his pen to take us on a different, downbeat tack:

My short stay on the Island was a most unpleasant one. For one thing, I wasn't supposed to be there! My Royal Marine Major CO had said I wasn't to leave Egypt and go to Malta with the Squadron. But when it came to the point, my replacement unfortunately went sick and failed to show up for three weeks. so, instead of home leave, I had to fly my old Flight over to the Island.

Once there, I was rather surprised immediately to be put on operations – a torpedo strike on shipping one day, mining Sousse harbour by night the next and subsequently a search for a lost plane at sea ... However, thanks to a sympathetic Squadron doctor, the CO let me return to Egypt and thence back to the U.K. ...

My lasting impression of Malta is of a lack of basic food, the awful emergence of Choat as the Sunday joint and the destruction of buildings. This was compensated for by some fun moments with Lt Bertie Hardman at the Union Club in Valletta ...

But for all the acts of derring-do (and, as our Canadian comrades were apt to put it, derring-don't), there was not a word for the record. It was ever the Fleet Air Arm's way in those torrid Mediterranean days of 1942.

# 24

# COMMAND

I repeat . . . that all power is a trust – that we are
accountable for its exercise

*Benjamin Disraeli*

The AOC shot straight from the shoulder in the talk he
gave some of us about the Island's position following the
arrival of what was left of the June convoy. He laid bare the
gravity of the situation, but tempered it with his conviction
that, despite the perils that remained, Malta would prevail.
He made it plain that there was no likelihood of another
convoy attempt being made from east or west till around
the middle of August, another six weeks away.

For those of us who had lived through the times of
steadily increasing privations since early in the year, the
prospect of shorter rations, summer flies and mosquitoes,
sweltering heat on the airfield and recurrent bouts of Malta
Dog, was hardly uplifting.

Water, as well as food, was now severely rationed, and
the restrictions strictly enforced. Officers, NCOs and airmen
all lived on the same meagre rations. It would have been
unthinkable for aircrew to have fed better than the groundcrews such was the contribution which the fitters, riggers,
armourers, signals and wireless tradesmen and the rest were
making, day after day, in the blazing heat. The pilots would
never have stood for it.

The need to conserve fuel further was reflected in the
banning of the use of electric lights in the Mess after dark.
Summer evenings were thus spent sitting out on the bastions
in Mdina or on the terrace of the Xara Palace, talking

among ourselves, trading anecdotes and experiences and moaning good-naturedly at our lot. Conversation was uninhibited. In the darkness, we watched the probing fingers of the searchlights stabbing and sweeping the sky, and the activities of the night fighters, equipped now with airborne radar in their Beaufighters. They were beginning to exact a critical toll of the enemy's bombers which had started to operate in greater numbers at night.

Moose Fumerton, the Canadian master, and Pat Bing, his capable radar operator and observer, were now clawing down Axis raiders at a gathering rate. Gradually this pair were becoming to Malta what John Cunningham and Jimmy Rawnsley had already become to Fighter Command in the night skies over England. They were setting a mark for their comrades to strive for.

These evening discussions brought home to me how close we had all become. The togetherness extended beyond squadron boundaries. 249, 603 and 126, messing together in Mdina, were units made up of a galaxy of English-speaking nationalities, whose countries spanned the globe – the United Kingdom, the Commonwealth and the United States. Yet we felt as one. There were no divisions between us. Opinions, accents and attitudes might vary, but we spoke the same language, thought in much the same way and did the same job. We didn't regard ourselves as being 'different'.

This common identity produced an extraordinary sense of comradeship. Friendships, smelted in the Malta cauldron, could readily be picked out. Pairs became noticeable. Nos 1 and 2, flying as a habit in the air, were inseparable on the ground. For this reason, losses in Malta tended to be felt more keenly than in the operational commands at home. Ours was in every sense an insular existence, contained within a small and tightly circumscribed area, from which, by and large, there was no escape, no release. It was an unnatural life for boisterously heterosexual young men, largely devoid of female company, to be living. Yet it promoted a feeling of unity such as I never found repeated elsewhere in the war. We were a close-knit family. Our relationships were such that survivors, meeting again decades later, were able to pick up the game at once just as it had been left on the bastions of Mdina.

For the islanders, and their families, living in the concentrated and heavily bombed areas, the conditions were, of course, even worse. We wondered how they stuck it and still remained so resolute. The fact was that, in Malta, civilians and military felt as one and acted as such. Hunger, privations and dangers were great levellers. The three, taken together, provided a common denominator.

Our isolation was now such that the arrival of a fresh batch of pilots and aircraft from *Eagle* was awaited as An Event. Newcomers were set upon and probed for every scrap of news from home . . . What was going on in 11 Group of Fighter Command? . . . Who had got what squadron or wing? . . . Who had 'bought it' recently? . . . What sort of resistance was the Luftwaffe putting up against the sweeps over France? . . . Who was making a mark? . . . What was the night bombing like? . . . How were the people taking it? . . .

There was a thirst for information and news. We wanted to read the Stop Press first and be brought up to date . . .

There was bad news from the first of the two June reinforcements from *Eagle*. Wing Commander McLean, still in Gibraltar masterminding the fly-offs from the carrier, had finally lost his unbeaten record of successful deliveries – as we knew he eventually must.

Of the last batch of thirty-one Spitfires, four had failed to reach the Island, the result of a sharp skirmish with the Me 109s from the Axis-held island of Pantelleria, lurking along the route. Those of us who had taken part in the May reinforcements had felt that McLean's luck couldn't last for ever. Such were the obvious hazards of these operations that his run was bound to end soon. The marvel was that it had lasted so long.

We heard about the loss from a greatly shaken Johnny Plagis, who, before he left the Island after an outstanding spell, would take over a Flight in No. 185 Squadron at Halfar. With his compatriot Buchanan, he had been sent back to Gibraltar on 23 May to lead in the next month's reinforcements.

'With about 150 miles of the 700 miles' flight still to go – and petrol reserves "dodgy" – this was no time to stay around and mix it with the 109s. We were lucky, I suppose, not to have lost more. If the Huns or the Eyetyes are really going to start making an effort to disrupt these flights from the carrier, we've got another think coming . . .'

We listened, with some unease, to Johnny's story. There, but for the Grace of God, we thought, might have gone a few more of us who had flown off *Eagle* during the May operations.

For me personally, however, events were presently about to take an unexpected turn. Stanley Grant had now led 249 for three months and scored an unquestioned success. But he was tired, and Lloyd and Woodhall, commendably vigilant when it came to watching the well-being of squadron and flight commanders, knew it. It was demonstrably time for a change.

Other things also were happening. The earlier loss of both Norman MacQueen and Pete Nash had deprived the Squadron of two outstanding performers – and potential leaders. Moreover, stalwarts like Philip Heppell, our Northumbrian joker, Jeff West, the New Zealander, and the two Canadians, Bud Connell and Buck McNair, who had been in the thick of the earlier fighting, were due for one reason or another – wounds, illness or just plain tiredness – for release and a rest. Ronnie West, also, who had been a linchpin in the unit since March, adding all the time to his record and stature, was deservedly picked out, like Johnny Plagis before him, to move over from Takali to Halfar, and take on a Flight in 185. The backbone of the Squadron was thus changing. But in place of these well-tried campaigners, a new intake of real ability and potential was beginning to assert itself in the 249 tradition.

Characters like Frank Jones, Ozzie Linton, Mickey Butler, Gerry de Nancrede, Chuck McLean, John McElroy and Bob Middlemiss – all from Canada – Alan Yates from Australia, and Jack Rae and Laurie Verrall from New Zealand, Tex Spradley from the United States and Les Watts from the United Kingdom, had all lifted their sights since joining the Squadron, and were now ready to form what might be called the unit's 'middle management' team. They were full of spirit and colour and well capable of filling the gaps which were beginning to open. No. 249 Squadron had the signal advantage of possessing strength in depth and it showed through in the Squadron's performance in the air. We now had a high-calibre lot. In cricketing terms, we batted down to No. 11. The Canadian star in our firmament, George Beurling – 'Screwball' to 249 – had yet to show . . .

The June convoy was only just behind us when Group Captain Woodhall paid another of his visits to the Mess at Mdina. The hectic fighting of the last days had relented and we were back to a rather lighter routine. For the time being, the Regia Aeronautica, rather than the Luftwaffe, appeared to be making much of the running.

Jumbo Gracie had told me at lunch-time, as my Flight came off readiness, that Woody wanted to see me. 'Nothing serious, old boy, so don't worry.' Jumbo had a way of leaving a piece of news, dangling in the air, half completed. I used to think he rather enjoyed making people quizzical and giving the impression that he knew more than he was saying.

I was talking to Paul Brennan and Ray Hesslyn on the terrace of the Xara Palace when Woody appeared with Gracie. Paul and Ray, inseparable on the ground and in the air, had had an outstandingly successful run since the early spring as NCOs, and had just been commissioned. They were bubbling with unconcealed pleasure at their new state. Woody, pink gin in one hand, cigarette in the other, lifted his glass to them. 'Good show, you boys. You thoroughly deserve it.' With that, he put his hand on my arm. 'Give me a few moments, will you?' He then took me aside, leaving Jumbo with the newly commissioned 'twins'.

Woodhall pulled a piece of paper from his pocket as he motioned me to sit down. I noticed there were several names written on it. Then, popping the monocle he used for reading in his right eye, he said his piece.

'I've got good news for you.' As he hesitated, I thought for a moment he was going to say that I was posted back to the United Kingdom. Like some of the older inhabitants, I was, in fact, due for a rest. But no, that wasn't it. Instead he started on about how he and the AOC had decided that there must now be changes on the Island – in 249 as well as 126 and 185. Four months in these conditions were considered to be enough – three, if things had gone on as they were in March and April. Those who had been with 249 in Malta since early in the year, and seen the heaviest fighting, must soon be stood down. We could afford to make changes now with the build-up of new pilots and aircraft.

Woody went through the list, finishing with Buck McNair who was already on his way. 'As you know,' he said, 'Norman Lee has got Buck's Flight. I gather from the CO that that's what he and you both wanted.'

Then he came to Stan Grant himself. 'We've never, as you are aware, used wing commanders flying, as such, here. We've had to work with much smaller formations – squadrons, flights and sections – so we haven't needed them. But there's an establishment at Takali for a wing commander flying, and when Stan Turner gave up 249, he was made up to wing co, but he did little or no flying. The AOC rightly wanted him rested from ops and, soon after, he came and joined us at AHQ in Valletta. Now the AOC has decided that Stan Grant, who has done such a fine job with 249, should also be rested. He is therefore being posted to fill the vacant wing co flying's job at Takali, but like Stan Turner he'll be doing little or no flying.'

I wondered whatever was coming next. I could not imagine 249 without Stan Grant at its head. I had got on so well with him, and I felt he was there for keeps – certainly until my time was up.

Woody then dropped 'the good news'. 'I'm very pleased to say the AOC has decided that you should take over 249 from Stan with immediate effect . . .'

I could hardly credit what I heard. It had genuinely never occurred to me that I might get the Squadron. I had always thought that if, for some reason, Stan had had to be replaced, someone else from outside would have been appointed. I had never coveted the job. I was quite happy as I was, fully aware that I was lucky to have a Flight in one of the Royal Air Force's exceptional squadrons. But this . . .! I couldn't believe it.

I was barely conscious of the rest of what Woody as saying – going on, as he was, generously about my handling of the Flight during the roughest times, having now had the experience, and being ready for the job . . . But I came back to earth with a bump as he put his glass down on the table, let his monocle flop down from his eye to be suspended from his neck, and stood up. He held out his hand.

'I'm so pleased, Laddie, you've got the Squadron. They're an exceptional bunch. I know you'll do a good job, carrying on where Stan has left it. If you ever want anything, you know you can always telephone me. Good luck!'

Woody stopped as he turned to go off and rejoin Jumbo Gracie. 'By the way, who do you want to take over your Flight in the Squadron? If you want to think about it overnight, give me a ring in the morning.'

'Sir,' I said, 'I'm in no doubt. I'd like Flying Officer Daddo-Langlois to take it on. I know he's still a bit young, but . . .'

The Group Captain wouldn't let me finish. 'Tell him to put his stripe up tonight.'

I felt a strange sense of relief at being given the Squadron – relief mixed with pride to think that I was getting not only the Island's top-scoring squadron, but one which was now recognized as being one of the Royal Air Force's outstanding units. When once I had got over the initial shock at the news and had begun to think about what the responsibility entailed, a sense of calm came over me. Although I had no right to think it, I was absolutely confident I could do the job. I had no qualms, no apprehensions.

I found this feeling of confidence difficult to understand. It was still no more than two years since, in June 1940, I had walked out of the *Express* building in Fleet Street for the last time to go away to war. But I had, I knew, one or two special advantages. I had been fortunate both at school, at Stowe, and at Cambridge, to have had to carry responsibility – as head of the school and captain of the XI and the XV and, at the University, as president of the Hawks Club, the highly regarded establishment of which the games-playing élite were mostly members. Having to carry the can in adolescence and early manhood if things go wrong teaches hard lessons; but once learnt, they are never forgotten.

I knew, moreover, that I had been prepared for the job by having served under a succession of first-rate mentors in my brief time in the Service. I had, even then, begun to admire straightforward professionalism (and to feel irked by command which showed a lack of it). One learns from example, which is why leadership – outstanding leadership – when it is offered is so important to subordinates.

Beyond this, I had now survived almost five months of combat, against all the odds, in one of the hottest theatres of the war. And, all the time, Stan Grant had left me to get on and run my Flight virtually without interference. 'I always thought,' he said, after Woodhall had given me the news, 'that you should get 249 after me.'

It occurred to me afterwards that this Cranwell-trained officer, of unusual quality, probably had this in mind when he deliberately left me alone with my Flight. A lesser commander would have been nosing about and the proof of ability or otherwise would not have been so plain. Some do not find delegation easy.

The sense of relief, I concluded, came from realizing that, at least, I would now be virtually my own master. There was no other command in the Royal Air Force in wartime quite like it. As a squadron commander, provided you did the job and made a success of it, it was your show, your affair to make what you could of it. It was an enviable remit.

I was certain I would get the response I needed from the two Flight Commanders. They were efficient and I trusted them. As for the Squadron, I knew its members well, their characteristics and their strengths. There were few weaknesses. Again, I was convinced they would follow an adult, common-sense lead on the ground and one which, in the air, eschewed selfishness and gave Nos 2, 3 and 4 in the sections a chance. We all knew each other's flying capabilities so well now, and the principles of our success were so clear-cut, that I couldn't see difficulties there.

As I went to bed that night a feeling of tranquillity came over me. Twenty-six years and nine months old, and a bit older than the rest, I was sure I would be able to manage, come what might. Half a century on, I hardly dare own up to the gross affront to the poet contained in the little comment I wrote in my log book the next day: 'Made OC 249 Squadron. Stan Grant becomes Wing Commander [Flying]. Raoul gets my Flight. This blessed plot . . . This seat of majesty . . . this Malta!'

# PART FOUR

# MASTERING THE AXIS

# 25

# PURE GENIUS

*When every morning brought a noble chance
And every chance brought out a noble knight*
*Alfred, Lord Tennyson*

George Beurling had been on the Island little more than a fortnight when we settled on his nickname. He had, by then, flown infrequently but quite enough for me to see that in this way-out individualist and eccentric, with flying and fighting qualities far above the general run, we had a find – and an oddball with it.

Accompanying an unkempt exterior of tropical shorts which were too long, stockings which were seldom properly pulled up and secured, and an open-neck, sleeveless khaki shirt, worn normally without any insignia, there was a head of fair, tousled hair, a rather sallow face, betraying a Scandinavian ancestry, and a pair of uncompromisingly blue eyes which pierced everyone and everything like a gimlet.

On this spell of early morning readiness at 249's dispersal, Beurling had his Mae West draped loosely over his shoulders, its untied strands hanging down almost to his knees. With his dusty flying boots, it all compounded the untidiness of his appearance.

Although he was by nature fairly brash and outspoken, he had been quite silent since we came down at dawn two or three hours before. He was always something of a loner and, early on with the Squadron, he tended to keep his thoughts very much to himself. Later, he wasn't averse from allowing his opinions full rein. This day, he was alert and restless, preferring to remain on his feet instead of finding, like the rest of us, an empty, upturned drum, an old sandbag or a heap of rubble to sit on. As he moved about, those searching blue eyes were forever traversing the sky. Had there been any 109s approaching, high up in the hazy heavens, he would have spotted them seconds before the rest of us. His eyesight was uncanny, even by the best Air Force standards.

The breakfast cart, bringing tea and the usual bully beef sandwiches and hard biscuits, had come and gone. Beurling had chucked a piece of half-eaten bully beef down on the dusty ground. Pulling up a rickety chair beside this morsel, his eyes were fastened on the mass of flies which were swarming about and settling on it. The sun, warming the temperature into the seventies and eighties, had brought them out in their hundreds. Transfixed by this spectacle, he would raise his foot every few moments, stealthily and slowly, hold it suspended for a second and whoomph! down it would crash on to this squirming target. As he surveyed the casualties from each attack, he muttered to himself 'The goddam screwballs!'

It became a well-worked phrase in the Canadian's vocabulary. It served every purpose . . . The flies, the Maltese, the Messerschmitts, the drivers of the tea cart – all became 'the goddam screwballs'. So Screwball he was named. It suited him and I think he rather liked it. It encouraged his ego to feel that he was being noticed and thought about, even with affection, by a squadron in which he had quickly developed a pride. He hadn't been treated like that, he told me, in England.

Screwball Beurling had come to us in a bizarre way. He had arrived with the second batch of reinforcements in June. When it came to allocating the new arrivals to 249 and 603 Squadrons at Takali, the adjutant had prepared an alphabetical list. Sergeant Beurling's name was at the top.

I had not then taken over 249 so Stan Grant had entrusted the selections to his two Flight Commanders, to Buck McNair and to me. David Douglas-Hamilton, on the other hand, wanted to pick his own candidates for 603. He was determined on the point.

'Let's toss,' I said, 'for who'll have first pick.' The coin favoured 249. One of the Squadron had served with George Beurling in England. Seeing his name on the list, he had given me a run-down. 'I was with him in 41. He was a loner who was always getting separated from the Squadron on the sweeps and going off on his own. A dim view was taken of it and he didn't seem to be prepared to learn. But, make no mistake, he can fly aeroplanes, has got flair and can shoot.'

'Would he fit in with us?' I asked. 'Remember the flying here is very different from the wing operations in England.'

The retort was equivocal. 'It's hard to say, might do, might not. But one thing's for sure. He'll either "buy it" very quickly here or shoot some down.'

Buck clearly didn't want him for his Flight. He had got the message from 403, the Canadian Squadron, which Beurling had joined first of all.

'OK,' I said, 'it's 249's pick first, so I'll have Sergeant Beurling for our 'A' Flight.'

Screwball somehow discovered later that I had picked him first. It obviously helped our relationship and probably made things easier when it came to the crunch. I think he was quite surprised that anyone should actually want him such had been his experience in Fighter Command in England.

I had a talk with him the day after he joined us. I told him straightly that I knew of the reputation he had made for himself in 41 Squadron and the problems this had brought. At the same time, I had been told that he had flair, could fly well and could shoot, all of which appealed to me. I added that he would start with a clean slate here and provided that he toed the line, stuck as a pair with whoever he was flying with and didn't go chasing off on his own, he would get every chance.

As soon as I took over command of 249 and Raoul Daddo-Langlois got my Flight, I asked him to take the Canadian sergeant pilot under his wing, watch him closely, make sure that he played things our way, but give him his chance. Raoul was just the one for that kind of assignment; he was, with all his other attributes, a fair-minded man.

A few days later, he came to me. 'This chap Beurling,' he said, 'is potentially very good. He flies well, seems to shoot very accurately and has particularly good eyes. He also seems to have a natural flair. But he goes off on his own and leaves his number one and he doesn't seem to want to learn. For this reason he could be a real risk if he goes on with it.'

I saw the Canadian the same day. I told him that by behaving like this in the air, no matter how confident he might be himself, he was letting the Squadron down and increasing the risks for others which were high enough already.

I added a rider. I said from what I had heard from his flight commander and the little I had seen myself, he had the ability to make a success of his time on the Island if he played things 249's way rather than selfishly for what he thought were his own ends. I then laid it on the line. 'However, Screwball,' I said, 'if you don't toe the 249 line then let's be quite clear about this. You'll be on the next aeroplane into the Middle East.'

Those blue eyes were still fixed on mine. 'Boss,' he said (he never called me 'sir', in my recollection), 'that's OK by me. I'll play it your way.' What's more, I felt sure that he would.

Screwball never let me down nor, so far as I am aware,

did Daddo-Langlois ever have another cross word with him. Treated firmly but reasonably, and in an adult way, he became a figure in his own right.

I had a feeling about George Beurling the moment I met him and as soon as I had seen enough of his work as a fighter pilot. Something told me that he was made for this rarefied form of island warfare, whereas he was unlikely to be suitable for the large, set-piece wing operations with which we were so familiar at home.

In the event, he proved to be, in this environment, a genius. Malta was made for him.

What few realized was that Beurling regarded flying as a precise science. He coaxed an aeroplane with gentle hands to do his bidding and he flew it accurately. He got the maximum out of a Spitfire as a steady gun platform because he was an accurate pilot – contrary to the general belief. He was agile in the air and this, allied to an innate judgement of distance and position, and exceptional eyesight, gave him the operational edge over his adversaries. He went for the kill fast, he got in close and he fired short bursts. He did not waste ammunition. But he was an individualist, not a team man. I felt pretty sure, the more I saw of him, that he was genuinely trying to fight this trait.

Ever since he was a teenager, being brought up at Verdun, in the province of Quebec, in eastern Canada, flying was an obsession with Beurling. He learnt to fly pre-war and he was well taught. His flying largely took the place of scholarship. His education was said to be below the standard which the Royal Canadian Air Force required in a potential pilot when he offered his services at the outbreak of war. In any case they were inundated with volunteers and could afford to be choosy; and this was as plausible a reason for rejection as any.

Shunned by the Canadian Air Force, he worked his passage to England to volunteer for the Royal Air Force. He worked it twice, as a matter of fact, both ways, because the first time he had left his birth certificate behind and had to go back for it. With that in his pocket, the Royal Air Force was glad to take him – just as the Service had taken Marmaduke Thomas St John Pattle – 'Pat' Pattle, the brilliant South African, in 1936, after the Air Force in his native land had turned him down.

Thereafter, Screwball, like Pattle, got the finest flying training in the world. His good luck was that he met up with James ('Ginger') Lacey at his operational training unit, the last stop *en route* for a squadron. Ginger Lacey, who could shoot straighter than most, taught him the art of knocking aeroplanes out of the sky.

Beurling shot down twenty-seven aircraft in his four months in Malta – twenty-seven out of his wartime total of $31\frac{1}{3}$. About his claims and everything else, he was, I believe, honest to a point. In my experience, I never heard the remotest suggestion in 249 that he overclaimed. A squadron will always mark down a fighter pilot who is thought to be prone, now and then, to 'stretching a point'. There was none of that in 249 or with Screwball, in particular.

We had some discerning intelligence officers at Takali during the battle, John Lodge and Keith Aitken among them. With all the practice, they developed a second sense with pilots and their claims. Where surging adrenalin, tense emotions, imagination and the possibility of duplication came into it, it was not always easy for an IO to establish beyond doubt the accuracy of a pilot's submission. Enemy aircraft crashing on land was one thing; falling into the sea, and leaving no trace, was another.

I remember John Lodge saying to me that after he had come to know him, and listened frequently to his reports after combat, he never doubted the accuracy of Beurling's claims. The Canadian was meticulous about them to the extent sometimes of being finicky because there might be some doubt about a 'damaged' claim being updated to a 'probable'; or a 'probable' to a 'destroyed'.

This did not surprise me, for the sergeant pilot had been brought up in a large and strictly religious Plymouth Brethren family. While I doubt whether he was still maintaining his allegiance to the Brethren when he came out to Malta, he certainly remained rigidly teetotal and retained his natural faith in the Bible.

I recall Flight Sergeant L. G. Head, one of the crew of the Royal Air Force's High Speed Launch 128, which did such yeoman air-sea rescue service during the battle, telling me years later of the time they lifted Beurling out of the sea, some six miles east of the Island, after he had been shot down right at the end of his tour in Malta. He had picked off a 109 and, in the process, had been nailed by another – not his form at all.

'It was 14 October and we found the young pilot officer [he had been commissioned by then] floating in his dinghy. He had been wounded in the foot. He was greatly agitated and distressed because he had lost his Bible as he was disentangling himself from his parachute and getting into his dinghy.

Fortunately, we found it and handed it to him after which he calmed down. He said this small book had been given by his mother and that he never flew without it . . .'

I became convinced of the accuracy of Screwball Beurling's claims after a skirmish we had with a bunch of Me 109s and Italian Macchi 202s high up over St Paul's Bay one morning early in July 1942. An excessive number of enemy fighters were acting as cover for a small force of bombers targeted on one of the airfields.

I was leading eight aircraft of 249, split into two sections of four each. Screwball was flying way out on my right, 400 yards away in line abreast. Woodhall, controlling the interception, got us perfectly placed at around 25,000 feet, east of Grand Harbour, up-sun of the incoming raid. His resonant, measured voice, which always reminded me of the BBC's Howard Marshall describing a Test Match at Lord's pre-war, created the picture. 'Little jobs approaching St Paul's Bay, angels twenty. There are forty plus . . .'

And there they were. It was the ideal bounce, out of the mid-morning sun, with all the advantage which height can bestow. They never saw us. Having dealt with an unsuspecting Me 109 myself, I was just in time to see Screwball, with plenty of speed away on the right, pulling up fast under another 109 and closing to what looked like his usual 150 yards. A two- or three-second burst from a quarter-into-an-astern attack and the German aircraft flicked on to its back before starting to spin earthwards.

I saw no more of Beurling in the general mêlée which followed. Having dispatched his 109, he had then caught a Macchi 202 and sent that plummeting down.

We landed back at Takali. John Lodge was the duty IO taking down the pilots' reports. Screwball gave his in his usual clinical and analytical way. Both the 109 and the Macchi 202 had been confirmed, not least by the ack-ack batteries in the north-east of the Island. He then added a postscript. As he had disengaged, he had seen another Macchi 202 by itself, heading for home just north of St Paul's Bay and east of Gozo. Unseen by the Italian pilot, he had attacked from the port quarter, seeing strikes all along the fuselage, in the wing root and along the side of the engine. The aircraft had dived away to port, but he could only claim a damaged as he had then seen some more 109s approaching and discretion told him it was time to call it a day. No one else had witnessed his attack.

A couple of hours later, a report came through to say that

a Macchi had crashed on Gozo. Later still, it was confirmed that the aircraft had been heavily damaged by cannon fire along the port side of the fuselage, in the wing root and up to a point just short of the engine.

John Lodge reported the matter to Beurling, said that this was clearly the aircraft that he had shot at and that he would therefore be credited with its destruction. It could be no one else's. The strikes that he had reported tallied with what had been found except that they did not extend right up to the engine.

Screwball was quite put out. 'Dammit,' he exclaimed, deadpan, 'I was certain I had hit that goddam screwball in the engine!'

With Rommel now halted at El Alamein, after his breath-taking gallop through Libya and into Egypt, and with his supply lines dangerously extended, the Beauforts with their Beaufighter escorts from Malta were presently hammering at Axis shipping as it headed south across the Mediterranean to Tripoli, Benghazi and Tobruk. The Baltimores and the Wellingtons were likewise taking their toll of port facilities and land-based targets by night. In the short lull which had followed the June convoy, the Island had recovered much of its pristine offensive strength. The German High Command was therefore obliged to retaliate.

The stage was thus set for the Luftwaffe's return and for its last great throw of the summer. Few among the enemy would have dared to admit it, but already it had begun to look as though Raeder, Kesselring, Weichold and the Italian Supreme Command had been right and the Führer wrong. Costly though it would be, there was, in practice, no effective and enduring substitute for the invasion of Malta. Bombing alone would not rub it out.

The whole North African campaign was now critically poised. Never was this isolated Mediterranean jewel seen to sparkle more brightly. Never had the stand of the last awful months been shown to have been more worth while. Rough though things would continue to be for weeks, the feeling was now abroad that we were over the worst. If we could hold the line now in the face of Kesselring's latest onslaught, Malta and its rugged people would prevail.

# 26

# TIDAL FLOW

There is a tide in the affairs of men,
Which, taken at the flood, leads on to fortune; . . .
On such a full sea are we now afloat,
And we must take the current when it serves,
Or lose our venture.
*William Shakespeare*, Julius Caesar, *Act IV Scene iii*

My luck was now well in. I could feel that things were flowing my way. There are moments in life when you can sense that you're in a winning vein. July 1942 was such a time for me. Now in my sixth month on the Island, I thought it was, perhaps, some kind of a reward for having stuck it out, first, with the old Hurricanes against the 109Fs in February and, then again, in those dreadful spring days of March and April when our fortunes were hanging by a thread.

One morning, quite soon after Woodhall had stunned me with the news that I was to take over the Squadron, he rang me on the Ops line while we were at readiness at Takali. 'Laddie,' he began, and I thought he was about to brief us for some unexpected escapade, 'you've been awarded the DFC.* It's a good show. You deserve it. You'll be getting the formal signal at Station HQ today.'

Elated, I wrote off to tell my widowed mother a couple of days later, as soon as I knew that someone was flying back to England and could take a letter with him.

All through the battle, I had struck rigidly to my self-imposed practice of writing to my mother each week. Indeed, no matter where I was in World War II, or how

*Distinguished Flying Cross.

little the censor might allow us to say, I never once consciously broke this routine.

I had begun the habit at school and had followed it during my undergraduate years. I had never forgotten something which I had heard J. F. Roxburgh, the first and founding headmaster of Stowe, say in one of his regular addresses to the School.

Roxburgh, one of the truly great headmasters, was a man of compelling charm and personality. He had been for me a dominant influence during the adolescent years. My father had died prematurely of cancer when I was eleven to leave a massive void in my young life. J.F. had, therefore, by his example and kindly attentions, supplied for me a special need. He had provided an image which I and many other contemporary Stoics could look up to. It has travelled with me for a lifetime.

In this talk to some of the younger boys in the School, he had spoken about writing regular letters home to one's parents. I can still recall the gist of his words, 'I hope, while you are here at Stowe, and whenever you are away for long periods from your family, you will make a practice of writing a regular weekly letter to your parents. Sunday is a good day for it.

'I cannot overstate its importance. Each one of you means more to your father and mother than you will realize now. They long for your letters because they love you and are anxious about you.

'I wrote a letter weekly (and, at trying times, more frequently) during my school and university days and when I was in Flanders during the Great War. I do not think there was ever a week during this time when I didn't write to my mother. I hope you will feel able to emulate my practice.'

Now, in Malta, my DFC, which happily was announced on the same day as another for Ronnie West, 249's Scottish fighter, who had now settled easily into command of a

Flight in 185, absorbed a complete letter, so overjoyed was I at my good fortune.

I knew how proud my mother would be in all her anxiety for my well-being. Reading its text again these fifty years on, I have no doubt whatever that it represented truthfully my feelings at the time. I never had any compunction in expressing my thoughts in writing to my mother – and she likewise to me.

Officers' Mess
RAF Station
Takali
Malta

9 vii 42

My dear Mother,

The big news since I last wrote is that the AOC, Malta, recommended me for the DFC and that his recommendation was granted the day before yesterday.

I received a signal in the evening which read: 'On the recommendation of the Air Officer Commanding, HQ Mediterranean, His Majesty The King has been graciously pleased to grant the award of the Distinguished Flying Cross to Acting Squadron Leader Percy Belgrave Lucas for courage, determination and devotion to duty. Message ends.'

I question really whether I was ever so pleased in all my life. Colours at Stowe, a 'Blue' at Cambridge, a job on the *Express*, winning the Boys' [Golf] Championship [at Carnoustie] – all these things gave inexpressable (sic) satisfaction. But I believe this DFC has pleased me more than any of these achievements. For I can say with truth that I've longed to get it and worked and tried like the devil to win it. And I believe the family will be a mite proud of the victory.

Perhaps you would write a note to John Gordon [editor of the *Sunday Express*: under Lord Beaverbrook, my immediate employer, pre-war]. The last thing he said to me when I left the *Express* to join the RAF as a pilot was: 'Come back here with nothing less than a DFC and we'll be satisfied.' Somehow that stuck in my memory.

Love, as ever, to you all
Laddie

One recent 'grandstand' interception, made right over the centre of the Island in the full gaze of the other squadrons and the local population, had probably tipped the scales in my favour. It had occurred on 4 July and it might have come straight out of a day-fighting text-book. It was a mission in a thousand, clear-cut and perfectly controlled by Woodhall from the ground – one of his skilled performances. He set up the contact and made it easy for us to score. Even so, it still required a well-drilled and aggressive piece of flying by 249 with the pilots right at the peak of their form.

The whole Squadron had been down on the airfield since dawn. Now, three hours later, with the sun climbing to its zenith, we had ten aeroplanes serviceable and at advance readiness.

Woody had given me the order to scramble on the Ops telephone. 'There's a big raid, it seems, building up over Sicily which is about to move south. From the plots on the table, it looks like a few big jobs* with a very strong escort – probably around seventy or eighty plus at angels seventeen thousand to twenty thousand.†

'Get the squadron off at once, climb fast away to the south to twenty-four or twenty-five thousand feet and stay up-sun to the south-east of Grand Harbour. I'll be giving you the usual progress commentary and tell you when to come in. Watch your tails. I fancy there'll be the customary squadron or two of 109s sweeping in ahead of the raid and trying to work round behind you before you can attack.

'Now get off right away and good luck.' Woody had a clear, uncomplicated mind. He invariably made the picture of a raid plain, and his instructions were always a model of simplicity and direction. This was a secret of his accom-

*Enemy bombers.　　† 17,000 to 20,000 feet.

plished controlling. He visualized everything so precisely and anticipated so accurately.

I deliberately pushed up the height above what Woody was recommending. I had the time to do it and one never lost anything in the day-fighting art with an excess of altitude. We were close to 27,000 feet, flying north, with the sun behind us, and nicely placed at about five o'clock from Grand Harbour, when Woody's sonorous bass voice gave the news we wanted.

'Tiger leader, eighty plus approaching St Paul's Bay now, angels seventeen to twenty thousand. You should see them very soon at twelve o'clock six or seven thousand feet below you. Come in now and come in fast. There are some little jobs* in your vicinity, but below you; so watch your tails.'

I was glad I had had time to add another 2000 or 3000 feet to our altitude. With such numerical odds stacked against us, it generated confidence in the Squadron to know the enemy was below.

The two section leaders and I spotted our prey almost simultaneously, dead ahead and some 6000 or 7000 feet below. Down-sun the gaggle was silhouetted against the hazy blue of the Mediterranean. 'OK, Woody,' I said, 'we see them. Thanks. Out.'

Three Italian Cant Z 1007 bombers, with a strong escort of Me 109s, flying beautifully in their usual wide-open formation of fours in line abreast, were in quite a tight VIC, a hallmark of the Regia Aeronautica. Well astern of them was a token force of Macchi 202s and Reggiane 2001s also flying a tighter formation than their Luftwaffe counterparts. The raid looked to be heading for the airfield at Halfar, with a saver for Luqa.

To an old Island hand, the three Cants were an obvious

*Enemy fighters.

decoy to tempt the defending Spitfires into battle while the superior forces of the Axis turned their guns on them. 249 weren't to be fooled with that kind of ruse. Surprise, born of height, sun and position, and a super-fast closing speed was the only plausible antidote for such a trap. With our extra height and the sun now blazing behind us, we clearly hadn't been spotted.

My instructions to the Squadron, with Raoul Daddo-Langlois leading Blue section to my left and Jack Rae and his No. 2, making Yellow section to my right, were necessarily concise. With such an experienced lot, they could have followed the tactics blindfold.

'OK, fellers,' I said, 'turning hard to port and going down now. My Red section will take the bomber to the port of the VIC. Raoul, you and Blue section take the starboard bomber. And Jack, you and your number two, cover Red and Blue sections as we go in. If you're not engaged, and have the chance, take a good poke at the leading big job. After the attack, all Tiger aircraft are to break downwards fast and go straight down to the deck. There are far too many 109s about to stay and mix it.

'OK, Raoul?'

'Roger.'*

'And Jack, OK?'

'Roger.'

'Right, fellers, going in now. Let's get in close to the bombers.'

The plan worked. With all the advantage of being unseen, and with height, sun and speed compounding the opportunity, we cut straight through the opposing fighters and closed quickly with three bombers, seconds before the escort spotted us. It was a diamond-sharp bounce, a chance in a thousand.

* Message understood.

My emotions, as we tore through a covey of unsuspecting 'dirty black crosses', and on to the three bombers, are vivid still. I had no feeling of apprehension or fear – only a buoyed-up excitement and determination to close right in with the port bomber and take a shot which might never recur. Every atom of concentration I possessed was riveted on the port Cant as Red section swung naturally in behind me and we turned a beam into a nicely curved quarter attack.

It was all over in seconds as these interceptions always were. But it had produced, for me, exactly the sense of exhilaration which I had become accustomed to on the rugby football field. The ball was out on our side of the scrum; a perfectly judged pass by the stand-off half, and here we were, the two centres, taking the ball flat out in our stride and cutting through a disorganized defence to leave the wing with the overlap and a straight run-in, of gathering speed, to the corner flag.

Here, for me, at the head of the Squadron, was the chance which every leader prayed for . . . with one difference. This was the first time since taking over 249 that I had had the opportunity of leading the whole Squadron into an attack. If ever there was a tide in the affairs of a squadron commander which led on to fortune, it was now mine. Ride in on such a current when it served and a mark would be made for ever.

A quick look in the rear mirror confirmed that only Red 2, 3 and 4, each immaculately positioned, were behind. Then, disregarding the Italian rear gunners' rather desultory fire, I pressed the attack on the port Cant until, at what seemed like point-blank range, I let the shells from the four cannons in my Spitfire VC rip into the port side of the aircraft's fuselage and engine. The bomber seemed almost to be disintegrating as I flew through a mass of debris severed from airframe and port motor.

As I broke away fast downwards, telling the rest of my section to follow, I could see the 109 escort spreadeagling all over the sky as the leaders suddenly became alive to the enormity of the affront to which 249 and Woodhall had subjected them. A *schwärme* of four Messerschmitts gave a face-saving chase after my section, but they were too late. As our speed built up in the dive for the deck, and we turned now and then towards them, they never had a hope of getting inside us with a worthwhile deflection shot.

Meanwhile, an upward glance or two told me that the three Cants, in various states of disrepair, were falling out of the sky. The port aircraft, which I had attacked, was ablaze and smoking, shortly to plunge into the sea 5 miles or so from Delimara Point. I was glad to see two parachutes open from it.

The starboard aircraft, which Daddo-Langlois and his aggressive Canadian No. 2, Bob Middlemiss, had sent smoking earthwards, looked as if it must crash within gunshot of Halfar.

Finally, the leading bomber, which had been Jack Rae's responsibility with his No. 2, was streaming black smoke as it went into a terminal dive southwards before hitting the sea a few miles from Kalafrana. More parachutes were floating down from it. Jack's attack on it, precisely timed to synchronize with those of Red and Blue sections on the two flanking bombers, was a professionally executed assault. He could, for all the world, have been a New Zealand All-Black centre threequarter, selling the dummy and thrusting through an opening in midfield to score the try of the match under the posts.

My section was the first to land back at Takali. As I jumped down from my aircraft, my groundcrew – fitter, rigger and armourer – were clustered round the dispersal with some of their mates. Stripped to the waist, their torsos nut brown from days spent working on aircraft in the burning sun, they had seen much of the engagement from the ground. My leading aircraft was 'our kite' to them and I, 'our pilot'. They were as elated as I was. It had been their victory on the ground just as much as ours in the air.

I walked back to our broken-down dispersal hut where John Lodge, our devoted IO, was waiting, notebook in hand, to pick up the score. Screwball Beurling, on one of his rare days off, was standing beside him. He had waited for us to land. With his acute eyesight and tactical brain, he had been reading the skirmish, blow-by-blow, for the groundcrews in a continuous aerial commentary.

As I walked up to the two of them, Screwball, blue eyes sparkling, and tousled hair flopping about, held out his hand. 'Boss,' he said, with touching sincerity, 'I couldn't fault that one.'

Coming from George Beurling, it was the ultimate accolade.

There was a disturbing sequel to 249's moment of triumph. The following day, I took Raoul Daddo-Langlois and two of our pilots who had taken part in the destruction of the three Cants to see the survivors in the military hospital at St Patrick's Barracks, just south of Fort Madalena in the east of the Island.

It was explained to the representatives of the Regia Aeronautica by an Italian-speaking officer on our station HQ staff who had come with us that I was the CO of the squadron which had shot the Cants down on the previous day and that my section had attacked the port aircraft in the VIC of three from which, we believed, there had been two survivors.

As I walked over to the bed occupied by one of the two survivors, a good-looking Italian in his middle to late twenties looked up at me with sad, plaintive dark eyes which seemed to be appealing for sympathy. As he gazed at me, he slowly and painfully lifted a heavily bandaged arm. The hand and a part of it had been blown off by a cannon shell during the attack.

Sickened, I bent down and held the Italian's other hand in mine, shaking my head in sympathetic disbelief as I did so. I then turned away and at once withdrew to wait at the door of the ward while my other Squadron colleagues finished their conversations with the Italians through the interpreter.

They told me that my victim had been a violinist in civilian life. The pleading, pitiful look in those dark Latin eyes was to haunt me for weeks. I can see it still. The same evening, I told my two flight commanders that the Squadron's practice of visiting badly wounded prisoners – German or Italian – in hospital must cease forthwith. Those with commonplace and non-evocative wounds were a different matter. I explained that a repetition of my emotive experience that afternoon could only harm morale.

I never found it easy to hate our opponents in wartime, even with all the brutalities. I wasn't, I admit, as hidebound or as unyielding as most in my attitude to the enemy. I could never bring myself to be otherwise. The rough, day-fighting role in Malta, with its intimate, hand-to-hand characteristics, always struck me as having far more of the elements of *la chasse* than those of the sordid, life-and-death business which was war.

I was, I recognize, in a minority. I used to think, however, that chivalry in the air, particularly in victory, was a nobler and more gallant posture to adopt than the bull-necked and insensitive stance which many – at least outwardly – affected to deploy.

# 27

# MARAUDERS RETURN

Does the road wind up-hill all the way?
    Yes, to the very end.
Will the day's journey take the whole long day?
    From morn to night, my friend.
                    *Christina Georgina Rossetti*

New Zealand's Harry Coldbeck, supported by the evidence of the cameras in his blue photographic Spitfire, warned us, early in July, to expect a resurgence of Luftwaffe activity. Kesselring's freshly strengthened forces on the airfields of Sicily and southern Italy confirmed our hunch that June's relative lull in the fighting would not last.

As the noonday temperatures at the aircraft dispersals nudged the mid-90s, and uninterrupted sunshine turned the Island into a parched expanse of dust, blown about by the hot winds from Africa, there began an ominous rise in enemy pressure. We were back again on the old and familiar treadmill. Only the odds were different.

The contrasts which operational flying now presented, as we scaled the summer peak, were exacting. The day temperatures demanded that only the lightest uniform – khaki shorts and sleeveless open-necked shirt to match, with fawn stockings – be worn. But the rigours of operations required that, in the air, the body be properly covered – khaki battledress top and trousers, flying boots and helmet, Mae West and silk gloves offered more protection against misfortune. Yet to sit for a few minutes in the cockpit of a Spitfire in that dress, at advance readiness, and in the glare and heat of the sun at its zenith, waiting for the order to scramble, came close to physical torture.

Half an hour or so later, after a fast battle climb to 25,000 or 30,000 feet away to the south of the Island, there to await the moment to strike, the air temperature could fall to a frigid minus 55°. A young mind, set inside a hardened frame, could take a lot; but these great extremes of heat and cold were, we felt, knocking at human limits.

It was rough going for the pilots, but how the ground-crews stuck it in that cruel airfield heat, when even to touch the wing surface of an aeroplane could produce a nasty burn, passed belief. Their courage and loyalty, as they worked on the aircraft, exceeded anything I thought it reasonable to expect.

High summer and the renewed attacks on the Island provided an opportunity for comparing the contrasting styles of the two Axis air forces. From early in the year, we had become all too familiar with the Luftwaffe's aggressive form ... The dive-bombing of the Ju 87s and 88s, pressed resolutely from 16,000 or 17,000 feet, through the ack-ack barrage, to low altitudes, were invariably covered by the high and fast flying of the Me 109s. Streaking across Malta's sky in their wide-open, line-abreast formations, they made the *rotte** and the *schwärme*† basic to everything they did. Their fighters moved about the heavens with all the speed and fluidity of a well-disciplined German World Cup football team, crossing over and back again in the turns, and seldom losing station. They were a finely practised lot.

The Regia Aeronautica's style, by comparison, was quite different. High-level bombing in relatively small and tight formations was accompanied by the similarly close and correct flying of the Macchi 202 and Reggiane 2001 escorts.

---

* A pair of aircraft.    † A section of four aircraft.

The Italians seemed to draw strength and confidence from the proximity of one aircraft with another.

Their fighters often used to entertain the defending Spitfires with some particularly spirited aerobatic flying such as they might have displayed at any peacetime air pageant back home. Their pilots were a fancy, artistic lot. What they lacked in aggression by comparison with their German counterparts, they more than made up with the extrovert, *joie de vivre* of their flying.

I used to find it necessary to warn the Squadron against any complacency in opposing the Italians. A nation, I said, which could produce, pre-war, racing drivers of the quality and courage of Enzo Ferrari and Tazio Nuvolari could surely be relied upon to possess some fighter pilots of comparable skills and flair. And when I think now of combatants of the quality of Gianni Caracciolo, Adriano Visconti, Franco Lucchini, Antonio Larsimont, Fernando Malvezzi, Aldo Remondino, Leonardo Ferulli, Teresio Martinoli and Tullio Martinelli, and, again, of the emergent Francesco Cavalera who, years later, would rise to the summit of the Italian Air Force and to the office of his country's Chief of the Defence Staff, it is then that I realize how salutory was my warning.

No one in 249 had the truth of this confirmed more potently than Jack Rae, then fast developing into one of New Zealand's outstanding pilots, and his able No. 2, the Australian, Alan Yates. These two sons of the Commonwealth made an accomplished and tenacious pair.

On 13 July, with the Axis seemingly throwing in everything they'd got against the Island, the Squadron had been embroiled high up with a mixed force of German and Italian fighters. Jack and Alan had had their share of the fun. Despite being low in ammunition, they had finally set upon a lone Reggiane 2001 as it was about to disengage and head for home. What then followed gave Jack such a shock that the incident has stuck starkly in his mind for half a century.

To my amazement the Italian proved to be an extremely competent opponent. I had never before been involved in such a complex sequence of aerobatics as I pursued him. Twice I nearly 'spun off' as I stayed with him; I found it difficult to get any sort of worthwhile deflection shot at his aircraft with what remained of my machine-gun ammunition. At times he got dangerously close to getting a bead on me.

Eventually, he started to evade and edge back to Sicily, but by this time we were, anyway, halfway across the Straits. He had started to smoke and I knew that his tail unit was damaged. So I called up Alan and told him to leave the Eyetye and head for home. Our own position was getting dangerous as we were now low in fuel and would be in real difficulty if we were ourselves attacked.

As we turned back to base, leaving our opponent's aircraft smoking strongly, the Italian, to my amazement, turned with us and made one final and defiant attack upon our section – as if to show what he thought of a pair of Spitfires!

This man was quite a pilot and, I suspect, quite a guy with it. I hope he survived!*

---

* I feel it right, for the sake of history, to record here an authoritative opinion expressed to me years later by my friend, Oberst Eduard Neumann, the widely popular Kommodore of Jagdgeschwader 27 in the desert fighting in 1942, about the proficiency of the Regia Aeronautica's fighter pilots. Both in Libya and, afterwards, in northern Italy, Edu had first-hand experience of their performance in the months when he was in close contact with their units, offering their leaders the benefit of his own expertise and extensive experience. Indeed, it is doubtful whether any of the Luftwaffe's senior commanders were as well placed as he to form such a judgement.

'Most of them were thoroughly able pilots who were born to fly and had been well trained. They were exceptionally skilful and their actual flying created a very good impression. I personally had a high regard for them. They made, I believe, much better operational pilots, in terms of flying ability, than history has accorded them.

'When the Italian senior officers allowed our 109 Staffeln to mix with them, our pilots got on well with them and respected them.'

The Luftwaffe's renewed blitz against the Island in July underscored the closeness of the relationship which existed between the island battle and the progress of Erwin Rommel's forces in the Libyan Desert. The lull in aerial activity over Malta in June, when the Afrika Korps was tearing across Cyrenaica to the Egyptian frontier in pursuit of the 8th Army, had given the garrison time to recuperate from the Luftwaffe's earlier hammering. It had allowed the Royal Air Force to regain much of its offensive strength.

Once again, the torpedo-carrying Beauforts with Patrick Gibbs now in the van, and with their Beaufighter escorts in attendance, could continue to extract, in daylight, a terrible toll of Axis shipping moving southwards across the Mediterranean at a crucial time for Rommel when his supply lines were becoming dangerously stretched.

With Baltimore and Wellington aircraft flying supporting

---

With his fair mind and ability to penetrate to the heart of an issue, Neumann made another point which is not generally understood. Although Italian pride would never allow them to admit it, the Regia Aeronautica's aircraft were, on the whole, always inferior to both those of their Axis partner and the British. When, in the early days in North Africa, the fighting was between biplanes, the Royal Air Force's Gladiator was superior to the CR 42. Then came the Hurricane to maintain, and even extend, the supremacy. The advent of the Messerschmitt 109 on the Axis side widened still further the discrepancy between the German and the Italian product. When the Spitfire Vs appeared in Malta, the gap between British and Italian equipment was extended again.

'Put yourself in the position of the Italian pilots,' said Neumann, 'and ask what this must have done for morale in their squadrons. It's not easy to be aggressive if the other man has a better aeroplane. Defensive aerobatics come much more readily. But I personally never had any doubt that there were plenty of tough customers in the Italian fighter squadrons. Only Tullio de Prato, one of Italy's ablest pilots, has been prepared to deal with this issue openly in his books and magazine articles. Yet it is most important in a proper appreciation of the capability of the respective air forces.'

missions against the enemy's North African ports and installations, and with the Royal Navy's submarines once more active, Malta could again maintain its aggressive stance.

Easy to see now, with Auchinleck and the 8th Army stabilizing a line at Alamein, and the Afrika Korps fully extended and crying out for supplies, why the German High Command ordered this fresh assault on the Island. But Malta, in July 1942, possessed a defensive capability quite different from that which had confronted the Luftwaffe in March and April and the first week or so of May. Furious air battles still had to be fought to preserve the Island's offensive strength, but preserved it was, with all that this meant to Rommel and the supplying of his troops.

When, in the first days of September, the *Feldmarschall* made his last determined thrust for Cairo, only to be thwarted by the newly-appointed Montgomery at the head of the 8th Army in the battle of Alam Halfa, Malta's contribution to the course of events in North Africa was plain to see.

All the same arguments could be applied to Rommel's shattering reverse six or seven weeks later in the great Battle of Alamein. Kesselring, from his special vantage point, could see as well as anyone the price which Hitler and the German High Command paid for the earlier failure to invade Malta and so remove this festering thorn from Rommel's side.

To guarantee supplies [to the Afrika Korps in Libya], the capture of Malta was necessary and at the time [July] this was no longer possible. The abandonment of this project was the first death blow to the whole undertaking in North Africa ... Strategically, the one fatal blunder was the abandoning of the plan to invade Malta. When this happened, the subsequent course of events was almost inevitable*

* *The War in the Mediterranean* Part I by Field Marshal Albert Kesselring. AHB 6 Trans No. VII/104.

Such, then, was the part that the Island played in the Desert victory. And such, too, was the reason behind the Axis powers' July onslaught against the central Mediterranean outpost.

As the July fighting escalated to its peak, tales of luck – and misfortune – abounded. Bob Middlemiss, now contributing strongly to the Squadron's work, was one who could well claim at this time that his Maker was protecting him in the face of mortal danger.

Flying No. 2 to his Flight Commander one morning, Bob had picked off a 109 from Raoul Daddo-Langlois's tail as the section leader was attacking, and destroying, a Ju 88. But Bob's victim also had an attentive No. 2 who, in the mêlée that followed, let drive a volley of cannon fire into the cockpit of the Spitfire, badly wounding Middlemiss's right hand and arm as he gripped the control column. The traumas he suffered, first, in extricating himself from his spinning aircraft and then, after the bale-out over the sea, getting into his dinghy with his left hand alone, would have overwhelmed all but the stoutest heart.

Worse was yet to come for the Squadron had hunted in vain west of the Island for the dinghy believing that this had been the area of Bob's descent. We had concluded, sadly, that we could do no more. We were resigned to having to stomach another severe loss.

It was then that the Almighty stretched out a hand and touched the Canadian's shoulder. In one of the day's later patrols, 249's Paul Brennan, the Australian, and his No. 2, L. E. C. de Lara, who had only recently joined us from 185 Squadron at Halfar, were covering a minesweeping operation, not to the west but to the east of Malta. In a chance in a thousand, Brennan spotted a dinghy in the water. A radio fix was given, one of Air-Sea Rescue's High Speed Launches was ordered to sea and, within a few hours, Middlemiss was being operated on in the general hospital at M'tarfa.

There, he discovered from the surgeon that the Deity had extended His patronage to the moment when the 109 struck. Shrapnel from the cannon shells had penetrated his torso to within a quarter of an inch of his lungs. Had Bob not been leaning forward in his seat and looking round at the time of the attack, he wouldn't have been troubling the surgeon.

Nor was that the end of his surprises. When, ultimately, he came to after being returned to the ward from the operating theatre, he found his squadron mate and fellow countryman, Gerry de Nancrede, lying toe-to-toe in another bed. Gerry, quickly climbing the 249 ladder, had baled out the same day ... Quite a bag for the Luftwaffe to have collected, for here was a pair of Canadians whom the Squadron had come to number among the strongest of its midfield players.

It was axiomatic in the Malta battle, with the adverse odds being what they were, that the more thrustful a squadron became and the more aggressive its pilots, the greater tended to be the likelihood of casualties. The principle of 'seeking out and destroying the enemy wherever he may be found' was a tenet to which 249 pinned its colours. But extreme aggression could provoke greater retaliation in a resolute enemy.

Still, losses, when they came, had to be met head-on – and then quickly forgotten. No matter how grievous, they had to be forced from the mind or morale suffered. There was no other way.

The Squadron was, however, now well past its hundredth enemy aircraft destroyed since it had re-equipped with Spitfires in March. What's more, our ratio of victories to losses compared very favourably with that of the other fighter squadrons on the Island. We had by this time developed an undeniable conceit in ourselves and our ability. We felt we were on top of the game.

But let no one suppose that we reached this enviable state without having 'worked our passage'. There could hardly have been a pilot in the Squadron – officer or NCO – who had not, at some moment since the spring, faced, as he must have thought, 'the supreme test'.

Take the case of Jack Rae, who had already been surprised by the Regia Aeronautica. In circumstances which can best be left unsaid, Jack was going about his business one day at 27,000 feet when a Me 109 planted a 'well-aimed cannon shell' in the cockpit of his Spitfire removing, among other things, the control column and causing the pilot deep and troublesome wounds. He felt, as he put it at the time, 'rather like a motorist must feel if someone, for no special reason, removes his steering wheel'.

Add to this a punctured fuel tank, with petrol sloshing about the place, 'the odd nick at the top of my helmet', and 'another slight furrow on the top of my head', and, in no time, Rae was spinning down out of control touching 500 m.p.h. or thereabouts as he went. Just as he was 'preparing for the customary interview with St Peter', he made a series of superhuman efforts to free himself from his aircraft. Having succeeded, he then became 'quite calm' and remembered 'the good book form logic "when trying to find the ripcord [of the parachute], *look for it*"'.

As he floated down to the only sound of Rolls-Royce Merlin and Daimler-Benz engines, another piece of luck struck. 'The wind was with me, blowing me towards the Island. It looked so small a place to hit from that height.'

Jack had kept his date with Destiny, and found his reward.

Few, if any, in the Squadron ever spoke about their spiritual beliefs. On the whole, such talk would have been embarrassing. We weren't on that kind of wavelength. Private thoughts retained their privacy. Yet I remained fairly sure that, within each one of us, there was a simple underlying faith which rested upon an equally uncomplicated premise: it was your job, if you were the leader, to do the best you could for the Squadron, for your comrades and for yourself – in that order. You had to take care, as far as you could, to ensure that those who were relying upon you were suitably prepared to meet the likely and known risks . . .

All this was your responsibility. But having discharged it, the rest was up to the Almighty. He held the future in His hand. If He had a continuing job for you to do on the Island and, maybe, thereafter on this earth, then you would survive. If not, and there was work to do in Another Place, so be it. It was His will.

Any other approach to the daily dangers would have been for me – and, I suspect, for many others – intolerable.

In the five commands I held in the Royal Air Force, I always made it a practice, if operations allowed, to give those for whom I was responsible a regular opportunity of worshipping together before God. Nothing was urged nor was anything made compulsory. Having provided the chance, I felt it was up to the individual officer, NCO or airman to react as he pleased. I regarded a man or a woman's religion as being a personal and private matter. The Anglican chaplain at Takali during the time I was commanding 249 was Padre Lamb – Squadron Leader the Revd G. H. C. Lamb – a man of common sense, understanding and undoubted resolve. He recognized my attitude to divine worship and invariably provided a regular chance for expression to be given to it, somewhere and somehow. The strength of the support there was on the station for the padre's weekly Communion service always surprised me.

The truth was, of course, that he was a brave man who could face war's trials alone . . .

# 28

# HUMAN RELATIONS

You're my friend –
What a thing friendship is, world without end!
*Robert Browning*

Personal relationships in the squadrons and on the stations were closer in Malta than I experienced them anywhere else in three tours of operational flying and six years of war. The divisions between officers, NCOs and airmen in the various units from the early spring to the late summer of 1942 were less marked and less particular than elsewhere, yet respect, authority and discipline never suffered.

I do not recall a place in wartime where good, common-sense discipline and comradeship came more easily. A squadron commander would have a brief, initial period on taking over when he was being sized up, notably by some of the more pungent and less inhibited critics from the Commonwealth. He could sense it instantly unless he was exceptionally thick-skinned. But once a CO or Flight Commander had established himself and been accepted by the unit – 'to have what it takes' – he was supported to the hilt.

Looking back, I have no doubt that these ready and close relationships sprang primarily from the fact that Malta was a diminutive island from which there was no escape and no leave. When the battle was at its height, the bombing virtually continuous, the hunger always present, the Dog and sand-fly fever recurrent, privations universal and the food the same for pilots and groundcrews, officers, NCOs and airmen, the levelling influence – the feeling of 'everyone being in it together' – was overwhelming. True, the black market in food outside, such as it was, was perhaps more easily obtained by aircrew than by others, but this was of minuscule proportions within the overall ethos which prevailed.

The inter-squadron relationship between 249 and 603 at Takali was, of itself, unusual. Each unit had its own character and personality – the one strikingly different from the other. But the preparedness by both to pool resources and help out in moments of crisis was remarkable.

It had begun soon after 603, led by Lord David Douglas-Hamilton, arrived on the Island from the US carrier *Wasp*, on 20 April. The inexperience of the Squadron, resulting from some absurd postings by Fighter Command only weeks before the unit left the United Kingdom, was quickly manifested in its first operations with us. Pitchforked, in that state, into a battle of that intensity and against such odds, it was inevitable that it would suffer.

Almost overnight, and for some days thereafter – until the Island drill had been learnt – Douglas-Hamilton mixed his pilots up with ours. They came and flew in sections led by our seasoned campaigners in a selfless show of magnanimity in which their CO, himself then relatively inexperienced, set an immediate example. Imagine such a thing happening in England!

Cynics will say that 'humble pie' was eaten to save 603's own skins. Believe none of it. Knowing their lot as I did, and remembering the Squadron's achievements after it had settled down, it would be hard to state the opposite of the truth more exactly.

I witnessed in wartime several instances of moral courage being shown by a commander in the face of unpalatable facts; but nothing that I saw in this context so became a leader as the unsung example which David Douglas-Hamilton set 603 at Takali in those last tortuous days of April 1942. Backed 100 per cent by characters of the quality of John Buckstone and Johnny Hurst, both soon to be killed, Bill Douglas, Tony Holland and others, he cut a noble figure, unspoilt, unpompous and unselfish.

It was convenient for me, when my turn came to lead 249, that I had already known Douglas-Hamilton in peacetime. Although, in the first couple of months that we were together on the Island he was a squadron leader and I a flight lieutenant, I had many dealings with him. Because my predecessor in office, Stan Grant, with the indelible stamp of Cranwell upon him, had left me happily free to get on and run my Flight in 249 without tiresome interference, I had often had to agree operational matters on the spot with the CO of 603 when he and I, with our respective units, were on readiness together. It had been an invariably easy relationship.

There was one issue, after I had been given command of 249, over which David and I had combined with some effect. The difference between the jobs which the officer and NCO pilots were doing, collectively, in the two squadrons was barely discernible. Indeed, in 249, the commissioned and non-commissioned officers operated in the air and on the ground as one, Christian and nicknames and all. It mattered not whether we came from New Zealand or Australia, South Africa or Rhodesia, Canada, the United States or the United Kingdom, we were members of one indivisible team.

It had stuck in my gullet, both as a flight commander and now as the CO, that we had NCOs in the Squadron who possessed all the personal and operational qualifications necessary for commissioned rank and yet had not been so recognized. People of the calibre of Brennan and Hesslyn, Rae, de Nancrede, Mickey Butler, Middlemiss and John Williams – all from the Commonwealth – and others, were manifestly commissionable. So, ultimately, was George

Beurling; but he, for reasons which I told him were thoroughly spurious, didn't want to become an officer. Eventually, he succumbed.

David Douglas-Hamilton had similar instances in 603 – Johnny Hurst, sadly to fall so soon, for one. In the special – indeed, almost unique – circumstances of Malta's environment, it made us both feel uneasy that so much good material remained uncommissioned. Stan Grant, before me, had felt just the same.

In due course, through a concerted approach, and backed ultimately by Woodhall and Hugh Pughe Lloyd, limited action was obtained although some of the surviving candidates had to wait for their return to England before the fruits of these efforts were seen.

I can't say, however, that Paul Brennan and Ray Hesslyn, for whose commissions Stan Grant had batted so strongly, made our task any easier. Some while before their 'elevations' came through in mid-June, this independent pair, with tongue in cheek, decided one evening to reconnoitre the officer-establishments in Valletta in disguised rank. The Union Club, in the main Strada Reale, was the first.

Wearing the insignia of flight lieutenants, they sauntered nonchalantly past the porterage, to the Club's well-named 'snake-pit' bar. There the two sergeants had the misfortune to encounter a mildly surprised Group Captain Woodhall. Woody played it, as he would, deadpan. 'Good evening, you fellows, I'm particularly glad to hear about your commissions. Let me buy you a drink on the strength of it.'

The Group Captain pressed two large pink gins into their hands. 'Now,' he said, 'I'd advise you to hook it . . .'

It bothered me also that we could do so little for the groundcrews at Takali to recognize their labours. Apart from the Maltese airmen, who worked spiritedly on general duties, all had originated from the United Kingdom and

Ireland and some had seen service elsewhere in the Middle East before fetching up in Malta's inferno. They had, in some cases, already been away from home for nearly two years. It would be all of another eighteen months, after the withdrawal of the Axis from North Africa, and the Allies' subsequent invasion of Sicily and then Italy, before they could look forward to a return to the homeland.

The scope for promotion was extremely limited and awards and 'mentions' were sparsely distributed even among the senior NCOs in the various trades. I was to admire my countrymen many times in war when they were truly up against it, with little hope for anything save a continuation of the *status quo*; but this lot with us at Takali, in the spring and summer of 1942, living for months under siege conditions, and often facing mortal peril, were special.

They had worked together in the exceptional rains and mud of February and in the scorching sun and heat of mid-summer. Their rations were meagre and yet they laboured with a single aim in mind – to keep what aircraft we had on the Island flying. At the height of the battle they toiled from pre-dawn to nightfall with a will and a courage which set them apart.

It was a commonplace at Takali to see an airframe fitter throwing in his lot with the engine fitters during an aeroplane's engine change in the caves cut into the hillside along the southern perimeter of the airfield. The crews were a wonderfully adaptable and versatile lot. Their ability and training had shown through with the arrival of the aircraft reinforcements from the carriers in the spring. Many of them had never worked on a Spitfire before and yet, within a few days, they had found their way round this aircraft and were quickly giving the impression that it was a long time since they had worked on anything else.

Moreover, with the critical shortage of spare parts, and, therefore, the need to cannibalize badly damaged aircraft to keep others serviceable, they developed, out of necessity, a facility for improvisation which astonished us. The case of Bill Moodie, from Aberdeen, one of Takali's rugged Scots, and an adept airframe fitter with the maintenance flight, was typical. Just before the Spitfires had arrived, Bill, who had been on the Island since November 1940, was dismantling the mainplane of a shot-up Hurricane to fit it to another to keep it 'on the line'. The details are still fixed in his mind.

'It was during one of those spells of maximum effort. Every fighter that we could muster had to be available. After fitting the mainplane and making all the connections, we discovered there were no suitable split-pins to provide the safety lock for the four main bolts. Rather than have the aircraft standing unserviceable, I fitted pins into the slotted nuts made from a piece of barbed wire. This in no way impaired the safety of the aircraft, in fact I personally thought the device was stronger than a split-pin. The aeroplane was brought on to the line and successive pilots completed their missions with it.

'At this time, we were working a thirty-hour inspection schedule. The way operations were going, no one in his right mind would place a bet on an aircraft lasting thirty flying hours. With the bombing on the ground and the action in the air, the chances were slim. However, this machine did last that long and when it came to the inspection the removal of the wing root fairing strip, of course, exposed the nuts.

'Reference to Form 700 showed that I was the fitter who had signed for the mainplane fitting . . . I was placed on a technical charge which was later quashed. I was then reprimanded for unorthodox procedures on the one hand, but complimented for initiative on the other!

'I never had any compunction about using bits of wrecked aircraft for skin repairs when no sheet metal was available.

Improvisation was the name of the game in Malta. It amazed me that when, a year or so later, prior to the Sicilian landings, a wing of USAAF Boston A20s operated from Takali on a softening-up, round-the-clock bombing operation, the Americans landed more supplies and spares in three weeks than we had seen in three years!'

When there were losses among the groundcrews during the enemy's heaviest assaults on the airfield, everyone felt their impact acutely. We had become inured to them in the air as an inevitable hazard of battle; but when they occurred among those who were giving everything on the ground to sustain the aircraft in the air, the effect was severe. For the crews themselves, these casualties hit very hard. To lose a comrade after working for months and years together under enemy attack was a lacerating experience. It happened to Moodie, I remember, just as I joined 249 Squadron in February 1942. The shock of the loss of the Scot, 249's Leading Aircraftsman A. D. Robinson from Aboyne, made a lasting impression upon him.

'Robbie and I, together with Tait and Bob Smith, had all served together in 612, the County of Aberdeen Auxiliary Squadron, before the war. He and I had volunteered together for overseas service. We had always been together. He was my great pal. There had, of course, been other casualties among the ground staff before he was killed and, God knows, heavy losses among the pilots, but when Robbie went it really struck me hard and told me what it was all about. Up till then, I had never worried much about survival. Like many others, I had adopted a sort of "it will never happen to me" attitude. I never professed to be a hero, but after Robbie had gone I must confess I had the shakes for a few weeks.

'One had to brace oneself every morning to face another day on the airfield and suppress one's fears and anxieties.

But thanks to the example which others of the lads set, friends like Somerville, Tait and Smith, I "got a grip" again. I think I then became a fatalist – what will be, will be.

'There seemed to be no light at the end of the tunnel. Week followed week and months turned into years. There was no let-up in the pressures. Frustration began to get us all down. The dreaded Dog, scabies, sand-fly fever, hunger, all took their toll . . .'

The airmen of 249 were billeted, for the most part, close to Takali at the time of the Luftwaffe's heaviest onslaught. With the disturbance and the lack of rest, this was most unsatisfactory. They were housed, first, at the Pottery (the AOC said of it, 'I hope I shall never see the like of it again as an airman's quarter') close to the edge of the airfield, then, in my first weeks with the Squadron, at Mosta, hard by the famous church, but still only a mile or so away from our operational base. Later, they moved on to Naxxar, Boschetto Gardens and, eventually, when the accommodation became available, to St Edward's College, not far from our Mess in Mdina.

Theirs was a testing experience, yet they turned to the task and never shirked a job even under the most intense enemy pressure. When, fifty years on, I think again of the calibre of these men who manned the runway and aircraft crews, and the two squadrons' maintenance flight at Takali in those days – men like Flight Sergeants Spiers, Tim Casey and 'Mollie' Morgan, Corporal Jim Somerville, who in this three-year stint on the Island, was to have three spells in hospital, Corporal Bill Moodie, the two Smiths – Corporal Bob and his namesake from London, Tait, 'Ginger' Neale and the rest – I still marvel at the collective character which they brought to our support.

The teams which they formed among themselves (often

pairing off just as the pilots at Takali did) were buoyant and dedicated to the achievement of the highest state of aircraft serviceability. They needed – and got – little supervision. Highly proficient by now, they were dominated by the governing thought – to keep their 'effing kites on the effing line'. The truth was that, by performance and practical experience, the airmen at Takali, by the late spring and summer of 1942, were as well versed in their jobs as the senior NCOs . . .

And when Jumbo Gracie, in his enlightened stroke, armed the crews with rifles, and allotted them machine-gun posts to man, they met the low-flying attackers from their slit-trenches with a vigour which matched the Squadron's spirit in the air. Many a Me 109 pilot was sent packing back to Sicily with a volley or three of machine-gun tracer warming up his jacksie.

Had invasion ever come I haven't the least doubt that the groundcrews at Takali would have fought to the last man.

The third and final blitz of the summer lasted for ten concentrated days from 4–14 July. If the Squadron lost five pilots in the sharp cut and thrust of this period, it also added significantly to its steadily rising total of victories. This was the time when Screwball Beurling began to come into his own. With four of the enemy falling to his guns in one day, the lethal accuracy of his shooting now became as obvious as the validity of his claims.

There was, however, another young Canadian who had joined 249 the same day as Beurling who was now making his mark. He had caught my practised eye the moment I saw him go to work. John McElroy, a pilot officer, with a circumspect and deliberate approach to the task, flew a couple of times with me during this July spell and each time collected a Macchi 202 with style. With his smooth co-ordination, he was another I could visualize as a game shot, stroking a high December cock pheasant out of the sky as it turned over the line of guns, borne on the wings of a brisk midwinter wind.

I remember saying to Norman Lee and Raoul Daddo-Langlois, my two flight commanders, quite early on in John's time with the Squadron, that if I was asked to pick a winner, apart from Beurling, from our newer talent, McElroy would get my vote. He finished his tour in Malta well after my tenure had ended, but he had, I believe, a dozen or so enemy aircraft standing to his name by the time he came to rule off the account.

An incident now arose which had the potential of sending shock waves chasing one another across the Island.

We had tried in the squadrons during the summer to give the longer-serving pilots, who had been through the spring fire, a day or two off at the Rest Camp which the Royal Air Force had established at St Paul's Bay. Forty-eight, or even twenty-four, hours away from the airfield's searing heat, swimming, picnicking and otherwise lazing about, could bring succour to a man's fractured nerves.

However, such was the scale of our operations that the facilities frequently remained under-used. We could not do justice to this idyllic haven.

One day, a trusted colleague – not of 249 – tapped me on the shoulder at lunch-time in the Xara Palace just as the Squadron had come off readiness. 'Could I,' he asked, 'have a word about one of your chaps whom I ran into down at St Paul's Bay last evening?'

My friend's news, given the wholly unnatural conditions we had been living under, did not at first concern me as much as perhaps it should. Brought up in a British public school, Oxbridge and Fleet Street environment, the sexual deviations of man (or woman) had always seemed to me to be fairly commonplace fare. Mark Twain had, I thought, got it about right in his famous comment on Coney Island. 'If you like that kind of thing, that's the kind of thing you like.'

Put straightly, the gist of my informant's story was that during the quiet of the previous night at the villa, he had chanced to find a member of my Squadron in bed with the officer of another. Somewhat taken aback, he had at once withdrawn.

'Were they drunk?' I asked, but the question was brushed perfunctorily aside. I could see my colleague was serious.

I believed the story. Here was a worldly man, a little older than the rest of us, widely experienced in fields far removed from the Service, who had been a continuing help to me, and to the Squadron, during our time together. I liked him and trusted him implicitly.

What to do? Having rumbled these two individuals (I wished devoutly that he hadn't!), one thing became quite clear. The matter couldn't be left. Something would have to be done quickly. The homosexual act (but not, of course, the condition) was an indictable offence in the Service, which, if proved, carried severe penalties. Today's civilian arrangement, whereby consenting adults (which is what these two were) can give expression to their desires in private, had (and has) no application for the Service. The ramifications of the thing began to appal me.

The men concerned, whom I had known well in Fighter Command in England, had each had an exemplary record in a relatively long run on the Island. They had been successful in the air, and brave with it. They were both very well liked and each was now nearing the end of his time in Malta. They were assets to their squadrons.

As I talked it over with my informant and wrestled with my conscience, two options became starkly clear to me. The proper, conventional course would be for me to see 'my chap' and, according to the outcome of the talk, then see the CO of the other's squadron. I had not the least doubt what his reaction would be: report the matter to our respective Station Commanders and let them get on with it. Again, I was quite sure I could prejudge the attitude of my Station Commander, subject to the story standing up: refer the case to the AOC. And the likely outcome of that would be for these two, after weeks of slogging it out with the enemy, to be dispatched on the next aircraft to the Middle East, there to await their fate.

I thought about the repercussions. No. 249 Squadron, in all its pride, would be stunned. So would the other unit involved. With such a bunch of boisterous, virile heterosexuals (with precious few chances of satisfying their thinly disguised desires), the effect – even if only temporarily – would be cataclysmic. My Squadron would suffer and so would its counterpart.

The other option was for me to handle the matter myself and accept full responsibility if things went wrong. I would tell my informant my decision, the reasons for it, and ask him to say nothing to anyone – an undertaking I was sure he would give and honour.

I would then see the two men separately as quickly as possible. According to their 'explanation', I would say what I thought, tell them in the special circumstances we were dealing with on the Island that I intended to take no further action on the report, but that I expected them to give me their word that nothing of the sort would ever be repeated while they were in Malta.

I would add a rider. I would say that the matter had been represented to me in strict confidence, that it would remain so and that no one else would ever be the wiser.

By the time I had weighed it all up, I was in no doubt whatever that, wrong though it was according to Service law, my job was to deal with the thing myself and face the music if I had to. What I cared about, on reflection, was my Squadron, its name and its continuing contribution to the battle. I also thought about the individuals concerned, and the effect on the careers of two first-class fighting patriots.

I resolved to act on the second option at once. I was determined that the sun should not be allowed to go down on the problem. I saw my informant again. He concurred immediately in my decision. At some difficulty, I then interviewed the two pilots separately, and in different places, before dinner. Neither attempted to deny what had happened and each gave the undertaking I had sought. It is of interest that each spontaneously volunteered the information that he was not a practising homosexual, and never contemplated such a liaison with another, and never would. I shook hands with each and never allowed the incident to cause subsequent awkwardness between us.

What happened to these two men?

One was killed later in the war, leading a unit in the face of the enemy. He had notably enhanced his operational record in the interim. The other went on to achieve fighting commands – with decorations to match. He played out the innings, married well, raised a happy family and eventually became a distinguished figure in the professional and public life of his native country . . .

The dividing line between conventional rectitude in a Service at war, and plain, human common sense, was paper thin. Judgement was the key.

# 29

# WHAT A WAY TO BLOW IT!

Knowledge is proud that he has learn'd so much;
Wisdom is humble that he knows no more.
*William Cowper*

Malta maintained its strictures to the end. Take an unwise
liberty in the air and the place bit you. The Island respected
no persons – certainly not an overconfident, almost-tour-
expired squadron commander. Like the few remaining survivors from the Class of February 1942, I was convinced, by
now, that the opposition would not lay a hand on me. We
had been at it too long and were too experienced for that.
Close shaves there had been – oh yes! But these were well
behind and, besides, I had learnt from them, otherwise I
wouldn't still be in play.

I had, moreover, the governing benefit of a magnificently
practised squadron about me. 249 knew the day-fighting art
from A to Z. Although we kept it strictly to ourselves, our
collective confidence on this, the last day but one of the
enemy's final summer blitz, was spilling over.

I possessed another personal plus. My habitual No. 2,
the Canadian, Frank Jones, from Montreal, was at his most
attentive. Broadly experienced, he had given up much –
leadership of sections, chances for himself to score – to
string along with me. Unselfish to a point, Jonesie, with his
sharp eyes, swift reflexes and sheer competence, had increased my own confidence still further. I felt comfortable
with him, although at times his high-pitched, nasal voice,
spoken not from the throat but from somewhere behind the
top of the bridge of his nose, suddenly reporting some

intrusion by the Luftwaffe, used to make me jump in the cockpit. This, too, had its advantages. Frank Jones was a quantifiable asset in the Squadron's balance sheet.

The entry in my log book for Monday, 13 July was factual: 'Spitfire Vc. Interception Patrol. 1 hour. Shot up by 109. Force-lobbed at Halfar. Mac [John McElroy] gets a Macchi.' It also cloaked an uncharacteristic blemish on the record sheet.

On this hot, cloudless morning, a high and fast-flying Axis fighter sweep, made up mostly of yellow-nosed Me 109s, with a leavening of Macchi 202s, was trying to clear Malta's sky of defenders ahead of an incoming raid. Working round, up-sun, well to the south-east of the Island, this force of some twenty to thirty fighters knew its business. But, then, likewise, so did 249's two sections of four aircraft apiece which had been alerted to take care of this enemy tactic.

We were at 25,000 to 26,000 feet and far south-east of Malta, with the sun behind, when I spotted the enemy's fast-moving force 1000 feet below at ten o'clock and heading towards us. I gave the Squadron the instructions, 'OK, fellers,' I said, 'stick, if you can, in pairs and watch out behind. Going in now.'

In no time, there was the usual explosion of aircraft, breaking, climbing, half-rolling, scattering all over the sky, guns flashing momentarily and smoking. Brief, staccato transmission studded the R/T.

The customary 'crowded hour of glorious life' was followed inevitably by quiet and emptiness, the blue canopy of the heavens, for the moment, being free of aeroplanes. But then, as I was looking round for a Spitfire to join up with, my eye lit on a lone Macchi 202, down-sun from me at eleven o'clock, a few hundred feet below. Heading north, like me, it was flying straight and level – the proverbial 'piece of cake'.

Hardly crediting my luck, I dived down out of the sun to attack, as I thought, unseen from underneath and astern. Instinct and drill made me give a last glance in my rear mirror as I closed in for the kill . . .

It always used to be said that if you could actually *recognize* a 109 in the mirror, it was too late. Now, I could identify not one but *four* of them in line astern, coming in from five o'clock and a little above in a fast closing curve. As I whipped my aircraft over into a tight diving turn towards the attack, a salvo of 20 mm cannon shells hammered into the starboard wing of the Spitfire with strikes from 7.9 mm machine-gun incendiaries along the side of the engine. Had I delayed another split second longer before looking in the mirror and breaking, the volley would have come straight up my backside, probably severing most of the controls and doing me even less good . . .

I had been caught in the most elementary trap of all. Taken in by this lone Italian aeroplane, while four of its German counterparts were waiting up-sun, poised to pounce, I had created for myself precisely the scenario that every pilot, on joining a squadron, was adjured to avoid.

What followed became a nightmare which would recur once or twice a week for the rest of the war, waking me up soaked in sweat. It persisted into the years of peace.

As the smoke and heat increased in the cockpit, tiny flames started to lick the engine cowlings along the top of the nose in front of me. I suspected there might be others which I couldn't see with the poor forward vision. I was still at 18,000 to 20,000 feet over the sea, 5 or 6 miles southeast of the Island, losing height in tight diving turns to thwart any attacker bent upon delivering the *coup de grâce*.

Cutting all the switches, I gave a fix over the R/T to Stan Turner, who was controlling in place of Woodhall. 'Stan,' I said, 'I've been hit. I'm pretty sure I'm going to have to step out.'

'Good luck,' he replied, and his voice was devoid of emotion.

With that, I tugged at the black rubber toggle at the top of the cockpit to release the canopy. The bobble came away in my hand. The hood was stuck fast. No two giants of Brobdingnag could have moved it. I guessed the runners had been hit in the attack.

I was now at about 15,000 feet, still over the sea, two or three miles out from Kalafrana Bay; the heat and the smoke were intensifying. My feelings at this unpleasant juncture were complex, quite different from what I might have anticipated. I was not overtaken by fear or panic. I was, in fact, surprisingly calm. I did not think I was going to die, which was probably the most likely outcome. I was somehow resigned to the implausible belief that, although the picture could hardly have looked blacker, in some inexplicable way things would come right. Hope clearly springs eternal even when close to the terminal point.

Interspersed with periodical thumps at the cockpit hood, I kept thinking what a damned shame it was that, after all that had gone before, I should have been caught in such a predicament – the result of a single elementary mistake which was untypical.

Then, astonishingly, as I went on diving and after what seemed like twenty minutes (it was probably nearer to two or three), the smoke in the cockpit began to thin and the heat perceptibly to lessen. The flickering flames at the side of the nose seemed to have gone out. The incendiaries, I thought, having done their worst had probably failed. With a dead stick, no engine and everything quite silent, I at once pulled out of the dive and used the excess speed to gain what height I could. A couple more despairing thumps on the hood had no effect. I could now see Halfar, the Island's southernmost airfield, through the hazy blue of the morning, three or four miles to the west. Could it be possible that, at this rate, I might make it? I felt I had the height to squeeze a glide.

I called Stan Turner. 'Stan,' I said, 'I'm going to try to make Halfar. Tell them it's an emergency. I'll have to force-lob.'

The retort was spoken deadpan in that quiet and serious transatlantic voice. 'OK, I'll tell them.'

I then had a totally irrational thought. At all costs I must try to save my aeroplane. Aircraft were precious in Malta. I obviously hadn't got the height to do a proper circuit of the airfield and try for a landing into wind. I would have to go straight in downwind.

I must, I felt, at least try the undercarriage. If it locked down as I landed and was going to overshoot, I could always whip it up. It was worth a try . . . Amazingly, it worked! Now, the flaps . . . Marvellously, they, too, came down! My speed fell instantly and so, mercifully, did the aircraft's nose for the landing angle. A jink or two and, as I was on the run-in over the boundary, two Swordfish of the Fleet Air Arm were taking off straight towards me amid an impressive pyrotechnic display of colour . . .

With the wheels on the ground, I gave the brakes the lightest touch and at once let go. They were still gripping! The aeroplane came to a stop 20 yards from what had once been a hangar or a store.

I must then have blacked out, with the noonday sun blazing down on the cockpit and the effect of the delayed shock, for the next thing I was conscious of was an airframe fitter on either side of me, with tools, trying to lever the canopy backwards along its runners to open it.

'OK, sir,' said the fitter on my right, 'you can get out now. Any luck?'

There was a pause as he looked at the mangled mainplane and fuselage. 'Cor, Christ, what an effing mess! Bleedin' shame.'

I had been a golfer since childhood. Golf, they had always said, was a humbling game. So, too, was wartime flying!

Of course, the Squadron didn't miss the trick. When once its members knew exactly how I had blown it, they had a field-day at the CO's expense.

'Never mind,' they said, echoing yet again Hugh Pughe Lloyd's historic quote. 'You will still be able to look back with pride and say, "I was there!"'

# 30

# THE LLOYD-PARK AXIS

In peace there's nothing so becomes a man
As modest stillness and humility:
But when the blast of war blows in our ears,
Then imitate the action of the tiger
*William Shakespeare*, King Henry V, *Act III Scene i*

Group Captain Woodhall came over to the Xara Palace for the last time early in July to tell us personally about the impending changes at Air HQ in Valletta. Stan Turner was with him. Air Vice-Marshal Hugh Lloyd, said Woody, would be relinquishing his command on 14 July after fourteen gruelling, but incontestably successful months at the summit. He would be followed the next day, as AOC, by the New Zealander Air Vice-Marshal Keith Park, the brilliant and opinionated commander of 11 Group, Fighter Command, in the Battle of Britain. It was a manifestation of the continuing importance which the Prime Minister and the Chiefs of Staff attached to Malta that this notable airman, a fighter pilot of World War I, should be brought in to fill what was bound to be, for the squadrons, a massive void.

Woody went further. He told us that he, too, would be going at the same time. We knew he was exhausted. After two hectic operational years at home, he had come out to Malta from Tangmere at the beginning of February 1942 and given everything – his spirit and his genius as a fighter controller – to the Island's cause. You could not lead the life that he had been enduring daily, or carry that kind of responsibility, without showing it. Six months down in 'the Ditch' in Valletta, coping with the strain of the heaviest fighting, had taken its toll. But Woody had made his mark as the Royal Air Force's outstanding fighter controller of the war. At this art, he was on his own. I incline to think that the battle of Malta would not have been won without him.

Much as we regretted it, there was another reason why it was timely for him now to move on. He had commanded the sector at Duxford, in Cambridgeshire, during the Battle of Britain when the legless Douglas Bader was stationed there as the CO of 242 Squadron, and leading the Wing. Woodhall had thus been in the thick of the vehement controversy which raged for much of the battle between Trafford Leigh-Mallory, AOC of 12 Group, in which Duxford lay, and Keith Park, his counterpart at 11.

He, like Bader himself and, for that matter, Stan Turner (also a member of Bader's squadron during the battle), was known to be an out-and-out supporter of Leigh-Mallory. As such, it was improbable that there could be an easy relationship with the incoming AOC. However, the question did not arise. Woodhall was all in and had to be replaced.

For Turner, whose name was not among the forthcoming changes, the substitution of the immaculate Park for Lloyd had an unsettling ring. Stan, who never hesitated to speak his mind – particularly about senior officers – was known to have been a critic of Park and an undisguised protagonist of Leigh-Mallory.

Now, propped up against the bar of the Mdina Mess, with a large gin in his hand, the Canadian contemplated Park's arrival. 'The guy will have me off the Island inside of a month.'

As things turned out, it took little more than a week!

Lloyd's contribution to the island story had been decisive. By his conduct of the battle in the critical months of March,

April and May 1942, when, with the fullest support of the Army and the Royal Navy, he had fashioned victory out of defeat, he had acquired for himself a place in history. He had turned the tables on Kesselring during the 'crunch' fortnight between 9 and 23 May. Anyone who fought through that key period knew that, thereafter, the feel of the place was completely different.

The German and Italian Air Forces would return in strength for short-lived blitzes until October, and desperate battles would be fought over the June and August convoys to stave off starvation and, with it, surrender, but May was the month when, with the US Navy's carrier *Wasp* making her second run down the Med, the battle was decisively turned. The crucial days were 9 and 10 May. Never again, after that, would Kesselring hold the whip hand.

The credit was Lloyd's.

It was my special fortune to serve two quite exceptional field commanders in wartime – Lloyd, in Malta, in 1942 and Basil Embry, with his 2 Group Mosquitoes, in France, in 1944 and 1945. The two AOCs, although well apart in temperament, had unmistakable features in common.

Each could be totally ruthless and yet both possessed a humanity and a kindness which endeared them to subordinates. They seemed to have a fine judgement of the extremities to which men could be driven in war – and then to know when it was right to ask them to go a little further.

Each would take calculated risks well beyond the general run – but only after a minute assessment of the dangers had justified their acceptance. Both gave the impression, which I am quite sure was not a pose, that they would never ask a subordinate to fly a mission which, in similar circumstances, they would not have undertaken themselves.

They both cared deeply about casualties just as if they had occurred in units they were commanding. The short telephone call which followed a hard reverse exposed the depth of that feeling – and the belief that it must be banished quickly from the mind. The same medium was used to convey a brief word of encouragement or to underscore the importance of some planned operation. Both could give the impression that they would not have entrusted the responsibility for such a mission to anyone else. (The fact that an identical feeling was left with another leader in the same sortie was of no consequence. It was the personal uplift which counted.)

Each was ready to buck authority if the need arose to do so, and both would be prepared to back you to the hilt if some unthinking attitude was adopted from above. However, if an error was committed which was shown to have been the result of slack planning or ill-disciplined thinking then the chances of retaining a command for long were slim.

Because each was a brave man, courage in the face of the enemy was everything to both. Conversely, the faintest trace of a lack of it was beyond the pale.

No two operational commanders in my personal experience had the same ability to make a man lift his sights and perform above his customary level.

In all the ups and downs of the island battle I enjoyed an even, steady relationship with Hugh Lloyd. For me, he became – just as Basil Embry did later in France – more than one's AOC. He was the symbol of the Service, and of my Squadron, in which I had, by now, developed an almost obsessive pride.

Keith Park visited Takali for the first time on 12 July, three days before taking over. This tall, slender and invariably well-groomed officer made me feel at once that had I been a newly-appointed squadron commander of his choice, starting out under him on some new crusade, he would have been a man to follow. As it was (and he couldn't have been more civil to me or more complimentary about the Squadron's success), he was patently aware that I and 249's two Flight Commanders were at the end of our tour of duty and would, perforce, soon be on our way.

What clearly (and naturally) concerned him now was the future. I could sense something of his intentions. First, whatever may have gone before, he was going to have things played his way. Second, offence would be the card he would play, with defence arguing for itself. He could afford the stance. There were now some 130 Spitfires on the Island's operational strength. In the spring we had been lucky to muster ten or a dozen. (It would have been interesting, incidentally, to see what he would have made of that!)

With such a hand, it was tactically quite possible – and, indeed, appropriate – to send a squadron or two across the 60 miles of Straits to engage the enemy formations as they built up over Sicily and set out on their south-westerly course. Our excellent radars would provide the necessary information. With another squadron held back in reserve to defend the base against the attacks which would inevitably get through, the aerial defence of Malta then became a kind of belt-and-braces job.

The tactic, supported by well-marshalled publicity, was vindicated by events.

Park, with all his flamboyance, was a first-rate publicist. Like Montgomery, with his 8th Army, he understood the value of publicity in war. With the eye of a peacetime Fleet Street reporter, I could see that he felt it important to cultivate it. The glaring red MG sports car in which he habitually drove about (when petrol was critically short, motor transport virtually banned and the Governor, Lord Gort, had long since 'got on his bike'), had something in common with the black beret and battledress of the General in the Desert, standing up in a jeep, acknowledging the plaudits of the troops as he passed by.

There was a piquant twist to what quickly became known

as Park's 'forward interception policy'. This was, as the new AOC conceived it, an almost exact play-back of the tactical ploy which Douglas Bader had wanted the Duxford Wing to perform in the Battle of Britain two years before.

Bader's concept, which he had planned and timed to the minute, distances and all, and which was backed all the way by Leigh-Mallory, provided for the 12 Group squadrons to be called off the ground as soon as our radars showed the Luftwaffe's formations to be building in strength over the Pas de Calais.

He could then, he said, have taken his Wing south, climbing straight ahead, to 20,000 feet over the Thames Estuary by the time the enemy was ready to set course from France. Another fifteen minutes on a south-easterly course and he would have been well forward on a line running roughly from Ashford to Dungeness with all the height and freedom he needed to take an aggressive first poke at the attackers as they approached the south-east coast.

This, Bader asserted, would, in turn, have given Park's 11 Group squadrons more time to gain the vital height they craved to strike at their prey as the bombers moved inland.

Park, who was conducting the day-to-day battle over south-east England, would have none of it and it became one of the issues which lay at the base of the running controversy between the two Groups. Yet there was no denying that this was the tactic on which the New Zealander embarked with such effect in almost identical circumstances during the first three months of his command in Malta.

Bader, fretting now in a prisoner-of-war camp in Germany, would have been entitled to smile . . .

It did not take us any time to see that Keith Park, who cut a fresh and invigorating figure in the torrid heat of late summer, would make his own idiosyncratic mark upon the

Island. He took on, with instant authority, where Lloyd had left off. As a great tactical commander, he gave a new impulse to the squadrons.

How, then, does history see the respective contributions of the two men to the Mediterranean battle?

The Royal Air Force's historians at the Ministry of Defence, in an absorbing analysis of the Malta conflict, and profiting, of course, from hindsight, have painted the picture in clear relief. Standing back and divorcing themselves from emotion and controversy, they have been concerned only with accuracy and fact.

This [Park's forward interception policy] was only possible because of the increased fighter strength in Spitfires in Malta. The new policy saved bombs and crashing aircraft from falling on the Island, but it is an exaggeration to claim, as has been done in some quarters, that the policy of forward interception 'saved' Malta. The battle for Malta had been won before Air Vice-Marshal Lloyd left the Island. After the enemy had called off the spring '*blitz*' of April, 1942 and Rommel became deeply committed to his offensive [in Libya], the existence of Malta as an air and naval base was never seriously threatened by concentrated air attack.*

The historians have had recourse to the former German commander of the Axis air forces in Sicily to furnish a comment upon the fighter squadrons' collective contribution to victory.

Perhaps the best tribute, [they write], to the quality of the Malta pilots is given by Field Marshall Kesselring when enumerating the difficulties encountered by his Luftflotte 2 in finally neutralizing Malta by air attack.

'The British fighter units [at Malta] deserve admiring recognition for their bravery, their manœuvrability in action and especially in their perfectly executed tactics of diving from a great

* Air Historical Branch Draft Narrative: Malta (unpublished).

height . . . through the close-flying formation of bombers . . . In Malta, the Luftwaffe had met a worthy opponent.'*

In returning the *Generalfeldmarschall*'s compliment, we would ourselves offer this humble salute:

In confronting the Luftwaffe and the Regia Aeronautica in the spring and summer of 1942, the Royal Air Force faced a well-disciplined, persistent and rugged foe in the rough give-and-take of battle . . .

*ibid. Quote from *The War in the Mediterranean* Part I by Field Marshal Kesselring. AHB 6 Trans. No. VII/104.

# 31

# LAST LAP

When you go home
Tell them of us and say
For your tomorrow
We gave our today
*Inscription on
the Kohima Memorial,
Eastern Assam*

The twilight was fading as we sat out on the bastions in Mdina exchanging the usual day's lies. The Island was quiet save for the distant sound of a Beaufighter's engines being run up at Luqa away to our right. The moon was already climbing in the sky to aid Moose Fumerton, the Canadian, and Pat Bing, his radar operator and navigator, on another of their nights of destruction. It was an entrancing setting as we looked down on Takali and east to the faint outline of Valletta and Grand Harbour and to the blackness which was the ocean beyond.

For evenings without number we had sat here during the summer, discussing the day's fighting and knowing that the morrow, and the day after, and the day after that would still be offering much the same fare. We knew, too, that we would still be feeling hungry.

One thing alone marred the tranquillity. I had acute toothache.

Squadron Leader H. E. Elthrington, Takali's well-covered and jovial Senior Administrative Officer, came hurrying down the street to find me. 'The Station Commander wants to see you at once. He's in the bar of the Mess.'

Jumbo Gracie, drink in one hand, cigarette burning in

the usual long holder in the other, came straight out with the news. 'The AOC has just been on. You're posted. So are your two Flight Commanders. And so am I. We're all going back to England. "Mitch" (Squadron Leader R. A. Mitchell), from 603, is taking over 249 from you right away. I shall be flying back to Gib tomorrow night. You, Raoul Daddo-Langlois and Norman Lee will be following a night or two later – as soon as another aircraft is available . . . Yippee! Now let's have a drink!'

Keith Park, with his decisive mind, had sized things up in 249 quickly. According to Gracie, he knew I had had a 'shaky do' a few days before and that only Daddo-Langlois and I, of the original February 'Spitfire' intake, were still operating with the Squadron. He had also established that the other Flight Commander, Norman Lee, like Jumbo himself, had come out in March, only a few weeks later. The rest of this early vintage had either 'bought it' or been posted away. There had been a heavy turnover. Park was now bent upon clearing out what remained.

Having got the drinks, Jumbo added a rider. 'The AOC thinks you've been kept on too long and were lucky not to have been "bumped" the other day. "Overconfident", he said! He wants to see you tomorrow morning. I'm to see him, too. We'll go in to Valletta together.'

To be fair to the AOC, I knew I had had my chips and ought to be taken off, but the news depressed me. I have never been any hand at saying goodbye. When, first, I was sent away to school as a small boy, the wrench at having to leave my home so young saddened me. I was always happy at school, but I loved my home. What I hated was the actual act of parting, the hugs, kisses and last glances . . .

History repeats itself through life. Leaving 249 which, for months, had been my life, and where I found friendship, kindness and loyalty, was just like going away to school. I longed suddenly to be picked up from the bar, parcelled up and, without anyone else noticing, deposited by some magic spirit in London without having to say any goodbyes. I didn't know how I was going to face them.

I was close to tears when I put my head on the pillow of my bed in the Xara Palace that night. Exhaustion leaves you with no resistance when once you let go.

Keith Park's line, when I saw him the next day, was unexpected. After some generous pleasantries, he quickly became quite serious. There was purpose in his voice. The substance of his words has stuck in my mind ever since.

'You have had an exceptional experience here in Malta. In particular, you have had the special privilege of leading an outstanding squadron made up of fine people of real quality from all parts of the Empire and Commonwealth and the United States. Add that to your upbringing and the experience you have had pre-war and there will be few operating and leading at home who will possess that kind of background.

'You're rather older than most of them (I was rising twenty-seven!), so, after all this, you have a responsibility to set an example. I hope, therefore, that, wherever they send you for your rest and whatever flying jobs you get afterwards, you'll do your best to make good use of this experience and give a lead.

'If I may say so, you owe it to the Service for the chance it has given you here in Malta.'

There was a handshake and a faint smile. 'Thank you, sir. Thank you very much.' With a strong salute, it was all that I could manage.

I was thankful there was no one waiting for me outside the door as I left . . .

It was just after midnight when the three of us, Raoul, Norman and I took off from Luqa for the last time. The Hudson transport was captained by the demonstrably competent Flying Officer Matthews, who had already flown Raoul and myself back to Gib in the spring for the fly-off from the carriers.

The moon was on the wane as we became airborne, but still the whiteness of the Island down below, framed by the darkness of the sea around it, stood out, boldly as ever. Drenched in nostalgia, none of us could credit that we were actually leaving Malta and going home. It was as if we had never known any other life and that our sojourn on the Island had lasted for an eternity.

My toothache, which I had been trying to quell with copious doses of aspirin for two days, was still raging. I hadn't dared to get anything done on the Island for fear it might have delayed my departure and prolonged the good-byes. Another six hours and thirty minutes of it through the night in extreme discomfort, and the moment we landed at Gib I collared a transport to take me at once to the dental centre.

There, a muscular Army dentist, in khaki shorts and bare torso, with a medical orderly, similarly clad, saw me immediately.

'By the look of your face, you've got an abscess.'

The assumption proved correct.

'There's only one thing for this now. The tooth must come out.' Anything, I thought, would be preferable to the pain.

Fifty minutes later, with the Army's dental surgeon, and his assistant, both running with sweat, and with my mouth and lips feeling as if they had been lacerated beyond repair, the offending molar was still there. A second dentist, obviously a more senior character, came and had a look. He assumed control of the extraction.

Five minutes later, and fifty-five after the session had originally started, the tooth yielded up the ghost. The victor held it up with a pair of forceps.

'Like to see the bugger?'

We were three days in Gib before leaving for England. I spent two of them in bed, flattened and unable to take anything but liquids. (I was already more than a stone underweight!) When, eventually, we rejoined the Hudson and Flying Officer Matthews and his crew, I could barely open my mouth to speak. My throat felt as if it had seized up and I could not turn my head.

Dawn was breaking as we made landfall at Land's End after the long, seven-hour flight from Gib. We passed over the airfield at Portreath at some 3000 feet . . . Portreath, where seven months before (if felt like seven years), 66 Squadron's adjutant had held up a signal from Group. 'Who wants a posting to Burma? Any takers? Two pilots wanted.'

Raoul Daddo-Langlois and I had lived a lifetime since then. And now, as we flew east over the Cornish peninsula, across Devon and Dorset, Wiltshire and Berkshire, and headed for Hendon and London, it was 'England's green and pleasant land' – the farmsteads with grazing cattle, the hedgerows, the big open fields, the downs, the hills, tiny valleys with little streams bubbling through them – that made the impact. It had been a wet summer and the contrast with the heat and the dry, dusty whiteness, and the myriad stone walls of the Island we had just left behind, had us fighting back our emotions. We didn't talk. All we wanted to do was gaze out of the aircraft's portholes at the novel scene below.

'God,' exclaimed Raoul, after a prolonged silence, 'what a country!'

'Yes,' put in Norman, 'and not a 109 in sight!'

I still had a week or so of my disembarkation leave left when the telephone rang at home. It was the secretary to E. J. Robertson, the managerial head of Beaverbrook Newspapers, my peacetime employers, on the line. Mr Robertson wondered whether I could go to a small luncheon party he was giving the next day? A few office friends would be there who wanted to welcome me home.

Despite his exalted position, Robbie, a generous and able Canadian, had become a friend and had often stopped in the office to offer a word of encouragement as I was starting out in the Group. Apart from Robbie himself, the 'few office friends' turned out to be Tom Blackburn, another helpful supporter, who would later head up the managerial side of the newspapers, and John Gordon and Arthur Christiansen, editors respectively of the *Sunday* and the *Daily Express*, for each of whom in peacetime I had developed an almost reverential respect. I felt humble in such company and a mite overawed by it.

Gordon, an uninhibited Scot and a first-class newspaperman, who had been my immediate pre-war boss and ever an objective critic of my copy, offered a toast at the end.

'You left us,' he said, raising his glass, 'as a reporter two years ago to go away and serve as an aircraftman in the Air Force. You have returned as a squadron leader with the DFC and a number of enemy aircraft destroyed. We welcome you home and drink to your continued good health and safety. But I would have you know you have missed a great opportunity to tell your Malta story!'

Better, perhaps, late than never?

# INDEX

# READ MORE IN PENGUIN

In every corner of the world, on every subject under the sun, Penguin represents quality and variety – the very best in publishing today.

For complete information about books available from Penguin – including Puffins, Penguin Classics and Arkana – and how to order them, write to us at the appropriate address below. Please note that for copyright reasons the selection of books varies from country to country.

**In the United Kingdom:** Please write to *Dept. JC, Penguin Books Ltd, FREEPOST, West Drayton, Middlesex UB7 0BR*

If you have any difficulty in obtaining a title, please send your order with the correct money, plus ten per cent for postage and packaging, to *PO Box No. 11, West Drayton, Middlesex UB7 0BR*

**In the United States:** Please write to *Penguin USA Inc., 375 Hudson Street, New York, NY 10014*

**In Canada:** Please write to *Penguin Books Canada Ltd, 10 Alcorn Avenue, Suite 300, Toronto, Ontario M4V 3B2*

**In Australia:** Please write to *Penguin Books Australia Ltd, 487 Maroondah Highway, Ringwood, Victoria 3134*

**In New Zealand:** Please write to *Penguin Books (NZ) Ltd, 182–190 Wairau Road, Private Bag, Takapuna, Auckland 9*

**In India:** Please write to *Penguin Books India Pvt Ltd, 706 Eros Apartments, 56 Nehru Place, New Delhi 110 019*

**In the Netherlands:** Please write to *Penguin Books Netherlands B.V., Keizersgracht 231 NL–1016 DV Amsterdam*

**In Germany:** Please write to *Penguin Books Deutschland GmbH, Friedrichstrasse 10–12, W–6000 Frankfurt/Main 1*

**In Spain:** Please write to *Penguin Books S. A., C. San Bernardo 117–6° E–28015 Madrid*

**In Italy:** Please write to *Penguin Italia s.r.l., Via Felice Casati 20, I–20124 Milano*

**In France:** Please write to *Penguin France S. A., 17 rue Lejeune, F–31000 Toulouse*

**In Japan:** Please write to *Penguin Books Japan, Ishikiribashi Building, 2–5–4, Suido, Tokyo 112*

**In Greece:** Please write to *Penguin Hellas Ltd, Dimocritou 3, GR–106 71 Athens*

**In South Africa:** Please write to *Longman Penguin Southern Africa (Pty) Ltd, Private Bag X08, Bertsham 2013*

# READ MORE IN PENGUIN

## HISTORY

**The World Since 1945**  T. E. Vadney
New edition

From the origins of the post-war world to the collapse of the Soviet Bloc in the late 1980s, this masterly book offers an authoritative yet highly readable one-volume account.

**Ecstasies**  Carlo Ginzburg

This dazzling work of historical detection excavates the essential truth about the witches' Sabbath. 'Ginzburg's learning is prodigious and his journey through two thousand years of Eurasian folklore a *tour de force*' – *Observer*

**The Nuremberg Raid**  Martin Middlebrook

'The best book, whether documentary or fictional, yet written about Bomber Command' – *Economist*. 'Martin Middlebrook's skill at description and reporting lift this book above the many memories that were written shortly after the war' – *The Times*

**A History of Christianity**  Paul Johnson

'Masterly … It is a huge and crowded canvas – a tremendous theme running through twenty centuries of history – a cosmic soap opera involving kings and beggars, philosophers and crackpots, scholars and illiterate exaltés, popes and pilgrims and wild anchorites in the wilderness'– Malcolm Muggeridge

**The Penguin History of Greece**  A. R. Burn

Readable, erudite, enthusiastic and balanced, this one-volume history of Hellas sweeps the reader along from the days of Mycenae and the splendours of Athens to the conquests of Alexander and the final dark decades.

**Modern Ireland 1600–1972**  R. F. Foster

'Takes its place with the finest historical writing of the twentieth century, whether about Ireland or anywhere else' – Conor Cruise O'Brien in the *Sunday Times*

# READ MORE IN PENGUIN

## HISTORY

**The Guillotine and the Terror** Daniel Arasse

'A brilliant and imaginative account of the punitive mentality of the revolution that restores to its cultural history its most forbidding and powerful symbol' – Simon Schama.

**The Second World War** A J P Taylor

A brilliant and detailed illustrated history, enlivened by all Professor Taylor's customary iconoclasm and wit.

**Daily Life in Ancient Rome** Jerome Carcopino

This classic study, which includes a bibliography and notes by Professor Rowell, describes the streets, houses and multi-storeyed apartments of the city of over a million inhabitants, the social classes from senators to slaves, and the Roman family and the position of women, causing *The Times Literary Supplement* to hail it as a 'thorough, lively and readable book'.

**The Anglo-Saxons** Edited by James Campbell

'For anyone who wishes to understand the broad sweep of English history, Anglo-Saxon society is an important and fascinating subject. And Campbell's is an important and fascinating book. It is also a finely produced and, at times, a very beautiful book' – *London Review of Books*

**The Making of the English Working Class** E. P. Thompson

Probably the most imaginative – and the most famous – post-war work of English social history. 'A magnificent, lucid, angry historian … E. P. Thompson has performed a revolution of historical perspective' – *The Times*

**The Habsburg Monarchy 1809–1918** A J P Taylor

Dissolved in 1918, the Habsburg Empire 'had a unique character, out of time and out of place'. Scholarly and vividly accessible, this 'very good book indeed' (*Spectator*) elucidates the problems always inherent in the attempt to give peace, stability and a common loyalty to a heterogeneous population.